William Anderson, Samuel Parlby

Sketch of the mode of manufacturing gunpowder at the Ishapore mills in Bengal

With a record of the experiments carried on to ascertain the value of charge

William Anderson, Samuel Parlby

Sketch of the mode of manufacturing gunpowder at the Ishapore mills in Bengal
With a record of the experiments carried on to ascertain the value of charge

ISBN/EAN: 9783337173876

Printed in Europe, USA, Canada, Australia, Japan

Cover: Foto ©Andreas Hilbeck / pixelio.de

More available books at **www.hansebooks.com**

SKETCH OF THE MODE

OF

MANUFACTURING GUNPOWDER.

Copies of Col. Anderson's *Work can be supplied to British and Foreign Governments, to Military and Naval Officers and others, by the Booksellers in the following named cities in Europe, Asia, Africa and America.*

Country of—	Cities.	Name of Bookseller.
ALGIERS, Africa	Algiers	Bernard, Dubos, & Co.
AMERICA, Confederate States	Richmond	Randolph.
,, Federal States	New York	Van Nostrand.
AUSTRIA	Vienna	Gerold.
,, Venetia	Venice	Antonelli.
BAVARIA	Munich	Baron Cotta & Co.
BELGIUM	Brussels	Muqnardt.
BRAZILS	Rio de Janeiro	Belin, Le Prieur & Co.
CANADA, Lower	Montreal	Dawson.
CAPE OF GOOD HOPE	Cape Town	Geo. Greig & Co.
DENMARK	Copenhagen	Gyldendal.
FRANCE	Paris	Dunod.
GERMANY, Central	Frankfort	Jügel.
GREECE	Athens	Antoniades.
HANOVER	Hanover	Hahn.
HESSE-DARMSTADT	Darmstadt	Kuchler.
HOLLAND	Rotterdam	Kramers.
HUNGARY	Pesth	Gerold.
INDIA	Calcutta	Le Page & Co.
	Madras	Pharoah & Co.
	Bombay	Thacker & Co.
IRELAND, United Kingdom	Dublin	Hodges & Smith.
ITALY, Piedmont	Turin	Bocca Brothers.
,, Central	Florence	Goodban.
MECKLENBOURG-SCHWERIN	Mecklenbourg	Hinstoff.
MEXICO	Mexico	Allouard & Co.
NORWAY	Christiania	Wulfsberg & Co.
POLAND	Warsaw	Gluecksberg.
PORTUGAL, Peninsula	Lisbon	Silva.
PRUSSIA	Berlin	Asher & Co.
RUSSIA	St. Petersburg	Messrs. Issakoff.
SAXONY	Leipsig	Weigel.
SCOTLAND, Great Britain	Edinburgh	Menzies.
SPAIN, Peninsula	Madrid	Fr. de Mellado.
SWEDEN	Stockholm	Bonnier.
TURKEY, in Asia	Smyrna	Castellan.
,, in Europe	Constantinople	Kœhler & Co.
WIRTEMBERG	Stuttgardt	Bach.

SKETCH OF THE MODE

OF

MANUFACTURING GUNPOWDER

AT THE

ISHAPORE MILLS IN BENGAL.

WITH

A RECORD OF THE EXPERIMENTS CARRIED ON TO ASCERTAIN THE
VALUE OF CHARGE, WINDAGE, VENT AND WEIGHT, ETC.,

IN MORTARS AND MUSKETS;

ALSO

REPORTS OF THE VARIOUS PROOFS OF POWDER.

BY

COL. WILLIAM ANDERSON, C.B.,
LATE AGENT AT ISHAPORE.

WITH NOTES AND ADDITIONS BY LIEUT.-COL. PARLBY,
RETIRED BENGAL ARTILLERY.

LONDON:
JOHN WEALE, 59, HIGH HOLBORN.
1862.

LONDON:
BRADBURY AND EVANS, PRINTERS, WHITEFRIARS.

TO

THE OFFICERS

OF

THE INDIAN ARTILLERY,

IN

RECOLLECTION OF OLDEN TIMES.

1862.

PREFACE.

THE following pages result from an earnest study to acquire an insight into the theory of Gunpowder, and from much labour in making numerous experiments to test and fortify the art of manipulation as practised at the Ishapore Mills.

No subject can easily be mentioned which is more difficult to bound by fixed laws.

Danger attends all operations with Gunpowder. The results are flashed forth in so momentary a period as to elude all scrutiny into the mode by which such extraordinary power is produced: the means have vanished while the end is often to be gathered from destruction.

In teaching myself the art, I was necessitated to investigate the facts and make the numerous experiments which form the basis of this sketch; the record of them may save much trouble to future agents.

Every trial carried on, and every experiment made, are truly and faithfully recorded, without deviation to meet any preconceived theory. The greatest possible care was taken to have all the circumstances identical except the one under consideration, to the end that attention might not be withdrawn from the point under investigation.

Much credit is due to the patience and perseverance of the conductor of the works, and of the overseers of the establishment.

The records are true ; the deductions may be unsatisfactory. They were carried on in the attempt to satisfy my own mind, but often lead to no very perfect conclusion ; such is particularly the case in all the reasonings and arguments on the various points of charges, weight, windage, or distances, as connected with mortars or muskets.

The simple art of powder-making is probably more correctly worked out, being based on the Memoir of Colonel Galloway ; of which a by no means incompetent judge once observed, "If any person would but implicitly follow the rules established by Colonel Galloway, he could not fail of fabricating excellent powder."

Every officer understanding the subject must acknowledge the labour and ingenuity which first established the present works at Ishapore ; and although some trifling alterations have been since introduced, the system will long remain a monument of no common ability.

A few years in the present race of improvements and scientific investigation may aid in obtaining greater perfection, even as the good high roads succeeding mere tracks were in their turn improved by Macadam, to be rendered almost useless for the means of rapid conveyance by the introduction of railroads.

The chemical portion of the sketch has received not the sanction or approbation of that eminent chemist Mr. O'Shaughnessy,* but his mere simple affirmation that it is fully sufficient and amply accurate for the required purpose.

The historical part is the best that my authorities would afford, the greater portion being but a new version of the old story.

W. ANDERSON.

ISHAPORE,
January, 1849.

* Now Sir William.

PREFACE BY THE EDITOR.

THERE never was a period, since the discovery of gunpowder, and its application to artillery and fire-arms, when nations anxious to maintain their status and integrity, could less afford to be inattentive to the improvement of their war equipments than the present.

Every civilised country is unceasingly labouring, by invention, experiment, and practice, to improve, regulate, and extend the ranges and effectiveness of their artillery and fire-arms ; and if we may judge from the number of new patents which have been taken out of late years for improvements in them, and in the important processes of the manufacture of gunpowder, from which material all the mechanical power of fire-arms is derived, individuals of the British nation have not been backward in the race for improvement and superiority.

As long as other nations remained content with the weapons of inferior power and construction, which served their purposes in former wars, it was well for Great Britain, having no aggressive intentions, but directed solely by the noble and patriotic principle of being prepared for self-defence, to remain quiet and inactive ; but a few years have brought about such important changes in the materials employed in war, and the apparently trifling event of the formidable effect, in naval warfare, of an iron-plated ship in the American waters has produced so powerful an influence, as necessarily to lead to the complete alteration and construction of our navy, and to the certain necessity that we must alter the old system of fortification, and give increased power to a portion at least of our ordnance.

Under this necessity, which is of momentous national importance, the nation must willingly submit to increased military expenditure; for we should recollect that in the time of peace we can most quietly and economically prepare for all contingencies: and it needs no argument to prove that what we can thus do with forethought and with just scientific grounds, for improvement and experiment is so much in advance in placing our country in such permanent security as to meet the immediate contingencies of war in the most decided manner, not with the least intention of threatening our neighbours, but with the valuable certainty that such an established preparation is the best guarantee for the happy continuance of peace. And if the philanthropist will allow the many historical proofs, that wars have become less deadly, less destructive, and less numerous, since the discovery of gunpowder and its application to cannon and fire-arms, than when battles were fought by numerous hosts in close combat with each other, the consideration ought to reconcile any one of right mind, that unless, happily, wars could be made to cease altogether, the study of the science, and of written information on the subject, are neither so unnecessary nor repulsive, as many estimable persons are disposed to consider them to be.

The historian well knows, as all who pursue the study of history will find, that the records of wars, and the progress of military science, are intimately connected with the past and present, as they will be with the future conditions of nations; and it is hoped that the gleanings from this volume may not be found wanting to supply a due portion of interest to some, and of advantage to others, objects which every person in placing a new book before the public should have in view.

The circumstances, however, which have been chiefly instrumental in bringing this volume forward, are as follows :—

Colonel William Anderson, C.B., late of the Bengal Artillery, having, with great professional talent and industry, drawn up voluminous MSS. on the subject of gunpowder, containing much that is curious and instructive, placed them in my hands, to prepare them for publication; and it will be impossible to examine the patient and laborious experiments here recorded, with his scientific deductions from the same, without according to him the chief merit of the present publication.

From my own experience as an Artillery officer, and for some years agent for the Manufactory of Gunpowder and War-Rockets, at Allahabad, in Bengal, I have endeavoured to add to the information given, and to bring down the progress of improvements to the present time.

Not having had access to the mine of very valuable information which is, no doubt, stored in the records of the Select Committee, on the subject of experiments with modern artillery and fire-arms at Woolwich and Shoeburyness, my statements on these subjects must be shorter and more incomplete than I should wish them to have been; and this deficiency is an additional argument in favour of the patriotic opinion of Sir Frederic Smith, M.P., in his place in Parliament, on the 16th of May last, that these reports of experiments made at the national expense, should be made public, for the benefit and advantage of inventors, and others interested in the subject of improving our national power in the most important arm of artillery.

How very useful it would be, if the causes of *the failure* in every projected improvement were publicly known and explained. It is well known how many celebrated men, from the great Newton to Watt, and others of later dates, have obtained useful knowledge and experience from *failures*, and it has been related of the last eminent man, to whose talents the world is so deeply indebted, that when some friend was complimenting him upon his extraordinary powers of invention and mechanical skill, his modest reply was, " You are regarding what I have succeeded in, but you are little aware in how many instances I have failed in perfecting what I aspired to do."

All experiments in improving artillery and projectiles are attended with expenses that few individuals can support or attempt; such improvement is a national benefit, and when there is reasonable ground for expenditure, it should be at the national expense. At the present time, when patriotism has embodied so large and noble an army of volunteers, in whose hands gunpowder, fire-arms, and artillery are widely distributed, the present volume may fill a void which, I understand, has been generally felt. In the small additions I have been able to make to Colonel Anderson's meritorious labours, I have sought to render the pages additionally interesting and instructive; and if my thoughts upon the chemical effects of the combustion of gunpowder are correct, they will serve to explain some circumstances as yet incorrectly understood, and probably awaken inquiry, which must tend to valuable results in using gunpowder as a projectile force.

SAMUEL PARLBY.

LONDON, *August*, 1862.

CONTENTS.

	PAGE
COLONEL ANDERSON'S PREFACE	vii
EDITOR'S PREFACE	ix
HISTORY OF GUNPOWDER	1

Opinions of Mons. Dutens—Early employment of rockets and fire-darts—Roger Bacon—Bartholdus Schwartz—Gunpowder used by the Moors, 1343—Strength of gunpowder gradually increased—China or India place of first invention—Early use of fireworks by the Chinese—Ghungeez Khan—Tatar magicians—Institutes of Teemoor—Battle of Muhmood at Delhi—Elephants and rockets—Smyrna taken, 1402, by Bayuzeed—First mention of matchlocks in Indian history—Cannon probably introduced from Europe—Ustad Uli Kull as gun-founder—Military despatch of the Emperor Babur—Fire-arms and cannon in common use with the decline of bows and arrows—Use of bombs by Sheer Shah—His death—Park of artillery drawn by men—The Ayeen Akbarree—Price of saltpetre—The Emperor Akebar's attention to artillery—Mons. Manouchi—Curious account of European gunners employed by Akebar—Ancient artillery supposed to have been made by the Chinese invaders of India—Akebar's numerous artillery—Conclusion of sketch—Note by Editor—Colonel Chesney's and Mr. Robert Mallet's works referred to for further information—China and India produced the first gunpowder—Difficulty of the inquiry—Extract from Mr. Halhed's translation of the code of Gentoo laws, proving the antiquity of cannon and fire-arms in India.

ESTABLISHMENT OF THE MANUFACTURE OF GUNPOWDER IN BENGAL . . . 21

Native manufactories—Removed from Baugh Bazaar to Ackra, in 1784—In 1794, Mr. John Farquhar obtained a Government contract—Established works at Baukee Bazaar, now Ishapore—New building erected in 1820—Machinery improved by Colonel Galloway—Allahabad Works established by Captain Taylor, at Poppa Mhow, in 1799.

FIRST ESTABLISHMENT OF POWDER WORKS IN ENGLAND 23

By the Evelyn family—Various licences granted in different reigns to dig for saltpetre and make gunpowder—Scarcity of gunpowder and saltpetre—The East India Company established works in Surrey in 1626—Bound to furnish the Government with 500 tons of saltpetre annually by charter of 1693.

	PAGE
GENERAL PRINCIPLES OF GUNPOWDER	31
CHEMICAL PRINCIPLES OF GUNPOWDER	32
TABULAR STATEMENT of proportions of ingredients used in different countries.	36

SALTPETRE: Abundant in India—Attempts to produce it artificially in France—Mr. Stevenson's account of the native process in Bengal—The Culmee saltpetre of the Calcutta market—Prices, &c.

SALTPETRE REFINERY AT ISHAPORE . . 41

Process described—First boiling—Second boiling—Fusing, grinding and sifting—At Madras and in English works large crystals prevented by agitation of solution—Tests to try the purity of—Table of prices—Improved process of refining as now pursued at Waltham Abbey Powder-Works.

CHARCOAL 49

Prepared in pits—Mode of preparing by cylinders at Ishapore—Woods used—Specific gravities of various kinds—Amount of charring, its effects upon the density of powder—Quantity produced—Average cost at Ishapore—Test for purity of.

CONTENTS.

SULPHUR 58
Whence obtained — Varied prices and impurity—Mode of refining—By melting—Subliming—Cost of new mode of refining by distillation, as pursued at Waltham Abbey—Mode of ascertaining its purity.

MODE OF MANUFACTURE OF GUNPOWDER . 62
Dry-mixing—Mixing barrels—Experiments with different times of revolution—Trials of the same.

INCORPORATION OF THE MATERIALS . . 69
Early mode by foot mills—Pilon mills—Colonel Galloway's grinding mill—His description and mode of working as used at Ishapore—Calculation of the power of the mills—Considerations of their action in grinding, mixing, pressing—Mr. Braddock's remarks on the mills at Waltham Abbey and Madras—Experiments in France with pilon mills—Madras process of milling—Tabular comparisons of effect of milling in England, Bengal, and Madras—Advantages and disadvantages of long milling—Trials of powder to determine these—Quantity of mill charge—Rate of moving—Water for wetting—Question of light or heavy cylinders—Cost of the present mills at Ishapore—Colonel Tennant's opinion that powder made by pilon mills is better than that made by cylinders—His reasons—Heat of India requires less velocity to mills than in Europe—Quantity of pounding from the old pilon mills.

BRUISING 86
To prepare the mill cake for the press—Process used at Ishapore—One man's labour required for each mill—Trials of mill cake charges made with different numbers of revolutions.

PRESSING 90
Formerly used only to be pressed in the mill—Description of press, by Colonel Galloway, as used at Ishapore—Degree of pressure — Power of the press—Press boxes contain 320 lbs.—Calculation of the power of the Ishapore presses—Specific gravities of mill cake—Of solid gunpowder at Ishapore, England (Hutton)—Mr. Braddock's opinion of pressing and glazing—The Hon. Mr. Napier's experiments—Table of varieties of density of powder— Loss of weight by evaporation—Men required to work the press to produce twenty barrels in twelve hours—Cost of the presses.

GRANULATION 100
Old process— Continued till 1824—New corning machine described — Twelve hours work to 100 barrels of powder.

SIFTING 103
By sieves suspended from roof—Where labour is dear a machine might be used with advantage—Sizes of sieves used at Ishapore.

GLAZING 104
English large-grained powder probably not glazed—Process pursued at Ishapore—Glazing reels described.

DRYING 105
In Europe artificial means are used—Solar heat considered sufficient in India—Ishapore drying terraces described—Process of drying —Heat of the powder—After third day weighed and barrelled—After a month powder is proved—Barrels closed up and marked.

PACKING, TRANSPORTING, STORING . . 108
Cost of transport—Barrels constantly rolled over in magazines—Advantage of occasionally exposing to sun—A pucka terrace convenient.

COST OF THE ISHAPORE POWDER . . . 109
Calculation of items—Average price from 1841 to 1848—Prices of English powder—Mr. Farquhar's contract—Cost of Colonel Galloway's—Of Bombay powder of 1846-47—Of Madras powder of 1846-47.

MOTIVE POWER TO WORK THE MILLS . 111
Running water best power— Steam much used—At Ishapore the power of bullocks only—Number of cattle required—Cost of cattle and pay of attendants—Bullocks of present day not strong—Average expense on this head.

HYGROMETRIC PROOF 113
Hygrometric reports—French experiment—Table of trial.

PROOF OF POWDER AT THE AGENCY . . 115
Various modes adopted—At Ishapore a Gomer chambered mortar used—Officers' proof—Pendulum gun éprouvette lately introduced—Table of agency proof—Proof for commandant of artillery—Table of ranges—Court of directors' proof—Trials of Bengal, Madras, and Bombay powders—Triennial reports—Experiments—Madras observations.

EXTRA GLAZING 127
Question of effects of glazing—Madras observations—Mr. Braddock's opinions

CONTENTS.

—Table of results of prolonged glazing—Hygrometric reports—Effects of density on range, of facility of ignition—Calculation—Effect of heat on gunpowder—Effect of overcharge—Density—Density measure described, with woodcut.

BARREL DEPARTMENT 137
Powder barrels should be made of dry, well-seasoned wood—Bengal barrels—Mr. Walker's patent barrels—Native Dubbas for packing powder—Dimensions of Ishapore barrels—Weight—Loss in resetting up—Manufacture of—Common barrels not water proof—Experiment, with woodcut to explain—Cost of the barrels—Colonel Anderson's proposal for a new dimension of barrel—Useful for transport by camels—Hoops and staves—Experiment to try the strength of staves and hoops—Experiment to prove strength of barrel.

TO ANALYSE POWDER 144
Process described.

SIKH GUNPOWDER 145
Sekh gunpowder from Kabul 1842—Examined in 1849—With small ball proved superior to Bengal powder—Curious fact with the "Trident's" powder—Proof of Bengal and Sekh powder—Singular experiment of a Sekh Sirdar with shell.

BUILDINGS 147
Distances between—Size—Construction.

EXPERIMENTS ON MORTARS 148
Necessity in proving powder to be very exact in mortar and ball—Experiments by reducing weight of ball—With regard to size and of grain in the charge—Table of ranges by progressive increase of charge—Comparative proof table—Calculations of charges and ranges—Force of powder to blow out clay, by Sir John Burgoyne—Table of effects of reducing weight of ball—Question of the advantages of hollow projectiles. WINDAGE: Effects of—The first tenth of windage has the greatest effect on range—Tables showing ranges and loss by windage. ELEVATION: Experiments and calculations of effect of elevation. RECOIL: Table of Experiment.

MUSKETRY EXPERIMENTS 165
Penetration of shot through boards—Tables of proof—Effect of windage—Colonel Anderson's ingenious theory to explain the effect of windage—Large charges of inferior powder compensate for loss by windage—Experiment with shot of different windages in 1759, related by Antoni—Table of experiments—Colonel Anderson's deductions—Considers a certain quantity of air necessary to complete the explosion of a charge—Difficulty of the question—Ranges of muskets of olden days longer than at present— Effect of length of barrel—Table of experiments—Disadvantage of superfluous length—Different lengths required for different qualities of powder — Experiments related by Antoni — Comparison of the effect of Antoni's charge with that of Bengal powder—Proper proportion of charge to length of barrel—Colonel Anderson's diagram to show the measure of the exploding force of powder on different parts of a barrel. TOUCH-HOLE: Tabular proof with different sized touch-holes—Difference of size of vent greatly affects range—Antoni's experiment—With no vent less powder of a charge is fired—Unburnt grains of powder driven out of a vent—Up to ·3 of an inch of no material consequence—Less than is usually considered by European writers—Supposed effects of the vent. DISTANCE: Effects of in diminishing initial velocity of a ball—Calculations of the resistance of the air — Differences of charge and of length of barrel give different results in the computation—The resistance is as the velocity impressed, and as the square root nearly of the distance. INCREASE OF CHARGE: Table of experiments — An excess of powder useless above a certain point—Size of grain—Table of experiments in favour of mixing sizes — Large grains evolve fluid slower than smaller—The higher gunpowder is pressed, the smaller should be the grain—Effect of placing different weights before the ball, useful in short barrels, questionable if long.

VARIOUS PROOFS OF POWDERS . . . 193
Table of proofs—Comparison of boards and range.

RECORDED RANGES OF GUNPOWDER FROM DIFFERENT AUTHORITIES . . . 195

APPENDIX 199
Experiments on varied proportions of ingredients—Table of proof—Remarks on the same—Unpulverised compositions in milling worthy of extended consideration — Remarks on the iron

CONTENTS.

mill — New proportions of ingredients suggested—Other changes.

CARE OF POWDER IN MAGAZINES . . . 203
Barrels to be carefully inspected — Barrels to be constantly rolled about — Hoops carefully set home — Occasional exposure to the sun useful.

DAMAGED POWDER 204
May be rendered serviceable for common purposes—Care required.

RECOVERY OF SALTPETRE . . . . ib.
Apparatus required — The saltpetre useful for magazine purposes.

EMPTY BARRELS 205
Care in taking them to pieces—Mode of packing the hoops, heads, and staves.

REPORT ON THE IRON MILL . . . 206
Constructed by Messrs. Hall at Dartford —Comparative cost of iron and gun metal mills—Apparent advantages of—Alteration of form of bed suggested—Reduction of cost of powder by its adoption —Quality of powders of iron and gunmetal mills—Table of proof.

REMOVAL OF THE POWDER WORKS PROPOSED 208
Admirable report of Colonel Anderson on the subject, with woodcut-sketch.

ANALYSIS OF ISHAPORE POWDER MATERIALS BY SIR W. B. O'SHAUGHNESSY . 212

REMARKS ON THE TEMPERATURE OF THE DRYING TERRACES. TABLES OF HEAT BY THERMOMETER, ETC. . . . 214
Temperature from 80° to 130°—Appearance of powder during three days' exposure—Register of thermometer during eight months 1843-44, 1844-45, 1845-46, and 1848-49.

EXPERIMENT ON THE EVAPORATION OF WATER BY SOLAR HEAT AT ISHAPORE 216
Danger of sun's rays in India.

INQUIRY INTO THE CIRCUMSTANCES ARISING FROM THE CHEMICAL EFFECTS OF THE PRODUCTS OF GUNPOWDER WHEN FIRED IN CLOSE CHAMBERS . . 217
Importance of this inquiry—Effects of carbonic acid in extinguishing flame—Known fact of grains of gunpowder being blown out of the vent and muzzle unconsumed — Cause explained — Mistake in supposing that a gun filled with powder, and plugged up at the muzzle, is exposed to the severest strain of a charge of gunpowder—How to extend the ranges of cannon shot—Mr. Vallance's patent experiment with a musket barrel — Mr. Cochrane's gun.

GUN COTTON, OR PYROXYLE . . . 225

Investigation by Dr. W. B. O'Shaughnessy of Calcutta Mint— Rationale of the explosion of—Experiment at Dum-Dum with a mortar and guns as to its projectile force—Major Mordecai's experiments at the Washington arsenal—Unfavourable to its adoption—Supposed to be equally unfavourable at Woolwich —Advantages of good gunpowder—New invention to supersede gunpowder—Supposed disadvantages of.

OTHER SUBSTITUTES FOR GUNPOWDER . 229
Powders made with nitrate of soda—Nitrate of ammonia—Chlorate of potash —Danger of the last — Experiments made with it in France—Use of it abandoned—Supposed to have been used by Bonaparte in one of his campaigns—White fulminating powder—For others, chemical works may be consulted.

REMARKS ON CHARCOAL 233
Quality of charcoal of the first importance in making good gunpowder—Too much charcoal in the English proportions —Mr. Cruickshank's experiments — Serious importance of residue in rifles —Chemical analysis of powders of little use in determining the best proportions of ingredients — Different results of analysis by chemists as to nitrate of potash—Earnest attention of the manufacturer should be directed to the charcoal used—Nature and properties of charcoal — Slow burning compositions will not satisfy inquiry—Question well worthy the attention of Government—Trials of gas and residue of various charcoals in France — The "charbon rouge" of Mons. Violette.

REMARKS ON SIFTING AND SIZES OF GRAIN 237
Tabular statements of the different sizes of grain of Madras, Bombay, Bengal, England—Comparative proofs with various mixtures of grain—Eprouvette proofs—Fall in the arc of measurement with density and larger grain—With mortars the arc rises with these—Trial of English and Ishapore powders—Superiority of English powder may be from weakness of Bengal charcoal.

ACCIDENTS 240
May be expected in making gunpowder —With the old pilon mills in Bengal were constantly occurring —Care and prudence required—Accident when the gloom stove was used—Accident at Allahabad in 1823, from the falling of a barrel—Accidents at Ishapore in the

CONTENTS.

Corning House—In the mixing barrels and mills—Colonel Anderson's inquiry into the causes—Explosions of gunpowder caused by striking with a hammer before a committee—Tabular statement of explosions in the mills—Inquiry into time and cause of explosions—All the explosions took place in the day—Supposed causes—The greater number in the hottest season—Why Nos. 2 and 3 mills should have exploded more than the others — Time of working, and quantities of powder produced — Reason why no old copper or brass should ever be worked up.

ON THE MODERN IMPROVEMENTS IN ARTILLERY AND FIRE-ARMS . . . 246
Improvements in America preceded those of Europe—Iron-plated vessels—Storms's breech-loading rifle—Colonel Colt—In France under Napoleon I.—In the reign of Louis Philippe—Under the Duke of Orleans—Monsieur Tamisier's rifled mortar—The Duke de Montpensier's encouragement—Not the first inventor of rifled guns—Patent of James Bodmer, 1813—In 1850—Under Napoleon III.—200 rifled guns with the Army of Italy—Prussia had 60,000 men armed with rifles in 1848—Continued improvements in cannon—All the continental nations engaged in these—Great Britain of late years not behind others—Varieties of arms in the International Exhibition—Impossible to state their relative values justly, without the necessary trials under the action of gunpowder—Necessity of not neglecting every improvement—Progress of events has changed the science and *matériel* of war both by sea and land—Important points of controversy and experiment as to solid or built-up guns—Rifling or smooth bore, &c.—Can only be settled by trial and experience—Advantages of the results of experiments being publicly known—Improvements in the manufacture of iron under the Mersey Steel and Iron Works Company—Bessemer and other processes of late years—Meritorious labours of Captain Blakeley—Robins's experiment on the deflection of round balls in the Charter House Garden—Mr. Dashley Britton's valuable improvements—The advantages gained in the flight of rifled balls—Curious phenomenon of the velocity and momentum of a rifle ball increasing for a short distance after leaving the muzzle—Attempt to explain it—Smooth bores best for heavy guns—Advantages of the breech-loading construction—Best plan of sustaining the recoil of the breech-plug—Singular variety, but nearly equal accuracy in range in the Enfield, Jacob, Lancaster, and Whitworth systems of rifling—Advantages of forming shot tapering to the rear, as Nature teaches us in the shape of birds and fish—Mr. Whitworth's testimony to its advantages—Time and experience will establish it—For heavy guns the form of rifle grooves requires serious consideration—The best form not yet determined—Advantage of having an excess of metal about the breech, applicable to all cannon as well as fire-arms—General Jacob's opinion—Advantages of modern improvements—The question of the best gun not yet settled — Failure of the 120-pounder Armstrong gun at Shoeburyness—Table of comparative trial of the Armstrong and Whitworth guns—Captain Blakeley's gun highly approved of in Spain—Severely proved at Woolwich — Expectations from Sir William Armstrong's 600-pounder gun — A 400-pounder by Mr. Lynall Thomas — Another by Mr. Whitworth.

EXPERIMENTS ON THE FORCE AND PENETRATION OF SHOT, WOOLWICH, 1651 261
Statement of the trials against timber butts—Remarks on the strength of the powder and great penetration of shot more than 200 years ago.

ALLAHABAD EXPERIMENTAL POWDER DRIED BY STEAM HEAT 263
My reasons for making this trial—Permitted by Military Board—Description of the temporary means I used—Materials carefully prepared—Attribute the superiority of this powder greatly to carefully selected charcoal—Proof reports of this powder as compared with that of Ishapore—Madras and Bombay.

WAR ROCKETS 270
Antiquity of this weapon—Attempts to improve, as an officer of the Bengal Artillery—Offered my services to the Earl of Moira in 1814 to make rockets for the Nepaul War—Offer declined, as the Congreve rocket had been sent for

b

CONTENTS.

from Europe—Returned to Europe—Made apparatus at my own expense, and on my own plan and invention, to take to India on my return—The value of the rocket as an aid to Artillery—Advantages—Explanation of the cause of flight—An error as to this cause long maintained; endeavoured to correct it in the "Encyclopædia Britannica," but error still continued—Marshal Marmont's opinion of the value of rockets—Faults of construction and combination in the Congreve rocket—Continued to the present day, as shown by the specimens in the International Exhibition—In consequence of the irregularity of flight of the Congreve rocket the weapon is held in contempt—Colonel Boxer's statement of their great irregularity of flight—Failure of the rocket in India during the mutiny 22nd May, 1858—Many other failures in Bengal, Madras, and Bombay could be detailed—Late failure with the army in China—Large sums have been expended on the Congreve rocket—Effect of the intimidation of rockets on a Royal Regiment of Dragoons at Meerut in 1821 or 1822—Not allowed to make any rockets in India until Mr. Adam was acting Governor-General—In consequence of the failure and defects of the Congreve rockets I was ordered to prepare 70 for a comparative trial—The trial took place at Dum-Dum May 31st, 1834—Report of the Commandant of Artillery—Extract from "John Bull" newspaper, showing that my rockets had a rotary motion—Rocket manufactory established under me at Allahabad in 1826—Reports of Captains Graham and Blake on the rockets produced—Gunpowder works and rocket ditto closed by Lord William Bentinck — Return to Europe — Mr. Hale's patent for a rotary principle in rockets taken out in 1844, twenty years after I had invented it—Repeated offers to the Government of this country to show how to improve the weapon declined—Large rockets made by the Birmese for fireworks—The most formidable vertical fire can be produced by large rockets which no other projectile can equal—Would be of the utmost advantage in aid of the Volunteers in resisting invasion—No other ammunition so safe in store—Late offer to the War Office declined—Effect of heat in the combustion of a rocket — The reverberatory action causes the great intensity of heat and force in large charges of gunpowder in cannon.

ON THE VELOCITY WITH WHICH AIR RUSHES INTO A VACUUM 283
An interesting inquiry to an artillerist—No vacuum can take place behind a shot—Inquiries on this subject in the year 1686—The celebrated Dr. Papin's communication to Royal Society—Error in considering the resistance of the air as acting only in front of the shot—The friction of the air on the surface of the ball is the great cause of resistance—Cause of the report of a gun—No vacuum is formed — Not even in the passage of a current of lightning—The striking on the air causes the thunder, the friction the lightning—A cannon ball would produce the same if it moved fast enough.

MEMORANDA BY COLONEL ANDERSON . . 287
Power required to start the cylinder mills at Ishapore—Detail of experiment.

EXPERIMENTS ON THE HEATING PROPERTIES OF COAL AND FIREWOOD. . . . 288
Quantity of each required to evaporate mother waters—Relative cost of wood and coal—Statement of prices.

EXPLOSIONS OF MILLS 290
Explosion of No. 2 mill—Experiments to try the causes of explosions.

FIREWOOD AT ISHAPORE 291
Trial of weight when wet and dry.

EXPERIMENTS WITH COMPOSITIONS OF NITRE AND CHARCOAL . . . . . ib.
Detail of experiment—Table of results.

PENDULUM GUN EPROUVETTE . . . 293
Description of woodcut — Principle of construction — Claim of Chevalier D'Arcy to the invention—Trial of result of increase of charge—Trial with large and small grains of powder.

VARIOUS PATENTS FOR IMPROVEMENTS IN MAKING GUNPOWDER 296
Remarks upon them—Private manufacturers should search for information from the best sources—Iron mills will probably supersede stone or gun-metal—The advantage of experience in all circumstances connected with this manufacture.

LIST OF PLATES.
WITH REFERENCE TO PAGES.

PLATE		PAGE
I.—Charcoal Furnaces for charring with Iron Cylinders.	to face	50
II.—Mixing-barrel, and Sieve to extract Bullets (Referred to in pages 63—65.)	,,	63
III.—Plan of Mixing-house with one Barrel	,,	65
IV.—Mixing-barrels and Glazing-reels, with the Adaptation of Cog-wheels to save Manual Labour	,,	68
V.—Incorporating of Grinding-mill used at Ishapore	,,	69
VI.—Press for Gunpowder, as used at Ishapore	,,	90
VII.—Plan, Section, and Elevation of Press-house	,,	ib.
VIII.—Corning-machine, used at Ishapore	,,	101
IX.—Glazing-reel, Filter for damaged Powder. Packing of Hoops and Staves of Barrels. (Referred to in pages 104, 205, 206.)	,,	104
X.—Section of a Charcoal or Sulphur-mill, with Sifting-reel, proposed to be erected at Madras	,,	206

Note omitted in Sir W. B. O'Shaughnessy's analyses of Ishapore powder, page 213, under CHARCOAL.

Density of selected Pieces.

Urhur . . . . ·138
Jointee . . . . ·213

Line 18 from top should be 100 grains of the coarse variety of gunpowder.

THE

HISTORY OF GUNPOWDER.

THE question yet remains to be determined, who were the first inventors and manufacturers of gunpowder.

Mr. Dutens, in his inquiry into the origin of the discoveries attributed to moderns, infers with a reasonable appearance of justice, that Gunpowder was known at a much earlier age than is usually supposed. This learned author thinks "that the attempts of Salmoneus, King of Elis, to imitate thunder and lightning, suggests to us that this prince used a composition of the nature of gunpowder. Eustathius (a commentator on Homer), in particular, speaks of him on this occasion as being so very expert in mechanism, that he formed machines which imitated the noise of thunder; and the writers of fable (whose surprise in this respect may be compared to that of the Mexicans when they first beheld the fire-arms of the Spaniards) gave out that Jupiter, incensed at the audacity of this prince, slew him with lightning as he was employing himself in launching his thunder." But it is much more natural to suppose that this unfortunate prince (an inventor of gunpowder) gave rise to these fables by having accidentally fallen a victim to his own experiments.

This supposition would carry the invention back to the fabulous age of Grecian history.

Dion Cassius, a native of Bithynia, who flourished about A.D. 230, reports of Caligula, that this emperor had machines which imitated thunder and lightning, and at the same time emitted stones. Joannes Antiochenus corroborates the same statement.

Philostratus, who lived about the year 244, wrote the life and travels of Appollonius Thyanœus, a philosopher who is considered to have made extended travels in the East and in Hindostan. On the authority of this traveller, it is recorded "that when the Indians of towns are attacked by their enemies, they do not rush into battle, but put them to flight by thunder and lightning." On the same authority it is said, "that Hercules and Bacchus, attempting to assail the Indians in a fort where they were intrenched, were so roughly received by rciterated strokes of thunder and lightning launched upon them from on high by the besieged, that they were obliged to retire."

Agatheus, an historian of the time of Justinian, reports also "that one Authemius having fallen out with his neighbour Zeno, the Rhetorician, set fire to his house with thunder and lightning." In the works of Julius Africanus, who flourished A.D. 220, Mr. Dutens mentions, that there is a receipt for an ingenious composition to be thrown upon an enemy which nearly resembles gunpowder. We now lose sight of the Latin authorities; more precise information being probably lost in the dark ages of the Gothic period. An Arabian physician, called Mesue, is the first author brought forward as evidence. He lived about the 9th century, and mentions an author, called Marcus Græcus. A work in manuscript exists under the name in the Royal Library at Paris, entitled "Liber Ignium." This author describes several ways of encountering an enemy by launching fire upon him; and among others gives the following: Mix together one pound of live sulphur, two of charcoal of willow, and six of saltpetre, reducing them to a very fine powder in a marble mortar. He adds that a certain quantity of this is to be put into a long narrow and well compacted cover, and so discharged into the air.

This is a clear description of a rocket; and the entire extract speaks of the composition and the effects of gunpowder. The composition was known as Greek Fire.*

* There were several kinds of Greek Fire spoken of by different authors.—EDITOR.

Rockets were also prepared during the reign of the Emperor Leo, about A.D. 880. The Greeks were exceedingly cautious to retain the secret of the composition, hence it may not have been mentioned in books. We have no positive trace of the use of this composition in rockets previous to the time of the Emperor Leo. The fire-engine, or siphon, mentioned by Thucydides is concluded to have been a species of pump, ejecting on the besiegers of towns naphtha, oil, and rosin, in a melted state. These were revived previous to the days of Leo by the earlier emperors of Constantinople, and may in some manner connect the rocket composition of this emperor with the composition in the time of Julius Africanus.

A.D. 1099, according to Maimbourg, in his " History of the Crusades," the Saracens defending Jerusalem against Duke Godfrey, "threw abundance of pots of fire and shot fire-darts against the machines to burn them.' On his side, the duke observing that the enemy had filled up the breaches with hay, wood, rags, and soft combustible matter, caused a great quantity of fire-darts to be shot, which set the whole in a blaze, and caused the fall of the city."

Frequent mention is made of these fire-darts.

Next, in 1216, we have mention of gunpowder by Friar Roger Bacon. "That from saltpetre and other ingredients we are able to make a fire that shall burn at what distance we please." The other ingredients appear to have been studiously concealed at first under a transposition of the letters : thus—*lura mope can ubrie* stood for carbonum pulveri. The friar told his secret, and the ingredients appeared by name in subsequent works. The French assert that *bouches à feu* existed at Amberg A.D. 1301, and were something of the form and shape of our present mortars, but made of wood hooped with iron, probably to cast balls of this Greek fire.

Some authors consider that Bartholdus Schwartz, or the Black, first discovered gunpowder in the year 1320, and that it was used by the Venetians during a war with the Genoese in the year 1380.

It was also employed against Lorenzo de Medici at a place called Fosso Cloidia, when all Italy made complaints against it, as a manifest contravention of fair warfare. When Mahommed the Second besieged Constantinople in 1455, he is said to have used metal mortars capable of throwing stone balls of 200lbs. weight.

Gunpowder also appears as a means of defence used by the Moors in 1343, when besieged by the King of Castile. The ships of Tunis had certain iron tubs or barrels wherewith they threw thunderbolts of fire.

As rockets had ample openings to the rear, and their flight was only opposed by the atmosphere, it is easy to understand that the stronger the composition, the quicker the rocket escaped away from the expanding fluid; but when the tube was fixed, and the basial opening closed up, with a view to propelling balls, it was soon found that the cases of the rockets were rent to atoms. Hence, in the first experiments on artillery as projecting shot, we find it mentioned that the very weakest powder was used, of equal parts of charcoal, nitre, and sulphur, the tubes for which were probably made of thin iron, leather, or wood. As the means were found for making these tubes of more tough materials and of greater magnitude and tenacity, the strength of powder was by degrees increased, until reaching the present relative proportions of ingredients. The quantity of saltpetre has been gradually increased.

A sort of universal belief has given to China or India the credit of being the birthplace of this destructive compound. As saltpetre, its chief ingredient, is largely found in Bengal and to the north-west of India, and probably on many of the vast plains eastward, in the direction of China, this assertion has a probability well founded. At the same time, until the passage round the Cape of Good Hope was discovered, gunpowder must have been an extremely expensive article of European warfare. A camel could hardly carry sufficient saltpetre for 300lbs. of gunpowder.

The nitre of Bahar may have reached the west coast of India, thence been shipped to some part of Arabia, and thence carried on camels across the desert to Egypt; or it may have been conveyed in coasting vessels either up the Red Sea to Suez, or the Persian Gulf to the capital of that country on the Euphrates. On the other side the nitre of Siestan would reach the Caspian, and thence be carried to the various districts of Asia Minor. From the heavy damp nature of the article, and its liability to be spoiled by rain, the cost of transport by land must have been excessive, almost reaching a point of prohibition, unless in small quantities as a matter of curiosity, or as a drug for medicinal purposes. We may thus infer that gunpowder could not have been in general use in Europe at a very early period, and that in all probability the knowledge of the manufacture and use did slowly progress from the East. In this mode may be accounted for the first appearance of gunpowder among the Turks, Venetians, and Moors; while their enemies, the Austrians, Genoese, and Spaniards, were taken unawares by its destructive effect.

John Bell, of Antermony, on his journey to Pekin, records, under date 1721, January 1st :—" The Emperor's General of Artillery, together with Father Fridelly, and a gentleman named Stadlin, an old German, and a watchmaker, dined at the Ambassador's. He was by birth a Tatar, and by his conversation it appeared he was by no means ignorant of his profession, particularly with respect to the various compositions of gunpowder used in artificial fireworks. I asked him how long the Chinese had known the use of gunpowder; he replied, above 2000 years in fireworks, according to their records, but that its application to the purposes of war was only a late introduction. As the veracity and candour of this gentleman were well known, there was no room to question the truth of what he advanced on this subject."

In the Ramayana it is stated, that the ban or rocket of Megnath, son of Rawun, which instrument was called Sangee, emitted a blaze of light equal to the flame from a thousand suns!

Several of these wonderful rockets were dignified by proper

names, and were hurled by their masters with great precision and effect.

If we turn to Persian history for any information on the subject, we do not find much bearing directly upon this explosive compound as propelling projectiles. Ferduosee, the author of the celebrated "Shah-namuh," had clearly heard something of the use of this compound; he describes the undoubted effects of rockets, but, like all the Arabian and Persian authors, attributes the effect to sorcery or jadoee. "One Sawuh Shah, a Tork, at the head of a large army, crossed the frontiers of Persia, and marched on the capital. Buhram Chuobeenah was appointed by the Persian King to command the army sent to oppose the invaders. The armies met on the plains of Herat. Ferduosee then introduces Sawuh Shah, ordering his *jadoee* to be commenced, that the Persian army might be dispirited, and his own preserved. On the command, Jadogurs set to work and launched fire into the air. The chief sorcerer, or head man, was mounted on a lion; in his right hand he grasped a snake, while his left controlled a dragon. He directed the work of destruction, causing the field of battle to be covered with flame; a wind arose, and dark clouds appeared, from which showers of arrows descended on the Persian army. Buhram entreated his band of warriors to believe the whole an ocular deception, to close their eyes, and charge. Sawuh Shah was killed in the battle, and all the Jadogurs taken prisoners were destroyed."

We may in this description clearly trace the rocket in its flight, the dark clouds of smoke, arising from some description of fireworks, under cover of which the soldiers shot forth their arrows: even the metaphors used by the poet for the implements of the chief sorcerer, or fire-master, are the very names long employed for ordnance of different kinds, as snake, bazilisk, serpent: none could better represent tubes vomiting forth flames.

These wonderful instruments are described as being with a Toorkee army, and entirely unknown to the warriors of Persia. Buhram puts the Jadoees to death, as workers of deeds of impiety.

Benjamin, of Todela, visited Persia in 1173 ; he mentions having seen suns and other fireworks.

When Teemoor Mulek, Prince of Khojund, fled in boats down the river Sehoon from his capital, ere it was captured by Chungeez Khan about A.D. 1219, Meer Khawend (Mirconde) in the "Ruozet al Sufa" thus relates :—

"As soon as the Moguls were in reach of the enemy, they hurled a vast quantity of darts, arrows, and fire at the barks of those of Khojund, but the brigantines, which were proof against these attacks, received no damage, for the leader had them plastered over with a certain composition, which was made of wet felt, kneaded with clay and vinegar ; and the nature thereof was such, that neither the arrows nor fire could hurt these vessels : again, upon a signal given to him that some brigantines full of tar and naphtha were got near the pontoons, of which the bridge was made, and were going to set fire to them, the Prince escaped in his boats."

The indication is of pots of burning composition, thrown to set the boats in flames : no fair inference of powder of a propellant nature can here be sustained. Fire-arms do not appear to be distinctly mentioned, or even hinted at, during the conquests of Chungeez Khan.

According to Carpini, "one Presbyter John (Ferishtuh Khan), a king of certain Christians of India Major, marched to oppose this Mogul conqueror, Chungeez Khan. Making men's images of copper, he sat them each upon a saddle on horseback, and put fire within them, and placed a man with a pair of bellows on the horse's back behind every image ; and so with many horses and images in such sort furnished, they marched to fight against the Moguls or Tartars, and coming near unto the place of battle, they first of all sent those horses in order one after the other, but the men that sat behind laid I wot not what upon the fire within the images, and blew strongly with their bellows, whereupon it came to pass that the men and the horses were burnt with the wild-fire, and the air was darkened with smoke."

This attempt may have been the first rocket troop, but more

probably consisted of combustible images like the Rawuns, constructed by the Indian soldiers, to be blown up on one of their grand holidays.

The use of vinegar as an antidote to fire is also mentioned in the history of the Crusades.

When Toolwec Khan, in 1228, after the death of Chungeez Khan marched from Central Asia to the southern districts of China, he is said by Persian historians to have betaken himself to Jadoee, for the purpose of discomfiting a large Chinese party.

"The Tatar magicians or sorcerers had a means, by the use of certain stones thrown into the air, of producing heavy clouds, thunder, lightning, and a discharge of rain or stones. Incantations, forms, and ceremonies, were previously in secret performed; among others, the stone called 'yudah' was to be well washed in the urine of a pure virgin." Perhaps in the stone we may trace the sulphur dug up from the earth, and in the saline taste of nitre the urine; the unburnt composition found on the fields of battle may have appeared dense as stones, and their concealed laboratory work in preparing the compositions been viewed as secret ceremonies. The other phenomena mentioned, may be those of rockets, having stones mixed with their exploding compositions, thrown into the air.

Real loss or injury by these instruments is seldom mentioned; the indication is as of something unreal, as before mentioned, some illusion which was perhaps more confined to terrifying the enemy by fire, noise, and smoke, than by any real projectiles; for had many of these been thrown, some must have been picked up on the field of battle.

A Toorkee Dictionary gives Juduh kash; Arabic, Hejr-al-metr; Persian, Sung-yuddah;—" a stone used by the Tork magicians, which, being thrown into the air, produces all sorts of convulsions of the elements, but which are often turned by the Almighty against those who employ such impious means."

D'Herbelot, in the "Bibliothèque Orientale," under the word Barud, says, " espèce de sel qui s'attache à la pierre nommée

Asius; les Arabes l'appellent encore Thelg Sini, Neige de la Chine, et les Persans Nemuk Tchine, sel de la Chine. Ce mot de Barud est aujourd'hui fort en usage dans les langues Arabique, Persienne et Turque, et se prend pour le nitre ou salpêtre et pour la poudre à canon qui en est composée."

In the metaphor snow of China we trace well-purified saltpetre, and fairly argue, from the adoption of a foreign name, that the substance named did not exist in any country nearer Arabia than a frontier station of China. This last appellation is constantly applied to articles reaching Persia from any stations eastward of the meridian of Herat; any produce of Bokhara would, under certain periods of history, have been considered Chinese.

In the "Institutes of Teemoor," written about the middle of the fourteenth century, are laid down many of the equipments for the soldiers of his army, but there is nothing indicative of the use of matchlocks or of gunpowder. The offensive weapons are bows, arrows, spears and daggers. One list of necessaries runs thus:— 1 bow; 1 quiver; 30 arrows; 1 spare horse, or yaboo, for carriage of baggage between every two men; 1 tent; 1 pickaxe; 1 billhook; 1 saw; 1 axe; 100 needles; 1 standard; half a mun of rope; 1 hide, and 1 cauldron to every ten men.

In the battle with Muhmood under the gates of Delhi, we cannot trace fire-arms being used by Teemoor, but on the side of Muhmood 120 elephants were drawn up, from the backs of which men scattered fireworks and flung rockets in every direction. It is true that Dow's "History of Hindostan," on the authority of Ferishtuh, states, " that on reaching Meerut, the Moguls having filled up the ditch, placed their scaling ladders, and fastened their hook ropes to the wall, in spite of all opposition, and without waiting for a breach by means of the mines, stormed the place, and put every soul within it to the sword. *The mines, however, having been finished, the king ordered them to be sprung, which blew the walls and bastions into pieces.*"

The word *sprung* used by the translator indicates the use of gunpowder in mines, but fire had always been adopted by the Asians in mining. Galleries were run into the walls, supported by poles and planks, and then filled with straw, which being fired destroyed the support, and allowed the rampart to sink. This attack upon Meerut took place A.D. 1398, at the close of the fourteenth century.

We have noticed above, that about fifty years previous to this date, viz., 1343, the Moors of Spain were using gunpowder against the King of Castile, while the Venetians had also been using it against the Turks. Hence, if Teemoor had not already possession of the secret from his birthplace, Sumurkhund, he may have acquired it in his first expedition into Asia Minor.

During his second campaign against Bayuzeed, it is recorded at the attack on the citadel of Damascus :—

"These platforms were built high enough to command it, from which fire-pots, arrows, and great stones were thrown, as thick as hail. The walls were shaken by *battering rams;* the large pieces of rock in the walls were heated, and shattered by vinegar being cast on them, and then broken by hammers. The walls were sapped, and one of the towers fell; the soldiers rushed into the breach, eighty Persians being crushed under the falling ruins. The troops halted; the breach was quickly filled up by the Syrians, but the wooden props which supported part of the walls being set on fire, the governor came out and surrendered."

During Teemoor's march, there preceded the army a rank of elephants, equipped magnificently, to serve as a rampart; their towers were filled with archers and flingers of *wild-fire*. These elephants were those captured at Delhi, or rather the remnant of them. Elephants appear never to have thriven to the north or west of India.

Up to this point we have no mention of gunpowder in the propellant uses understood by moderns. All is a species of Greek fire, burning but not impulsive.

The Greek emperors at Constantinople purchased peace by the promise of the tribute of the usual customs and duties. But of Smyrna it is thus related :—" There was an exceedingly strong place on the sea-shore, built of freestone, surrounded on three sides by the ocean, and on the fourth by a deep ditch ; it was inhabited by Europeans. It had never been taken by any Mahomedan, or paid tribute. Bayuzeed had besieged it in vain for seven years ; his zeal for his religion made him resolve to summon them to embrace that of Mahomed, or to pay tribute. This place contained a great number of the bravest Christian captains, or rather a band of desperate men who had laid up much ammunition. By means of sapping, battering rams, and fire, the place was stormed, and the inhabitants put to the sword. Two large ships, 'Curaccas,' arrived, and their commanders anchored. Teemoor ordered that some of the Christians' heads should be cast by machinery on board the vessels. This took place in December, 1402."

These machines may have been mortars, and here Teemoor may have obtained his first type of cannon ; for it has been shown that about forty years before this period, projectiles by powder were used in Europe.

We know from history that it was the invariable custom of Teemoor to secure craftsmen, workmen, manufacturers, artizans, add them to his camp followers, and ultimately locate them at his capital ; therefore, if the manufacture of gunpowder, matchlocks, and cannon, was prevalent in Asia Minor among the Christians, it is more than probable he carried back to Bokhara this art, which may hence take the date of its re-introduction into Asia. We find the matchlocks and guns were always considered Feringhee (or European), and that all the masters of the art of gunnery in Asia were denominated as Roomee, Feringhee, or Osmanlee-Torks ; and almost the whole of the terms used in the art by the Asiatics are of Toorkee derivation, as *Koor Khannuh* (magazine), *Shumkal* (hand cannon), *Kourchee, Toopchee, Bundookchee*, and *Topunchee* ; all are derived from the Moghul or Toorkee language.

About one hundred years after the period of the conquests of Teemoor, we have, at the close of the fifteenth century, the memoirs of Babur as a guide.

In his early rebellious forays, risings, and battles beyond the Oxus and the Juehoon, we do not trace any notice of gunpowder. Arrows from cross-bows are mentioned as *Teer-tutchsh*, which, the translator adds, may mean a war-rocket. One man is mentioned who shot from this machine exceedingly well, and wounded a great many people.

The defence of Sumurkhund against Shubanec Khan is detailed at some length. All sorts of weapons are mentioned, as well as operations offensive and defensive; some of them are so described as plainly to indicate that projectiles propelled by gunpowder were not used.

Neither in his attack upon the town of Kandahar, nor in the long detailed list of plunder taken, is there any trace of cannon or matchlock. But ten or twelve years after this, when Babur had obtained a permanent position in Kabul, he may have found in that capital some of the rude ordnance brought by Tecmoor from Asia Minor, and the art of gunnery may have remained with the descendants of the early *Toopchees*, brought captives from the same land; for we find, on a foray for plunder, the following record:—

"As the people of Bajoor had never seen any matchlocks, they at first were not the least apprehensive of them; so that when they heard the report of these fire-arms, they stood opposite to them, making many unseemly and improper gestures. That same day, **Ustad Uli Kuli** brought down five men with his matchlock, and Wale Khazeen also killed two; the rest of the matchlock men likewise showed great courage and behaved finely; quitting their shields, their mail, and cowheads, they plied their shot so well that before evening seven, eight, or ten Bajoorees were brought down by them, after which the men of the fort were so alarmed, for fear of the matchlocks, that not one of them would venture to show his head." Ustad Uli Kuli was also there again, and on that day too he managed his matchlock to a good purpose. The Feringhee piece was also twice discharged. Wale Khazeen also brought down a man with his matchlock.

I suspect the shield, mail, and cowheads, were used as a kind of stalking horse, behind which the men carried on the operations of loading and firing their pieces, which operations in those early days were most likely a secret service of time and danger. Ustad Uli Kuli is clearly a Persian name.

The translator remarks, " much has been written concerning the early use of gunpowder in the East. There is, however, no well-authenticated fact to prove the existence of anything like artillery there, till it was introduced from Europe. Babur here, and in other places, calls his larger ordnance *Feringhee*, a proof that they were then regarded as owing their origin to Europe. The Turks, in consequence of their constant intercourse with the nations of the West, have always excelled all the other Orientals in the use of artillery; and when heavy cannon were first used in India, Europeans and Turks were engaged to serve them."

After Babur was fairly established at Agra the capital of his dominions, and had obtained possession of the treasures collected in that fort, we notice the services of Ustad Uli Kuli called into play as a *gun-founder*.

" I had directed Ustad Uli Kuli to cast a large cannon for the purpose of battering Biana and some other places which had not submitted.

" Having prepared the forges and all the necessary implements, he sent a messenger to give me notice that everything was ready. On Monday, the 25th Mohurrum, we went to see Ustad Uli Kuli cast his gun. Around the place where it was to be cast were eight forges * and all the implements in readiness ; below each forge they had formed a channel which went down to the mould in which the gun was to be cast. On my arrival they opened the holes in all the different forges : the liquid metal flowed down each channel and entered the mould. After some time, the flowing of the metal from the various channels ceased, one after another, before the mould was full. There was some oversight in regard of the forges or the metal. Ustad Uli Kuli was in terrible

---

* The melting furnaces, from using bellows for blast, were called forges.—EDITOR.

distress; he was like to throw himself in the melted metal that was in the mould. Having cheered him up, and given him a dress of honour, we contrived to soften his shame. Two days after, when the mould was cool, they opened it. Usted Uli Kuli, with great delight, sent a person to let me know that the chamber of the gun for the shot was without a flaw, and that it would be easy to form the powder chamber. Having raised the bullet chamber of the gun, he set a party to work to set it to rights, while he betook himself to completing the powder chamber." *

With the unlimited command of the resources of India, and of the art above indicated, no emperor after Babur will be found without a means so conducive to dominion as a powerful battery.

Soon after this period we may safely allow to have been cast all the numerous immense pieces of artillery which used to be found in the various old forts of India. Many also have been carried away as trophies to Europe by the different nations who have effected conquests in Hindostan.

The early Portuguese visitors of India and China state, that they were received with rejoicings by fireworks and explosions like thunder by gunpowder contained in hollow cases.

The services of two *artillery officers* are thus spoken of in the despatches of Babur on his victory at Biana.

Previous to the battle, Babur fortified the guns in front and connected them by chains.

"Mustafa Rûmi had disposed his guns according to the Rûmi fashion. He was extremely active, intelligent, and skilful in the management of artillery. Ustad Uli Kuli was jealous of him.

" And the wonder of our times, Mustafa Rûmi, from the centre, directed by my excellent, upright, and fortunate son, who is regarded with favour in the sight of the Creating Majesty, and distinguished with the particular grace of the Mighty King who commands to do and not to do, having brought forward the

---

* This clearly describes that the founder must have had a pattern to follow, of a gun formed in separate pieces, having a powder-chamber perhaps similar to the ancient patterns of China and Europe.

cannon, broke the ranks of the Pagan army with matchlocks and guns (black), like their hearts."

"While the miracle of the times, Ustad Uli Kuli, who was stationed with his men in front of the centre, having exhibited great proofs of valour, discharged large bullets of such a size, that if one of them were placed in the scale of duty, then the man whose scale is heavy gains a name among the blessed ; and if thrown against a rooted hill or a lofty mountain, it would drive them from their foundations liked teazed wool. Such were the bullets he darted on the iron-clad lines of the heathen lands ; and from the discharge of balls, and guns, and matchlocks, many of the sons of the heathen were annihilated. The imperial matchlock-men, according to orders, having issued from behind the artillery, in the heat of the fight, each of them made many Pagans drink of the draught of death."

During the closing period of the Afghan dynasties, which ruled in India between the last of the Ghuzneevide chiefs and the first of the Mogul kings, we trace fire-arms and artillery coming into more common use with the concomitant decline of bows and arrows. Thus, two Afghan chiefs held out Chunar with great gallantry against the troops of Babur's son, Humayoon, the greater part of the besiegers falling by the fire of the artillery.

"Sheer Shah, in his attack upon a fort called Raisein, drew the artillery of other citadels to his camp, and planting it upon high scaffolds, pressed so hard on the fort, that the garrison had scarcely time to breathe ; besides that, he placed mine pipes filled with powder at the foot of the besieged place on all sides."

On these high scaffolds we may suppose wall-pieces or smaller cannon placed, rather than heavy guns.

Sheer Shah himself subsequently fell a victim to his own artillery devices, in an attack on the fort of Kalinger. It is related : "Sheer Shah upon this ascended the scaffolds, and having cast with his own hands some bombs into the forts, he descended, and going to the place where the bombs lay, gave orders for the bombardment to be kept up. At this moment a shell that was thrown against the wall rebounded, and fell down amongst the store of bombs, which, catching fire, all at once blew up.* Sheer Shah was carried away half burnt and died.

"When the Mogul party under Humayoon advanced from Kabul to expel the Afghans, Islam Shah, the Putan king, was urged to advance towards the frontier. On a representation that the bullocks for dragging the artillery were in the country, he ordered men to drag the guns instead of the animals. It is said that he had sixty guns with him, each of them drawn by one thousand men; notwithstanding which, he advanced every day twelve miles, the artillery always arriving in advance at the halting station."

About the year 1580 was written the "Ayeen Akbarree." In it we find less than might have been expected on these important subjects—gunpowder and artillery.

The price of saltpetre is stated at that time as from thirty seers to four maunds for the rupee, about one halfpenny per pound, for the finest quality. Under the head of artillery we read—"These are the locks and keys of the empire, and excepting Room (Constantinople), no kingdom can compare with this in the number and variety of its ordnance. Some pieces are so large as to carry a ball of twelve maunds (the Tabreez maund of eight pounds), and others require, each, several elephants and a thousand bullocks for their transportation.

"His majesty gives great attention to this department, and has appointed to it daroghas and clerks. He has invented several kinds; some of which are so contrived as to take to pieces for the convenience of carriage, and when the army halts are nicely put together again. Also seventeen pieces are so united together, as to be discharged by one match. There are others which can be easily transported by one elephant, and they are called gujnal; others can be carried by a single man, and they are called nurnal.

"It has been wisely ordered that a sufficient train of artillery be placed in each Soobuh. The cannon for battery, and for boats,

---

* Here we have the first mention of bombs with fuses, as used in Hindostan.
—Editor.

and those which are fit for journeys are kept separate. In this department omrahs and uhdeyans receive large salaries : the pay of the foot soldier (private) is from 100 to 400 dams," the last sum values ten rupees. The price of matchlocks is noted as varying from half a rupee to one mohur (sixteen rupees), and of war-rockets from two and a half to four rupees.

I now extract a passage from the History of the Mogul Emperors, stated to be a translation from an account written by a Monsieur Manouchi, a Venetian, who resided at the Court of Aurungzeeb for many years. The anecdote is amusing and illustrative of the customs of a class of persons—the European gunners, who were more numerous at the various Courts of Indian potentates than is usually supposed.

" The projects of war which Akebar was continually forming on one another obliged him to erect a school for cannoneers. There was artillery enough in the Indies, and there is reason to think that the Chinese, who doubtless had been formerly masters of Hindoostan, had left some pieces there of which it is impossible to discover the antiquity.

" It happened, unluckily, that there were but few in the Indies who knew how to make use of them with the same art that we do in Europe.

" Akebar, therefore, resolved to employ Europeans, and invite them by rewards to come to Agra. The English had made settlements not long before on the coast of Hindoostan, and soon acquired a great reputation of valour. In sea-fights they commonly had the advantage of the Portugals. They are since established at Suratte, where they begin to carry on a great trade. It was from the town of Suratte that Akebar procured Englishmen for his artillery. One of these gunners had an extraordinary reputation of skill among those of his own country, and was no less famous for drinking.

" He was at a strange loss, when he found himself in a Mahometan country, where taverns are forbid by the law. Mark the cunning of the man to have the liberty and conveniency of drinking. One day that the Emperor had a mind to see the trial of his skill, there was a large piece of cloth set up for a mark, at a reasonable distance on the other side of the river, where the gunner was to shoot. The Englishman levelled his piece so ill, that he did not come near so fair a mark. The King was surprised, and began to abuse him. 'Sire,' says the Englishman, 'ever since I have left off drinking wine, my sight is so weakened that I do not perceive the plainest object at a very small distance. Nothing but wine is capable of restoring the organs of my sight, and making me perceive objects as I used to do.' The place was never without wine. Akebar kept some for his own drinking, and the elephants had every day a certain quantity given them. The King ordered a bottle to be brought for the gunner, who drank it off at a draught. Then desiring that the mark might be changed (which after his wine seemed too large) for another not much broader than the diameter of the bullet, he hit it exactly, and had the King's applause.

"From that time Akebar allowed his European gunners to plant vineyards about Agra, and the wine they make there is excellent. This ordinance of the King's was inserted in the 'Chronicle' with this preamble: wine is as natural to Europeans as water to fish, and to forbid the use of it is in effect depriving them of life.

"This liberty of planting vineyards, which the strangers in the Mogul's service enjoy, is a vast profit to them, wine being scarce and very dear at Agra, and the vines are not subject in the Indies to the hazard of nipping frosts, as they are in Europe, so that it is a certain revenue.

"Nor did Akebar take only English gunners into his service. He sent for artists of all other kinds from Goa; as lapidaries, enamellers, goldsmiths, surgeons, and physicians, all of Europe."

Monsieur Manouchi closed his sketch of the Mogul armies with the following accounts of the artillery for the period closing the seventeenth century :—

"The Emperor has a numerous artillery, and the pieces of cannon which he makes use of in his armies are for the most part older than we have in Europe. Powder and cannon were certainly known in the Indies long before the conquest of Tamerlane. It is said the Chinese, who are supposed to be the first inventors, had cast some pieces of cannon at Delhi at the time of their being masters there. This is the tradition of the country. Every piece of cannon has its particular name according to the custom of the empire; one is called *Orang var*, that is to say, the strength of the throne; another *Bargissitan*, which signifies that which batters bulwarks. The gunners of the empire were almost all Europeans under the Emperors who preceded Aurungzeeb. The present Mogul's zeal for the Alcoran will permit him to employ none but Mahometans. There are hardly any Feringhees to be seen now at court, except physicians and goldsmiths. All the rest have quitted a country where the free exercise of religion is not allowed as formerly. The Emperor has but too well learnt to dispense with our gunners, and, generally speaking, with all our artisans of Europe."

In the preceding imperfect sketch may be seen the progress made by Eastern nations in the art of artillery; guided by practice and experience, they attained to the manufacturing of very large and very heavy pieces of ordnance, such as were capable of projecting balls fully as large as those in present use in Europe.

In the meantime, among the nations of the west, geometry and the higher portions of mathematic investigation have been applied to the art.

Certain laws and principles being demonstrated as true, the art of artillery took its place among the sciences, and books and treatises became common on the subject.

Note by the Editor.

There are so many excellent modern works, in which the early histories of gunpowder and cannon, as well as in our encyclopædias, have been investigated, or touched upon, that I feel it would be quite unnecessary to do more than refer to them in addition to Colonel Anderson's treatment of the subject; and I may recommend particularly Colonel Chesney's work, " Observations on the Past and Present state of Fire-arms," and Mr. Robert Mallet's truly scientific and valuable work " On the Physical Condition involved in the Construction of

Artillery," in which the notes on the above subjects contain much information and instruction.

Few, however, can doubt, at the present day, that to China and India the origin of gunpowder may be traced. It is most probable that the kindling of fires upon the surface of the earth, and using temporary earthen fireplaces, as well as the early use of pottery, which has ever been, and now is, the custom of eastern nations, may have led to the discovery of iron, gunpowder, and glass. The accidental use of ochreous, nitrous, or silicious earths on these occasions may sufficiently account for them; and we cannot wonder that, when no written records were kept, the impenetrable veil of antiquity stops our search. Let us consider the subject of iron alone; the most useful and most widely distributed metal on the earth's surface. We know, from the earliest and most sacred of writings,[*] that the use of iron may be traced back to the greatest antiquity of the race of man, but all is perfectly obscure as to the date of its first discovery, except that it was most extensively used and wonderfully worked up.

And that gunpowder and fire-arms were in use in India in the earliest ages, the following extract—which I am aware has been often quoted on the subject—from Mr. Halhed's translation of the code of Gentoo laws, supposed to have been compiled at the time of Moses, 1500 years before the Christian Era, is convincing proof: " The magistrate shall not make war with any deceitful machine, or with poisoned weapons, *or with cannon and guns, or any kind of fire-arms.*"

And thus, though the invaders of northern India may have brought these, the repressive influence of the laws of the Gentoo code, and their effect upon a superstitious, submissive, indolent, and uninventive people, may have caused their use to lie dormant for many centuries after their invaders retired.

[*] Gen. iv. 22.

EARLY ESTABLISHMENT OF THE MANUFACTURE OF GUNPOWDER IN BENGAL.

In the early records of the progressive conquests of England in India, I cannot find that there was any complaint against the quality of the gunpowder used, nor can I obtain any information of the sources from whence this article was supplied, or of the prices paid.

Fire-arms are so clearly the instruments in which the European excelled the native powers, that to them much of the English success is due; hence probably care was bestowed on the subject of furnishing a good description of powder from England, or in purchasing the best kinds from the native manufacturers.

The chief cause of inferiority in gunpowder is that, if the ingredients are not carefully refined, and carefully manipulated, the powder quickly deteriorates from its original strength of propellent force when fresh from the mills.

In the early days of European occupation, war and battle were too frequent to admit of the powder being long stored in the magazines.

With native armies the powder-makers followed the camp; the women of families often manufactured the article for the matchlocks of their husbands; such too at the present day is the custom in the wilds of Afghanistan, where the hand flour-mills of the huts are occasionally seen grinding the sulphur and saltpetre, to fabricate a coarse powder for the use of the men on their sporting occasions or plundering forays.

From the information I can collect it would appear, that up to the year 1784 there existed at Baugh bazaar, near Calcutta, several native manufactories of gunpowder, which supplied the article at a high price to Government. As the population of Calcutta increased, and as some attention was paid by the local authorities to municipal regulations for the protection and safety of lives and properties, these powder manufactories were declared unsafe and dangerous.

From Baugh bazaar the works were removed, in 1784, to Ackra, below Calcutta, where they continued for some years.

Though the situation was favourable as regards public safety, yet the place, as unprotected to the seaboard, was considered to be insecure from an invading enemy.

About the years 1740—50 the Dutch possessed a settlement on the Hooghly, with a fort and factory called Bankoo bazaar. These were located on the lands lying between the villages now called Ishapoor and Nawab Gungo; close to the grand ferry at Pultah Ghaut, and nearly opposite to the celebrated French Government house and settlement of Guerettee.

The Nawab Nazim of Moorshedabad appears to have defeated the Dutch in a battle, and regaining possession of Bankoe bazaar, to have assigned it to Rajah Nubookessen Bahadoor, on payment of a small yearly revenue.

The importance of manufacturing good gunpowder, and the profit to be obtained by such an article, did not escape the attention and scrutiny of the talented, able, but eccentric John Farquhar, then an assistant-surgeon in the service of the East India Company, subsequently better known for the large fortune which he acquired from the various speculations into which he entered, and from his penurious habits.

Few articles of country produce escaped his attention, from silk for the markets of Europe, to *pork* for the bazaars of Calcutta.

In 1794 Mr. Farquhar appears to have moved the Government to obtain from Rajah Nubookossen an exchange between the old Dutch factory and some lands at Satanooly, near Calcutta. This was done; and at Bankee bazaar, now called Ishapore, was laid down the nucleus of the present powder manufactory.

Mr. Farquhar appears to have held a contract with the Government. His powder was made in the native mode, by foot mills under mat houses, and sifted in leather sieves.

In 1796 the magazines of Pultah and Duckinsore were established as reserves for Fort William, by General Kidd, of the Engineers.

The old Dutch buildings, the Pultah magazines, and, indeed, the earlier parts of the different edifices erected by Colonel McLeod and Colonel Galloway, are of most excellent construction.

Land has been from time to time added to the old Dutch factory, until the works have reached their present extent.

In 1820 the agent's house was erected by Colonel McLeod. In the same year Colonel Galloway, returning from a trip to sea for the benefit of his health, fell in with a foreign gentleman at the Mauritius, who appeared well versed in the art of gun casting and metal founding; and he succeeded in bringing this gentleman to Calcutta, and by him, in Fort William, were cast in bronze metal the machinery of the eight mills now in use.

From this time, slowly and progressively, have various improvements been introduced by different agents until the works have attained their present magnitude.

Allahabad Works.

With a view to meet the extended dominion of the East India Company, and in consideration of the advantage of a central position, powder works were in the year 1799 established by Captain Taylor, of the Bengal Artillery, at Poppa Mhow, near Allahabad. From motives of state economy, during the first years of Lord William Bentinck's career as Governor-General, both the powder works at Allahabad and Ishapore were closed for three years, and the Allahabad works have not since been reopened; and it was fortunate that it was so determined, as in the late mutiny and occupation of Allahabad by the mutineers the most serious results would have followed.

The History of the first Establishment of Gunpowder Works in England.

Before quitting the subject of the establishment of powder works, I have deemed that it will be of considerable interest to give such information as I have been able to obtain on this subject through the kindness of Mr. Hart, of the Public Record

Office, which will in a considerable degree afford information as to whence we derived our supplies both of gunpowder and cannon.

The exact period when this important article of warfare, gunpowder, was first made use of by our ancestors cannot now be determined; but from the testimony of various records, as shown by the Rev. Joseph Hunter, in a paper printed in the "Archæologia," vol. 25, it is evident that it was used at the battle of Cressy, for in an account rendered by John Cook, the clerk of the king's great wardrobe, of the monies received and expended by him from the 22nd Dec., 19 Edward III. (1349), it is stated that 912 pounds of saltpetre, and 886 pounds of quick sulphur, were supplied to the king for his guns.

On the 25th November, 1346, the king issued a writ, commanding that all the saltpetre and sulphur that was anywhere to be sold should be bought. The total amount obtained was 750 pounds of saltpetre and 310 pounds of quick sulphur.

In the time of Henry VI. an enterprising merchant of London, John Judde, who was skilled in devising warlike instruments, made at his own expense sixty guns, called serpentines, and also "stuff for *gonnepowdre of saltpietre and sulphur*, to the weight of xx tonne," which he offered to deliver to the treasurer for the king's use under certain conditions, in consideration of which good service the king, by letters patent, dated 21st Dec., in the thirty-fifth year of his reign, constituted him Master-General of the Ordnance for life.

It was not, however, till the latter part of the reign of Elizabeth that public attention was drawn to the necessity of establishing at home the manufacture of gunpowder, which before had been chiefly supplied by importing from abroad. It had been up to that time an open trade; but the Government being compelled, by the menacing attitude which Spain assumed, to provide more efficient means of defence, commenced the granting of patents for the manufacture of gunpowder, which constituted it a monopoly in the hands of those whom the Government thought proper to trust with the privilege.

The first establishment of gunpowder mills of any importance appears to have been at Long Ditton, near Kingston, in Surrey, by George Evelyn, grandfather of the celebrated Sir John Evelyn. He had mills also at Leigh Place, near Godstone, in the same county. The Evelyn family is said to have brought the art over from Flanders. The mills at Faversham, in Kent, were in operation as far back as the time of Elizabeth; but those of the Evelyns, at Godstone, were at this time of the greatest importance.

It appears, also, that on the 28th January, 1589, the thirty-first of queen Elizabeth, was granted to George Evelyn, Esq., Richard Hills, and John Evelyn, gentlemen, licence and authority for the term of eleven years to dig, open, and work for saltpetre within the realms of England and Ireland, and all other dominions where the same should be found, as well as within the queen's own lands and grounds and those of her subjects, except in the city of London and two miles distant from the walls of the same, and the counties of York, Northumberland, Westmoreland, Cumberland, and the Bishopric of Durham, and all the saltpetre so found was to be made into powder for the queen's service.

And on the 26th April, 31 Elizabeth, George Constable, Esq., had similar licence to dig for saltpetre within the counties of York, Nottingham, Lancaster, Northumberland, Westmoreland, Cumberland, and the Bishopric of Durham, for the term of eleven years.

8th of January, 32 Elizabeth (1590), Thomas Robinson and Robert Robinson had a similar licence to dig for saltpetre within the cities of London and Westminster, and within two miles of the city of London, or from the old palace of Westminster, for the term of ten years.

By letters patent, dated 7th September, 41 Elizabeth, after reciting that John Evelyn, John Wrenham, gentlemen, Richard Hardinge, Esq., and Simeon Furner, gentleman, had undertaken to deliver yearly into the store of the Tower of London a greater quantity of good, perfect, and serviceable *corn* gunpowder, meet and serviceable for cannon and caliver shot, at a lower rate than was before paid, whereby the queen would not be driven to seek the said proportion of gunpowder out of any foreign countries, and that they had devised means of making saltpetre, whereby the excessive waste and spoil of woods and other inconveniences to the queen's subjects will be avoided, licence was granted them for the term of ten years to make and work for all and all manner of saltpetre and gunpowder within the realms of England and Ireland, and all other the queen's dominions, and to have the sole making of all manner of saltpetre and gunpowder within the realms of England and Ireland, except in the county of York, the city of York, the counties of Nottingham, Lancaster, Northumberland, Westmoreland, Cumberland, and the Bishopric of Durham; and they had from the last day of April similar licences for those excepted places for the same term of ten years.

These parties were bound, it appears, to deliver during the term 100 lasts of powder; good, serviceable *corn* powder, eight lasts; and eight hundred pounds weight every month, half of which was to be *cannon corn gunpowder*, and half to be caliver corn powder, at the price of sevenpence per pound; and they had permission to sell to the public.

Thus we have established on undisputed testimony that gunpowder of different sized grains, or corned—an art probably obtained from Flanders—was generally used at this time; and that before this date the greater quantity of gunpowder used in Great Britain had been imported from abroad.

It may be a wrong supposition, but with all this *digging* for saltpetre, to the great distress and worrying of the inhabitants of houses in the town and country, gardens, orchards, &c., which led to much discontent, probably our great Shakespeare took the expression—Act 1, Henry IV. :—

> " And that it was great pity, so it was,
> That villanous saltpetre should be *digg'd*
> Out of the bowels of this harmless earth."

Since the general practice in countries where it abounds is to obtain it by lixiviation of the upper soils.

It appears by letters patent, dated 24th January, 18 James I. (1621), that in consequence of the abuses and inconveniences which the inhabitants of this kingdom complained of as sustained from the servants of the above patentees, that the patent was revoked on the 17th December, and after reciting that there was in the kingdom a great quantity of the *mine of saltpetre*, it stated that the King had once determined again to furnish the store of gunpowder by importation, but still as there were inconveniences in this mode of obtaining the necessary supplies of gunpowder, the King thought it expedient to continue the manufacture in the kingdom, and to establish certain vigilance and care to repress all abuses complained of by his loving subjects.

The King then granted to George, Marquis of Buckingham, High Admiral of England; Lord George Carew, Master of the Ordnance; and Sir Lionel Cranfield, Knight, Master of the Court of Wards and Liveries, licence to make and work for saltpetre and gunpowder.

On the 16th of January, 20 James, a proclamation was issued which, after stating the great inconvenience of the sale of weak and defective gunpowder, ordered that no persons should make gunpowder in England and Wales, or any saltpetre, but by warrant of His Majesty's Commission, and that no saltpetre could be sold or bought but to and from the King's powder maker—and all gunpowder was to be proved and allowed by the sworn proof-master, and marked by him, for which he was to have a fee of sixpence the barrel. The marks of the proof-master were three crowns for the best, two crowns if new and strong, but O W and one crown for old powder new worked, but good and strong, and fit for ordnance for one year's service at least.

By an indenture, dated 26th April, 2 Charles I. (1626), made between the King on the one part and Sir John Brooke, Knight, and Thomas Russell, Esq., after reciting that there was never yet made, since the first making of saltpetre in the kingdom, being about the beginning of the reign of Queen Elizabeth, a third part of the saltpetre required for the service of the kingdom, but the King, as well as his subjects, were forced to procure the same from Barbary, France, Poland, Hamburgh, and other places in Germany; and that Brooke and Russell had discovered a new mode of making saltpetre, whereby the King should have whatever quantity was required; the King granted them a licence to exercise this invention for twenty-one years, and they were to be paid £3 3s. 4d. for every hundred-weight of saltpetre delivered into the store in the Tower.

The East India Company by this time had begun importing great quantities of saltpetre, and had erected gunpowder mills in the county of Surrey, but being in an inconvenient situation they were pulled down by the King's direction. The East India Company then petitioned for leave to erect mills in the counties of Surrey, Kent, and Sussex, or any or either of them, and accordingly by letters patent, dated 17th August, 2 Charles I. (1626), they were empowered to do so, and also to convert into powder all such saltpetre as should be imported by them from foreign parts, and to employ the same powder for their own use, or to the use of any of the King's subjects.

28th April, 5 Charles I. (1629), the King granted Richard Lord Weston, High Treasurer of England, and others, commissions to work for saltpetre; and on the 18th April, 10 Charles I. (1634), a similar commission was granted to Richard Earl of Portland and others.

No doubt the manufacture of gunpowder at this time was a very profitable investment of money, and we find by a commission dated 8th March, 12 Charles I. (1637), directed to the Bishop of London, and others, a contract was made with Samuel Cordwell and John Collins for the sole working and making into gunpowder all saltpetre made in England or imported.

A commission dated 26th April, Charles I. (1637), after reciting that grievances had arisen from the indiscriminate sale of gunpowder—Mountjoy, Earl of Newport, and others were ordered and authorised to make choice of and license persons who were desirous of buying and receiving gunpowder from any of the Royal magazines, and selling the same by retail.

7th June (1637), another commission was granted to the

Bishop of London and others, giving the licence to dig for saltpetre, and to make gunpowder.

17th March, 16 Charles II. (1663), was issued a proclamation prohibiting the exportation of saltpetre for three months.

June 5th, 18 Charles II. (1666), a commission was granted to John Lord Berkeley, Baron of Stratton, and Sir John Dunscombe, Knight, Thomas Chichely, Esq., commissioners for the execution of the office of Ordnance, William Legg, Lieutenant of the Ordnance, John Evelyn, of Deptford, E. Strong, Esq., Edward Sherborne, Esq., Clerk of the Ordnance, and Jonas Moore, Esq., to dig and work for saltpetre, and make the same into gunpowder for the King's service.

22nd July (1689), was issued another proclamation prohibiting the exportation of saltpetre.

Letters patent, dated 29th October, 1692, were granted to " Our trusty and well-beloved subjects—Richard Earl of Belmont, in our kingdom of Ireland ; Peregrine Bertie and Phillip Bertie, Esqs., sons of our trusty and right well-beloved cousin and councillor, Robert Earl of Lindsey, Sir John Huband, Bart., Sir Nicolas Pelham, and Sir John Bucknall, Knights ; William Gulston, William Tindal, Thomas Cox, Rupert Brown, Richard Dayrell, William Barnesby, John Hoskyns, Esqrs.; John Seger Widenfelt, Charles Cox, Thomas Malyn, John Sherman, Patrick Gordon, Samuel Antrim, Jonathan Smith, gentlemen ; Thomas Dawson, and James West, merchants ; and all such others as shall hereafter be admitted and made free of the Company by the name of the Governor and Company, for making and refining of saltpetre within the kingdoms of England and Ireland, and to have continuance for ever."

They were to sell and deliver into the office of the Ordnance two hundred tons of the best white saltpetre, duly refined, within one year from the date of the patent, and every year afterwards such quantities, not exceeding one thousand tons in any one year, as should be required by the Ordnance, at the price of £70 the ton, in case it bore that price in the market; or if not, then at the market price.

HISTORY OF GUNPOWDER.

"*They were also to pay, yearly, during the continuance of their grant, to the Treasurer of the Navy,* 1000*l. towards the relief and maintenance of maimed, aged, and decayed seamen, until a hospital should be built for them; after the erection of which, the money would go towards the support of the hospital.*"

There is no record, Mr. Hart states, that he has met with, of this remarkable charter of incorporation, in any works on the subject of gunpowder, nor is it known when the company was dissolved, or the charter surrendered.

There can be little doubt, however, that, as by the East India Company's Charter, the Company was bound to import a certain quantity of saltpetre annually, for the use of the Ordnance, probably quite sufficient for the Government purposes, that the supply from the Governor and Company was quite unnecessary, and that the discovery of William Tindal and Thomas Cox, Esqs., of a "new way of making saltpetre in great quantities," on which the company was formed, was of no commercial value, and thus the supply of Indian saltpetre led to the discontinuance of their project.*

I have thus, through the kindness of Mr. W. Hart, of the Public Record Office, been able to place before the readers of this volume some interesting facts which will establish the certainty that although the manufacture of gunpowder commenced in England in the time of Edward III. (1345), it was not until the reign of queen Elizabeth, when the improved art was imported from Flanders by the Evelyns, that it was fairly established; also that until the reign of Charles II. the quantity required for the King's service, and of saltpetre also, was not sufficient, and that large supplies were imported from various foreign countries. It will also account for the supply to the East Indian armies after the East India Company had established their manufactories in England, in aid of the quantity furnished to the Bengal Government by the native manufacturers, until the time of Mr. John Farquhar, in 1794.—EDITOR.

---

* According to the charter of 1693, A.D., the East India Company was bound to furnish the Government with 500 tons of saltpetre annually, at from £38 to £45 per ton.

General Principles of Gunpowder.

The first object in the manufacture of gunpowder is, to obtain, in small space and weight, a material which produces, when excited by chemical action, a high propellent force, possessing an expansive power which shall be gradual, progressive and under good control.

Such is gunpowder. Thus the weight of 2 oz. will, in its expansion when fired, propel 1088 oz., the weight of an iron ball placed before it in a mortar, the distance of 100 yards. We are thus supplied with a power the artillerist requires, infinitely superior to the mechanical contrivances of ancient times.

The expansion of gunpowder, though amazingly rapid, is by no means instantaneous, as, if so, it would be totally unfit for the purposes we apply it to, for the following reasons:—we can only apply it to artillery projectiles or fire-arms generally, by using chambers of metal to confine its expanding power, except on the side of the shot or projectile placed before it, in which we allow it to expand. Now all metals consist of particles held together by what is termed the power of cohesion, and that this is only a limited power of resistance, differing in different metals, we know by experiment. Thus fulminating powders, laid upon an open plate of metal, though confined only by the atmosphere, produce a perforation in the plate of metal from the *momentary impulse* of the force; and when applied to cannon or shot placed before it in a confined chamber, shatter both probably, without producing any intended projectile motion.

Hence the advantages of gunpowder; its expansion is progressive, and there is time given to overcome the *inertia* of a weight of matter placed before it, and to impart this force to the projectile, without the evil consequences of fulminating powders.

Gunpowder has also the advantage of being easily transported, and, under proper precautions, with perfect safety; and it is a singular circumstance, that notwithstanding the advance of science, and the wonderful chemical progress of moderns, there has been no substance yet produced that possesses all its advantages, and that the three materials used in its composition from the earliest times, viz., saltpetre, charcoal, and sulphur, have not been superseded by others.*

Chemical Principles of Gunpowder.

Chemistry teaches us that there exist certain properties in matter which, when different atoms of various kinds are brought into contact, will, under the influence of heat, produce the wonderful phenomena called sudden decomposition and consequent explosion, changing their condition from solid particles to an expansive gaseous or aëriform state. We cannot explain *the nature of the power*, but we can, by experiment with it, produce effects, and from these calculate the power we can produce, with other results.

There can be little doubt that, in the first formation of gunpowder, when the science of chemistry was comparatively unknown, accidental circumstances led to these properties being discovered in the mixture of saltpetre, charcoal and sulphur; probably, in the first instance, only saltpetre and charcoal were used.

But at the present day, from the science of chemistry, we find that in these ingredients the following properties exist, which render them so essential for the purpose of forming gunpowder.

In saltpetre, or nitrate of potash, we have a compound consisting of nitric acid and a base of potassium.

Chemists of the greatest celebrity have not given to their analysis the exactness of the proportions, but if we take the fair medium, we may consider saltpetre to consist of,

     Nitric acid 54
     Potassium 46 †

The charcoal and the sulphur may be considered as simple substances if pure; and though this is seldom the case, we must so consider them at present.

In the three components of gunpowder, we have, therefore, a compound and two simple combustibles.

---

* Gun cotton, and other proposed substitutes for gunpowder, will be noticed in the Appendix.—EDITOR.

† Celebrated chemists differ in the proportions. See Appendix.

The compound (the saltpetre) consists of nitric acid combined with a base of potash. The nitric acid consists of oxygen and nitrogen, six parts of oxygen to one of nitrogen; when saltpetre is exposed to a red heat, or above 800°, it decomposes gradually if there is no combustible present, and a portion of the oxygen and all the nitrogen will pass away into the atmosphere, the other portion of the oxygen will unite with the potash, and form oxide of potassium; but when we bring a combustible, as charcoal, into contact with the saltpetre at this heat, a violent and sudden decomposition takes place, and consequent explosion, from its striking the surrounding air so suddenly. The oxygen combines with the carbon, forming carbonic acid gas, and the nitrogen is set free. It is found from experiment that the volume of gaseous or aëriform fluid thus formed, occupies a space as a permanently elastic fluid, about 240 to 290 times that of the bulk of the gunpowder used, when cooled down to the state of the atmosphere; but at the time of explosion the heat generated is so great, that the expansion of this volume of gas is increased from four to eight times in bulk, varying according to quantity and quality of the gunpowder and the circumstances of the explosion. Such is the cause of the amazing power of fired gunpowder.

We have as yet taken no notice of the third material used in the composition of gunpowder, viz., sulphur; nor of the base of the saltpetre, potash. For neither the sulphur nor the potash are elements from which the expanding gas is formed; that proceeds alone from the combination of the oxygen of the nitre with the carbon, for gunpowder of equal strength can be formed with saltpetre and charcoal only; but the sulphur has many valuable properties, which render its mixture necessary and advantageous in the manufacture of good gunpowder; it is highly combustible at a lower temperature, about 550°, and in the combustion, no doubt, assists in the ignition of the charcoal and combines with the potash forming sulphuret of potassium. It has the valuable property, being unalterable itself in moisture, of closing the absorbent pores of the charcoal, and from its hardness and tenacity assists in adding firmness to the grain of gunpowder, qualities that are invaluable when powder is to be stored or transported. Good gunpowder cannot, therefore, be manufactured without a due portion of sulphur.

The question, therefore, now is, what are the best proportions of the three ingredients? Chemists have decided, in general terms, that the proportion of charcoal should be just sufficient to absorb the oxygen of the saltpetre, and the sulphur to saturate the potash. Then, according to the theory of chemical equivalents, the weight of the compound will be the sum of the weights of the equivalents, thus :—

				Equivalents.	
Nitre consists of . .	{ 1 proportion nitric acid .		54	} 102
	1 ,, potassa . .		48	
Nitric acid consists of .	{ 5 proportions of oxygen .	8	40	
	1 ,, nitrogen .	14	14	
Potassa consists of . .	{ 1 ,, oxygen .	8	8	} 102
	1 ,, potassium .	40	40	
	or			
Nitre consists of . .	{ 5 + 1 ,, oxygen .		48	
	1 ,, nitrogen .		14	} 102
	1 ,, potassium .		40	
Carbonic acid consists of	{ 1 ,, carbon . .	6	6	} 22
	2 ,, oxygen .	8	16	
Therefore to absorb it will require	{ 6 ,, oxygen . .	8	48	} 66
	3 ,, carbon . .	6	18	
Sulphuret of potassium will require . . .	{ 1 ,, sulphur . .	16	16	} 56
	1 ,, potassium .	40	40	

Supposing nothing lost in the transfer the result would be—

Nitrogen	14	} 136 or	10·3	} 100
Carbonic acid	66		48·6	
Sulphuret of potassium	56		41·1	

To obtain the three ingredients in these proportions would require—

    136 : 100 : : 102 : 75·08 saltpetre ⎫
                  18. 13·12 charcoal ⎬ per cent.
                  16. 11·8 sulphur   ⎭

Dr. Shaughnessy remarks on the above :—" There are, at least, seven definite compounds of sulphur and potassium, and there are,

---

* Carbonic acid gas was first discovered by Dr. Black in 1757; and Dr. Priestly discovered oxygen gas in 1774; and Dr. Cruickshanks, of Woolwich, made many experiments on gunpowder and these gases, for notice of which, see Appendix.—EDITOR.

at least, two of carbon and oxygen always formed on the explosion of gunpowder. The carbonic acid *in part* combines with potassa ; the sulphur is partly converted into sulphuric acid ; compounds of nitrogen and oxygen, especially nitric oxyde (N 1, O 2), are produced, and in some analyses cyanogen and its compounds have been detected ; all this is cited to show that the results cannot be enunciated in the above simple terms, and admit not of estimation in these simple formulæ."

There is a simplicity in the above calculations ; but as we find that the most celebrated chemists offer different results, and that it is easy to combine under given proportions atomic weights into other and different forms, we must pause ere we accept the above theory as complete.

As regards gunpowder, we may observe, and it is a curious circumstance, that the resulting proportions of chemistry are nearly those universally made use of by manufacturers of gunpowder in early times.

The quantity of gas, the temperature of the combustion, and the expansion under this temperature, are uncertain and varied quantities ; but the average may be taken, that one measure of gunpowder will yield from 240 to 290 equal measures of permanent elastic gas ;* that if the temperature during combustion is as high as 2196° Fahr., this will create an expansion or a propulsive force of about 1592 atmospheres ; taking the atmosphere at only $14\frac{1}{2}$ lbs., there results the astonishing pressure of $1592 \times 14\frac{1}{2} = 22,074$ lbs. on the square inch of surface at the moment of combustion.

NOTE.—I am well aware that many writers on the subject have estimated these measures, temperature and expansive forces, both in excess and below the average statement here given. Great variety will arise from the nature of the charcoal used in the composition, supposing the other ingredients pure, and also from the circumstances under which such experiments are tried, from the quality of the manufactured

* Gay Lussac estimated this quantity of permanently gaseous volume at 450. See Appendix on this subject.—EDITOR.

material and the proportions used. The subject will be further alluded to in the Appendix.—EDITOR.

The following tabular statement of the proportions of the ingredients to form gunpowder used in different countries may well find a place in this portion of our pages :—

	Names of Countries and Places, &c.	Saltpetre	Charcoal	Sulphur	Remarks.
		lbs.	lbs.	lbs.	
Indian	Bengal, Ishapore, and Allahabad	75	15	10	
	Madras	75	13⅓	11⅔	
	Bombay	75	15	10	
	Best Sikh powder	75	12·5	12·5	Probably derived from French officers.
English	England Royal mills, Waltham Abbey	75	15	10	
	Dartford	79·70	12·48	7·82	From French analysis.
	Hounslow	78	14	8	
	Mining powder	65	15	20	
	Government mills, 1808	75	12·5	12·5	
French	Mons. Champy	80	15	5	
	„ Bouchet (sporting)	78	12	10	
	„ Chaptal	77	14	9	
	De Berne	76	14	10	These proportions were made by the French chemists, in order to satisfy the Government which were the best proportions, and the three first were declared strongest, and the third proportion was then adopted, though it contained less charcoal and kept better; but of late years the proportions were adopted of 75', 12·5', 12·5, as the increase of sulphur was found to be a great preservative.
	Poudre ronde	76	14	10	
	Macquer	75	15·5	9·5	
	1794 of Bac	76	14	10	
	Grenelle	76	12	12	
	M. Merveau	76	9	9	
	Ditto	77·32	9·24	9·24	
	M. Keffault	77·50	7·50	7·50	
	Austria	76	13	11	
		75·5	11·3	13·2	
	United States	76	14	10	
		75	15	10	
	Prussia	75	13·5	11·5	
	Switzerland	76	14	10	Spherical grain.
	Hanover	71·2	13·2	10·9	
	Sweden	75	16	9	
	Spain	76·47	12·75	10·78	
	Belgium	75	12·5	12·5	
	Ditto, Carbine	78	12	10	
	Holland	75·6	12·5	12·5	
	Wirtemburg, Artillery	75	12	13	
	„ Infantry	74·6	10·7	14·7	
	Russia	70	18·5	11·5	
	For mining	65	15	20	
	Hesse Cassel	73·3	13·35	13·35	
	Chinese	75·7	14·4	9·9	

Other analyses of 1844 give different proportions to these powders with but slight alterations. But there are many circumstances which will cause variation, and much will depend upon the purity of the saltpetre employed by different manufacturers.

All the various powders agree in these points—to require nitrogen, oxygen, and carbon; to reject all substances attractive of moisture, as hydrogen and its compounds, or sulphuric acid and its salts. Hence it appears the object should be to bring those substances evolving the first desiderata free from all combinations of the latter; or when found together to separate them as far as possible, so as to neutralise the effects of the injurious ingredients.

Saltpetre is found in abundance in Siestan, and between Persia and India; but in Bengal this salt exists, perhaps, in greater abundance than in any other country. The great demand for it in the periods of European warfare, combined with the distance from whence brought, rendered saltpetre a truly valuable article. The greatest exertions were used in France to counteract the English monopoly, but they were not rewarded with the success desired, art being unable to compete with the natural production. Still the attempts led in some measure to a better understanding of the nature of the article.

In some cases advantage was taken of situations affording a portion of the required elements, and by the addition of the other portions the compound was produced.

Thus in cases of limestone containing nitric acid, the stone was pounded up and mixed with earth; to this was superadded ashes obtained from vegetable matter affording potassa; after which the whole mixture was watered. The nitric acid combined with the potassa and rose to the surface, whence, the water being evaporated, the saltpetre was deposited. The carbonic acid united to the lime was allowed to remain at the bottom.

In other cases decaying animal matter of every description was obtained as containing nitrogen and yielding ammonia. This was brought into contact with a mixture of earth and ashes with water, when the same result appeared in an efflorescence of nitre on the surface.

Thus from 433 lbs. of urine thus mixed were obtained 100 lbs. of crude saltpetre.

Experience pointed out that the following conditions required to be fulfilled :—

> The presence of a base ;
> ,, ,, of moisture ;
> ,, ,, temperature above 32° Fahr. ;
> ,, ,, matter containing nitrogen ;
> ,, ,, atmospheric air.

The great difficulty appeared to exist in the obtainment of the nitric acid.

Many other opinions were held. Some considered the presence of carbonic acid necessary, and that both the elements required for the nitric acid were obtained from the atmosphere, and were generated and recombined under certain laws, with reference to the moisture, temperature, and mode of union.

Unable to compete with the natural production, from the time that the material was brought to Europe by commercial enterprise, the manufacture of the article by such processes was abandoned.

The subsequent development of the process of manufacturing saltpetre in the provinces of Bengal indicates that a near approach had been made in France, under the clever chemists of that nation, to the correct elements of the compound, all that was further required being the vivifying energy of nature peculiar to certain locations.

According to Mr. Stevenson's account, all the soils of the districts of Tirhoot, Bahar, and Agra consist more or less of saline matter intermixed with sand and carbonate of lime.

The quantity of saline matter is extremely various, the salt of potash being chiefly found in places tainted with animal matter. There exist also large portions of saline ground, barren by reason of their saltness. During the periodical rains these districts are overflown, the various salts are dissolved and brought into contact, when new combinations follow, and fresh salts result; as the water evaporates or percolates the soil, these are found and collected; the lowest produce of saltpetre being, perhaps, three per cent. of the collection of surface soil, and the highest about thirty-eight per cent.

These products, by repeated washings, evaporations, and filterings, are collected in a mass, valued at three rupees per maund, and contain by analysis—

Moisture	10·6
Sand, mud	22·7
Sulphate of soda	23·8
Muriate of soda	4·2
Nitrate of potash	38·7
	100

This raw material next passes into the hands of the class who crystallise it in the form required by the Calcutta merchants. The crude mass above (called *dhoah*) is boiled in its weight of water; evaporation goes on, and it is skimmed on the surface. The liquor is then let off into a deep tub, where the insoluble matter sinks to the bottom; after that the solution is again transferred into a shallow vat, where in three days the crystals are formed.

These crystals are then well washed in pure spring water, and are then called the *culmee* saltpetre of the Calcutta market, and valued at 94 per cent. of pure nitre, which, however, is full 20 per cent. over estimated.

Mr. Stevenson gives the following result of an experiment to ascertain the quantity of *culmee* saltpetre, extraneous salts, and insoluble matter contained in 20 maunds of native *dhoah*, or crude saltpetre, purchased by the Gomastah at 3 *rs.* 8 *as.* per maund.

Dhoah saltpetre	20 maunds.
Water used in solution	20 ,,
Time in evaporating the solution to a crystallising state	3½ hours.
Fuel consumed (jungle grass)	3 maunds.
Time the liquid remained to crystallise	30 hours.
Temperature after standing 30 hours	84° Fahr.
Produce of *culmee* saltpetre	4 maunds 10 seers.

MOTHER LIQUOR OF FIRST BOILING.

Time in effecting the evaporation of this	3 hours.
Fuel consumed (jungle grass)	2 maunds.
Time setting to crystallise	30 hours.
Culmee saltpetre produced	3 maunds.

MOTHER LIQUOR OF SECOND BOILING.

Time in evaporating	$2\frac{1}{2}$ hours.
Fuel consumed (jungle grass)	2 maunds.
Time in crystallising	30 hours.
Culmee saltpetre produced	1 maund 33 seers.

LAST PORTION OF MOTHER LIQUOR EVAPORATED TO DRYNESS CONTAINED

	Md.	Seers.
Sulphate and chloride of soda	3	5
Insoluble matter, mud and sand	4	36

TOTAL QUANTITY FROM THE 20 MAUNDS OF DHOAH SALTPETRE.

	Md.	Seers.
Culmee saltpetre	9	3
Extraneous salts	3	10
Insoluble matter, mud and sand	4	36
Moisture in the *dhoah*	2	31
	20	0

THE ABOVE QUANTITIES REDUCED TO PER-CENTAGE.

Non-insoluble matter	25 per cent.
Extraneous salts	16 ,,
Moisture in the *dhoah*	14 ,,
Total impurity	55
Nitre or *culmee* saltpetre	45
	100

Such may be estimated as the result of the manufacture of the nitre or saltpetre of the Calcutta market; and, notwithstanding the recorded extraction of 16 per cent. of extraneous salts in the native processes, a large quantity—more than half the above per-centage—still remains, which must be extracted before the saltpetre is fit for the manufacture of gunpowder.

As the gunpowder agency holds forth a demand for a considerable supply of *culmee* saltpetre in its crude state, of course the dealers attempt to sell it to the best advantage, and the agent to buy on the same terms. Tenders are invited for the quantity required, and musters sent. Of each sample fifty pounds are taken, and boiled with an equal quantity of water. On the third day the produce of crystals is weighed, and that tender giving the best result, with reference to the price, is usually taken (provided the terms are in every other respect unexceptionable).

The price multiplied by 61, and divided by the produce of the 50 lbs., gives the rate per 100 lbs. on the price per maund.

In examination of an extended average of the loss in refining the saltpetre of the Calcutta market to the state of purity fit for powder, it may be put down as 32 per cent.

According to the charter of 1693 A.D., the East India Company was bound to furnish the Government with 500 tons of saltpetre at from £38 to £45 per ton. The price in London in April, 1849, was about £28 per ton. Of course, at the present day, the Government obtain their own supplies in the market. Bengal exported on an average of seven years, from 1840 to 1847, of saltpetre 570,300 maunds, valued in invoice at rupees 5 r. 6 a. 5 p. per maund, about £16 the ton.

SALTPETRE.

PREPARATION OF THE SALTPETRE FOR THE FORMATION OF GUNPOWDER AT ISHAPORE.

First Boiling.

In the evening 32 maunds of crude saltpetre of commerce was put with 40 maunds of tank water into each of the large boilers; a strong fire in the furnace below (having proper flues to carry the heat and flame round the boiler before it entered the chimney) was kept up all night, by which the solution was boiled until the morning, when the fire was withdrawn and all impurities that had risen to the surface were skimmed off. A small quantity of cold water was then thrown in to check the ebullition, and cause the lighter impurities to rise, and the muriate of soda and other impurities to subside.

The solution was then pumped off into large wooden vats, and there left to settle for three or four hours; after this the liquor was run off into large wooden vats, 16 ft. square by 18 in. deep, where it was allowed to remain three days to crystallise.

The mother liquor, remaining uncrystallised, was then drawn off, and returned to evaporating boilers, where it was boiled down to a state fit to form crystals, which state was easily ascertained by dipping in a small clean stick, and exposing a drop of the moisture upon it to cool in the air on a cold surface; if crystals form in cooling, the boiling has proceeded sufficiently.

The crystals are now drained from all moisture, and placed in the store as the first-boiled saltpetre.

Second Boiling.

The first-boiled saltpetre was treated in the same manner as in the first boiling, and then run off to cool in copper pans, to avoid any chance of impurity being imbibed from the wood of the vats. These pans were set on an incline, upon elevated troughs, to allow the crystals when formed to be well drained from moisture.

The crystals were then thrown on a canvas-covered platform, and broken up coarsely to allow all impure water in the cavities of the crystals to escape.

The bruised crystals were then put into a washing-tub and washed with cold tank-water, which, carrying with it a small portion of saltpetre as it runs off, will free the crystals from almost all the impure salts which may have remained.

After this the nitre was piled up in baskets over draining troughs, and sprinkled with distilled water from watering-pots. It was then tried with the test of a solution of nitrate of silver in distilled water; and if no cloudiness appeared as it dissolved, was received as pure nitre; and after draining in the baskets for two days, was carried to the fusing-house.

All the washing or draining waters, dirty or clean, were then returned to evaporating boilers; this liquor was kept constantly on the simmer, impurities skimmed off, and the evaporation carried on for about twenty-four hours, till crystals began to form in cooling. These crystals after being drained, were considered and stored as saltpetre of the first boiling. The crystals of the second boiling, after having been tested by the nitrate of silver, and drained in their basket for two days, were then carried to the fusing-house, where they were placed into iron pots, set in proper furnaces, and heated until melted, and then appeared perfectly fluid, and as clear as water. The heat may be continued until a little slip of paper dipped in occasionally begins to ignite; the fire must then be damped, and the liquid nitre ladled off into shallow copper pans, in which it cools in twenty-four hours into a solid cake, opaque, being the sal prunella of commerce, quite free from all water of crystallisation; and when broken and put under the mills, far more easily reduced to a fine powder than when in a crystallised state. The time required to heat a pot of 200 lbs. of saltpetre to the melting point, is about four hours: wood fuel was used in all the furnaces.

Care must be taken in this process that the heat does not reach that of redness, or 1050° Fahr., for then a portion of the nitre would be decomposed; but the test of the strip of paper will guard against this evil.

This process is by many considered unnecessary and useless; it can in no respect render the nitre more pure; and should the pot ever attain a red heat of 1050° Fahr., a portion of the nitre might be decomposed, part with some of its oxygen, and become hyponitrite of potash, a salt extremely attractive of moisture.

The advantage lies in leaving no water whatever in the nitre, and hence the weight given to the powder being quite correct, and always the same. But this difference might be easily calculated.

No very large amount of weight or loss of nitre should result from this operation, except that quantity incidental to all handling; still the fuel, the pots, buildings, labour, and loss, all add to the cost of the powder. Very dry first-boiled nitre, being fused, lost by weight 1·8 per cent., but from waste and other causes 2 per cent. may be considered as the loss.

The fused cakes of nitre, when cool, being broken up by hard mallets, their produce was then placed in the grinding mill of the common construction, viz., vertical wheels running round on a circular bed. These were of iron at the Ishapore Mills, the wheels 7 ft. diameter, with iron rims 16 in. in face, with a small bed of iron to work upon 2 in. thick, and their required weight was made up by filling up the openings of the wheels with blocks of wood.

Three or four bullocks worked the mill, and could turn out 75 lbs. of saltpetre finely ground in forty minutes, a man following the wheels round with a wooden spatula to prevent it caking under the process. Heavier wheels were tried; but though the effect was produced in a shorter time, the nitre was found to cake, and time was lost in breaking the lumps.

When the nitre was considered sufficiently pulverised, it was taken and dried over an iron stove, and afterwards passed to the sifting-house, and sifted in common hand-sieves, the bottoms of which are made of fine Tussore silk.

I am inclined to doubt if there exists any advantage in this very fine sifting; and to ask, if the impurities resulting from too much handling (especially in a hot climate, as India) may not counterbalance the advantage of this minute state. Indeed, pulverised and sifted nitre soon sets together under the dampness of the atmosphere, so that it will hardly pass a second time through the sieve with less labour than the first operation required. The expense of the silk sieve is great. A fine wire one would answer equally well, and save money. The old agency books go far to establish that unfused, coarsely pulverised nitre, and even first-boiled nitre, do not give inferior powder *when* fresh.

At Madras, and in some of the English works, the saltpetre is prevented from crystallising by causing the solution, in the boiling, to cool down and settle under constant agitation; the result being that no crystals of any size are formed, and the saltpetre is produced at once in a fine powder; and where great economy and quick production are required, the process might be followed without disadvantage, and considerable saving of expense.

The average quality of the saltpetre brought to the agency at Ishapore, yielded about 69 per cent. of pure nitre. Prices varied, but the cost of the 100 lbs. of nitre, after going through all the processes of refining and preparation for mixture, was from 13 to 14 *rs.* for the 100 lbs.

The analysis of saltpetre, as given by chemists, differs considerably; but we shall bring this under further consideration in the concluding pages of this book; and in this place will merely allude to

The Tests to try the Purity of Saltpetre as fitted for Gunpowder.

To ascertain the presence of muriates, common salt, &c., a solution of nitrate of silver in distilled water is the most convenient—4 grains of this substance being dissolved in 1 ounce of distilled water.

If a small portion of the refined saltpetre is to be examined, it may be dissolved in pure distilled water, and, if the saltpetre is pure, when a few drops of the solution of silver are mixed with it, no cloudiness or change of transparency will be observed; but if the contrary, and any white cloudiness appears, it denotes the presence of a muriate, and the saltpetre will require further refining. One drop of the solution of the nitrate of silver will indicate the presence of so minute a quantity of muriate as $\frac{1}{480}$.

By this test the quantity of the muriate present may be detected; for if 100 grains of crude saltpetre are dissolved in distilled water, then 2 drachms of the solution of nitrate will throw down a precipitate; and if more be not occasioned by a further addition, the saltpetre may be considered to contain $\frac{1}{4}$ per cent. of common salt: one drachm of the solution will detect $\frac{1}{8}$ per cent.

To ascertain the presence or absence of sulphate of soda, a similar process is followed with a solution of 4 grains of nitrate of barytes to 1 ounce of water; of which solution 2 drachms will indicate the presence of $\frac{1}{2}$ per cent. of sulphate of soda or Glauber salt.

Table of Saltpetre prices: average of six years.

	Bazaar price, per maund.			Bazaar price, 100 ℔.			Outturn reported to Military Board.				Reported cost per 100 ℔.			Loss on first-boiled per cent. of crude.				Residuum per cent.			First-boiled per cent. of crude obtained.				Cost of first-boiled.			Loss on second-boiled per cent. of first-boiled.			Cost of second-boiled.			Loss on refinel per cent. of second-boiled.		Cost of refined fit for powder.		
	r.	a.	p.	r.	a.	p.	℔.	oz.	d.	r.	a.	p.	℔.	oz.	d.	℔.	oz.	℔.	oz.	d.	r.	a.	p.	℔.	oz.	r.	a.	p.	℔.	oz.	r.	a.	p.
Average of six years {1841 to 1847}	6	10	4	8	1	6	65	12	5	12	5	8	20	4	6	10	9	79	11	9	10	8	7	8	12	13	11	4	0	13	15	3

The average run of our pure saltpetre is 69 per cent., which gives 11r. 10a. for the cost of nitre, and 2r. 5a. 3p. for the expense of pulverisation; which may be resolved into—

```
                               r.  a.  p.
Firewood        . .    . .     1   0   0  (about six maunds)
Labour          . .    . .     1   1   3
Wear and tear          . .     0   4   0
                              ─────────────
                               2   5   3
```

Improved Process of Refining Saltpetre.

The usual impurities of unrefined saltpetre—as nitrates and muriates of lime, with other salts having bases of magnesia and soda—dissolve and remain in solution equally in hot or cold waters, and saltpetre has the property of excess of solution as the temperature is increased : advantage has been for some years taken of this property, both in France and at Madras, as well as the saving of labour accruing, in preventing large crystals being formed by the slow process of cooling, by keeping the solution in agitation during the boiling, so as to obtain pure saltpetre in the state of fine meal at one operation. This new system of refining has now been improved upon, and adopted at the Royal Mills, Waltham Abbey, and by some other private manufactories.

A quantity of unrefined saltpetre, according to the size of the manufactory, say 40 cwt., is put into a copper boiler holding 500 gallons, with 270 lbs. of water, and brought to a boiling point ; the impurities are carefully skimmed off as they rise, and a small additional quantity of cold water is occasionally thrown in to assist in precipitating such salts, as not equally soluble with the nitre as the temperature rises. After boiling about $3\frac{1}{2}$ hours, the fire is damped, and those salts that have crystallised fall to the bottom. In about two hours a copper pump is used to pump off the solution into a trough, properly provided with cocks, to each of which a canvas bag of a jelly-bag shape is attached, and the solution runs off through the canvas into large troughs 10 ft. by 6 ft. wide, 9 in. deep, lined with sheet copper, and is kept in a state of agitation with wooden rakes until nearly cold. Thus a large quantity of very minute crystals are formed, which are drawn up by a wooden hoe, and thrown by a shovel on a framework wire sieve resting on the opposite sides of the trough ; here they are allowed time to drain, and have the appearance of fine white snow ; when drained sufficiently, the produce is raked over into a washing cistern conveniently placed, which is 6 ft. long by 4 ft. wide, and 3 ft. 6 in. deep, and fitted with a false bottom of wood, that can be removed at pleasure. A quantity of pure cold water is then allowed to run on the saltpetre into this cistern until it is nearly full; after remaining an hour in this bath, the first water is drained off, and fresh water is again added to fill the cistern. After an hour this is drained off by raising the bottom, and the saltpetre is found to be perfectly pure, and equal to that which used to be obtained in three crystallisations on the old plan of refining.

The water remaining in the cisterns where the solution had been kept in agitation is allowed to remain until the next morning, when a quantity of larger crystals will be found at the bottom and sides.

These are placed with the unrefined saltpetre, and the mother liquor from the agitating cistern is then drained off and evaporated to crystallising density as usual.

The water from each washing of the crystals is conveyed to cisterns, and used with the boiling of the unrefined nitre instead of other water; but, as it contains a small portion of saltpetre in solution, a lesser quantity of the unrefined saltpetre is used to make the proportions correct.

This saltpetre, having a snowy appearance, contains a degree of moisture, which is evaporated by its being placed in 2 copper trays, about 10 ft. 6 in. by 3 in. deep; and these trays are heated by being placed over flues heated by a furnace; 4 in. of dry sand being laid between the flues and the bottom of the trays. The saltpetre is spread about 2 in. thick in strata, and raked about till dry: 4 cwt. will dry in about 2 hours. The saltpetre is then barrelled for use.

Thus the whole process of refining takes place in one day, instead of six on the old plan, and with less than half the amount of labour and fuel.

The apparatus is trifling in quantity, and the space required in the refining building greatly reduced.

Thus, for a refinery to produce 23 cwt. of refined saltpetre per day, the following apparatus will be ample :—

    1 copper boiler, holding 500 gallons, set in a proper furnace, and provided with a wooden trough lined with copper or

lead, and 4 or 5 cocks with canvas filtering bags of the jelly-bag form.
50 copper crystallising pans.
2 copper cisterns, 10 ft. long by 6 ft. wide, and 9 in. deep.
2 wooden cisterns, 6 ft. by 4 ft. wide, 3 ft. 6 in. deep, having false wooden bottoms, easily fitting, and loops to lift by.
2 copper evaporating pots for the mother water, &c.
2 copper drying trays, 10 ft. by 6 ft., with 4 in. rims, and set over furnaces with flues, and a bed of 4 in. of sand, on which the trays are placed.
2 copper pumps, and troughs of the necessary length.
Wooden rakes, shovels, &c., as required, with cisterns to receive the washing water.
The floor of the refinery should be lined with flag-stones, and the sides and roof capable of free ventilation.—EDITOR.

CHARCOAL.

THE common mode of preparing charcoal is to fill a deep pit with the pieces of wood in regular layers, and then to apply fire. The water, gum, mucilage, and other volatile parts distil from the wood; the greater part falls from the upper to the lower strata; to these denser particles succeeds a gas, called carbonic acid, with portions of hydrogen gas. The lighter gaseous matters ascend to the upper strata. Both these exudations are ultimately evaporated, incinerated, or driven off by the fire.

When the carburetted hydrogen gas appears in its purest form coloured with a light tinge of red, and inflammable by a light being applied, the external air is excluded by closing up the pit; the fire dies out, and charcoal remains.

Such is the common and cheapest mode of preparing charcoal. By many authors it is considered equal to all other expensive ways of producing it, and to this day it is followed at the Madras manufactory of gunpowder.

The method used at Ishapore, as in the best manufactories in England, is to cut the wood into small sticks about 5 or 6 inches in length, and to separate them into parcels of nearly equal diameters; carefully taking off the bark of the wood, and separating all unsound pieces. The wood is then packed into a sheet-iron cylinder 6 feet long by 2 feet 5 inches diameter, and its cover fitted on. The cylinders will contain 150 pounds to double that quantity of wood with reference to its state of dryness and the size and close packing of the pieces.

The cylinder is then placed inside a thick cast-iron cylinder or retort, of a little larger diameter and length, fixed horizontally, and set, generally two or three together, in a proper brick furnace. The open end of the cylinder is then closed with an iron circular plate, fitting exactly to the neck of the retort, and luted up with clay. An iron shutter working on hinges below, and looped up at the top, covers the retort completely, and the edges of this shutter being turned inwards close against the brickwork of the furnace, the vacant space between the shutter and the mouth of the retort is filled up with damp sand.

There are four short projecting pipes cast on the opposite or rear end of the retort, two of which only are required to be used in the process, the other two being carefully luted up. The advantage of having the four pipes is, that after use for some time, the lower parts of the retort being exposed to the greatest heat of the furnace burn, when the whole retort being shifted $\frac{1}{4}$ round in the brickwork, will bring fresh parts of the exterior into equal exposure.

The two open pipes are so placed that one is above and the other directly below in a vertical line, and to these are attached copper pipes about 18 feet long, leading to cisterns of water, into which, after the denser vapours are passed off when the furnaces are first lighted, they are, by means of a bent nozzle, to be fitted on at the proper time, made to dip a little below the surface of the water, to prevent the admission into the retorts of any atmospheric air, which would cause the consumption of the charcoal. The fire is then applied to the grate below the

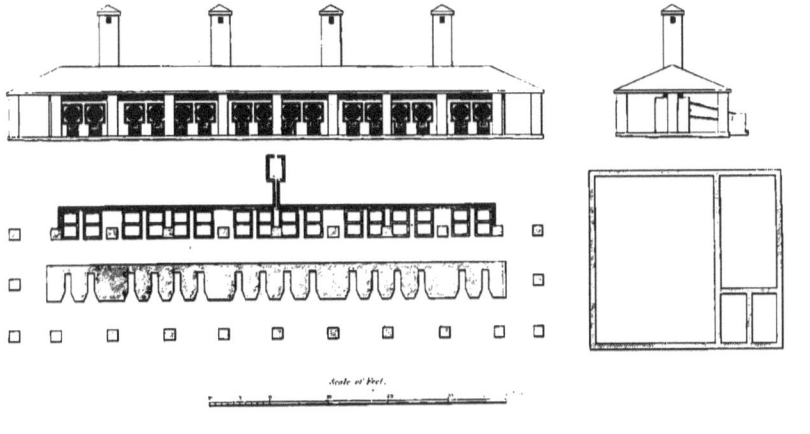
CHARCOAL FURNACE.

retort, which becomes nearly red-hot. In the process the heavier matter and vapours distilled off pass through the lower pipe, and are condensed in the waters of the cistern, and form the pyroligneous tar and acid much used in commerce. The lighter vapours escape from the upper pipe, first in the form of dense smoke, then follows carburetted hydrogen gas,* and, lastly, pure hydrogen, which is of a light red tinge, and inflames by the application of a candle. This is the time to apply the upper nozzle, to exclude the atmosphere, and to withdraw the fire of the furnaces, the process of carbonisation being completed.

After a time, when the retorts have cooled down a little, the doors may be opened, the internal cylinders withdrawn, and immediately carefully luted up with clay that no air may enter. It is very advantageous to have little circular pits to let these cylinders down into, and to cover them with a flat sheet-iron cover and sand—where they will cool gradually.

As the retorts are now hot, another set of the interior cylinders, with their loads of wood, may immediately take the place of those that are withdrawn, from which practice a saving of time and fuel will be obtained.

In twenty-four hours the new formed charcoal may be safely taken out.

The time of charring in these retorts is from three to four hours. The test of good charcoal for gunpowder is that it should not scratch copper, and that it should retain the complete organic forms of the fibres of the wood—any pieces that appear glazed on the outside should be rejected.

It is of the utmost importance to the goodness and quick ignition of the gunpowder, that the charcoal should be of the best quality, and recently made and pulverised.

In Bengal, the woods chiefly used are the—

		Sp. gr.
Urhur—Dhallbush	. (Cytisus Cajan)	. ·478
Jointee—Jayuntee .	. (Æschynomene Sesban)	. ·520
Bukus . .	. (Justicia Gundarusa) .	. ·657

* Many manufacturers consider that this gas should be retained, and that the first appearance of inflammable gas is the time to withdraw the fire.

In Europe, the Rhamnus frangula, or Alnus niger, is considered a good wood for gunpowder.

The Willow (Salix)—sp. g. 585—is also much used, as is the Alder (Betula alnus).

The Dhallbush, Urhur (Cytisus Cajan), has a growth of a few months, the seed is planted in April, and the grain ripens about the 1st of January the next year, when the bushes are cut down. The stalks are bought, and stacked for use at the Powder-works. The wood is white and soft, and contains much saccharine matter. Hence, insects breed internally, while externally it is attacked by various moths, which deposit their larva. The charcoal is good, its fibrous texture distinct, and it rings with a clear metallic sound, being at the same time soft and friable.

The Jointee grows from seed, and flowers after the first year; it then increases in size till it becomes a small tree; at three or four years old it makes the best charcoal, the fibres large, and defined, and well separated; the charcoal is of a lightish colour, and is not dense to the eye or touch. The tree flourishes best on the banks of the small nullahs. Jointee charcoal is not so soft as that of the Dhallbush; it is more dry, brittle, and hard. An average sized tree of three years' growth will occupy about five square yards, and produce about three maunds of wood, which will yield about thirty pounds of charcoal, the quantity required for two 100-lb. barrels of gunpowder.

Therefore 10,000 barrels would require about 60 beegahs of land under constant cultivation, one-third to be cut each year.

A beegah of Urhur wood is calculated to give about 200 maunds of wood in its yearly crop, or the charcoal for 160 barrels; hence 10,000 barrels would require a yearly cultivation of 60 beegahs.

The Bukus wood (Justicia Adhaloda) is exceedingly heavy, and full of juices; its leaves are a good vermifuge, and considered medicinal.

Native powder-makers esteem the Bukus as the best for charcoal. Of the Parkinsonia and Milkhedge, I have had no experience.

CHARCOAL. 53

In Affghanistan the cuttings from the vines make excellent charcoal.

The following is a list of woods and their charcoals, with their specific gravities as ascertained by me in experiments :—

Name of Wood.	Sp. gr. of wood.	Sp. gr. of charcoal.	
Lignum vitæ, twenty years old	1·3	·755	
Teak	·739	·236	
Bukus, four months dry	·657	·389	average
Jointee, three months dry	·520	·275	average
Urhur, fresh	·478	·302	average
Soondree	·922	·451	
Solah, almost a pith	...	·0159	
Mahogany, old	·780	·405	
Deal (Europe), old	·438	·299	
Saul, dry	·922	·401	
Seesoo	·724	·400	
Urhur wood, fresh, not split, 1¼ in. diameter	·602		
Do. do. ¾ in. diameter	·560		
Do. do. very small twigs, ¼ in. diameter	·377		
Urhur wood charcoal { 1 in. diameter	...	·303	}
{ ¾ in. diameter	...	·319	}
{ ¼ in. diameter	...	·285	} ·269
Urhur wood charcoal { large pieces	...	·321	}
{ smallest twigs	...	·322	}
Urhur wood, highly charred { middle size	...	·215	}
{ smaller size	...	·220	}
Bukus wood, cut { large	·713		
{ large	·703		
{ middling	·704		
{ small, 2 in. diameter	·572		
Bukus wood charcoal, branches 1½ in.	...	·389	}
Jointee wood, cut one month and split { large	·790	·230	}
{ small	·745	·281	} ·283
Do. do. { unclean	...	·292	}
{ roots	..	·329	}
Willow charcoal, fresh { 1 in. diameter	...	·266	}
{ small twigs	...	·231	}

How far the quality of the charcoal of these woods may follow that of their uncharred state, it is difficult to determine; but lasting, tough, astringent woods are selected in Europe, as if less likely to suffer under damp. Thus the Dogwood is used chiefly by the makers of the finest grained sporting and rifle powder. The density of this wood corresponding with the density of their cake.

It must be borne in mind that price and supply are regulating points to a large manufactory; that a superior wood for charcoal to that generally used may exist; but not so with respect to supply and cost.

The Urhur varies much, but the large chiefly predominates; while the Jointee is almost always of the same age and dimensions.

From the table it clearly appears, that the specific gravity of charcoals differs most considerably; next, that the wood of the larger branches, as well as the charcoals of the same, are denser as larger; and that the twigs of the Urhur are one-third less dense than the larger branches.

On the average, the specific gravity of the Jointee coal is perhaps less than that of the Urhur coal; while both are inferior in this respect to the Bukus. The density of the wood depends much on its age and dryness; not so the charcoal.

The amount of charring also clearly determines the specific gravity of the coal, as well as the carbon available. This is seen in the specific gravity of the highly-charred Urhur wood.

I placed 4oz. of pulverised charcoal in an open crucible which was heated in the furnace; the charcoal was reduced to 8 drachms, of a light slate-coloured ash.

An experiment was instituted with charcoal *over-charred* for one, and for two hours; there appeared little difference in their gunpowders. The result of over-charring would be, that when all the gas had disappeared, the carbon would combine with the oxygen of the air, and pass off as carbonic acid; but the saline and earthy matters of the portion passed off would be left with the remainder, round which it might vitrify, and thus render it less inflammable and more dense.

Still there must exist a point up to which the gases should be expelled, and when the process should be suspended. Uncharred wood is useless as applied to ignite nitre, as are the residues of ashes when all the gases are driven out.

Colonel Tennant, when agent, using equal measures of pulverised charcoal, compared his densities with those given by

Colonel Galloway a former agent, and concluded that the Jointee was a denser coal than the Urhur; that both being less charred in the days of Colonel Galloway, were therefore denser; and that the gunpowder of that period was denser; which proved to be the case, Colonel Galloway's powder being 280 to Colonel Tennant's 270 drams in the same measure:

	Pulverised Urhur Charcoal.	Pulverised Jointee.	Pulverised Bukus.	
Colonel Tennant .	162*	189	277	Weight of drams in the Ishapore density measure.
Colonel Galloway	202	236		
Difference in charcoal	40	47	...	

The produce from different woods is also very different. In England the manufacturers expect from 25 to 26 per cent. of charcoal in the 100 of wood used. From the Dogwood, full this quantity.

One of the Ishapore slip cylinders will contain 160 lbs. of the dry Urhur or Jointee wood, and will produce 40 lbs. of charcoal, or about 25 per cent.

The Madras Government sent up to Ishapore, in four barrels, 247 lbs. of dry Urhur wood to be charred; it was quite dry, and much eaten by worms. The result was:—

$$\text{Urhur} \begin{cases} \text{Thick} & 63\tfrac{1}{2} \\ \text{Thin} & 82 \\ \text{Rotten (useless)} & 80\tfrac{1}{2} \end{cases} 145\tfrac{1}{2} \Bigg\} 235. \quad \text{Loss, 12 in transit.}$$

The 145½ lbs. gave, after three hours' charring, 40 lbs. of charcoal.

It requires about 150 lbs. of Soondree firewood to char one cylinder, at a cost of five annas.

On a long average of years it is found, that 120 lbs. of *green fresh wood* will give 10 lbs. of charcoal, including every loss of drying, insects, and decay; the refuse is used as a portion of firing for the furnaces.

In the common mode of carbonising, by pits, no firing is used, the wood itself nourishing the fire during the process. This economical process thus saves the cost of the firewood cylinders and buildings, and is still pursued at Madras.

Captain Bishop, one of the agents at the Madras mills, recorded, that the Milkhedge, Euphorbia, yields a charcoal which requires 10 lbs. to make equal strength of powder to that of 8 lbs. of the Urhur charcoal.

Unpulverised charcoal, in its fresh carbonised state, is highly porous, and exceedingly attractive of moisture. The condensing power of its mass over gases, under very slight chemical affinity, is well established. Thus: 16 oz. of charcoal, fresh from the retort, became 17 oz. 6 drachms after exposure to the atmosphere for twenty-four hours; but during the next twenty-four hours it lost 9 drachms, which it had absorbed.

Fresh pulverised charcoal, even after it has been sifted through fine sieves, often inflames spontaneously when left exposed to the air; and when once lighted by the application of fire, or spontaneously, continues to burn for some time, smouldering away, and unless supplied with a current of air, dies out.*

After the charcoal is taken out of the cylinders, it is well rubbed between cloths, to clear away all particles of dirt, bark, &c.; and no more is made in one day than can be used the next. It is then ground in a mill similar to those used for the saltpetre and sulphur, only that the face and bed are of a whitish metal, termed Tutenague. This mill is worked by four bullocks; it requires 82 revolutions in half-an-hour to reduce one maund of charcoal to be fit for sifting. The sifting is performed with common

---

* It is probable that the carbonic acid gas formed by the charcoal combining with the oxygen of the atmosphere as it burns, being heavier than the latter, forms a screen, and prevents the combustion continuing by shutting off the supply of oxygen. Mr. Hall of the Dartford Gunpowder Works, who has done much to improve the machinery and the processes used in the manufacture of gunpowder, has produced a machine for reducing charcoal to fine powder on the principle of the coffee-grinding mill, thus superseding the usual milling for this purpose, and having other advantages.—EDITOR.

CHARCOAL. 57

sieves, the bottoms of which are made of fine wire cloth. This previous grinding and sifting is not performed in all the manufactories of Europe. At Madras, the charcoal is broken and pulverised between several pairs of rollers; which, having under them a sieve in a close box, sifts the charcoal at the same time, which is a saving of time and labour.

The Bengal supply of Urhur is exceedingly precarious; any increased quantity which necessity required could hardly be obtained. The average price is sixteen rupees per maund; but a very slight increase of the demand raises the price, as all now within limit of the Agency is brought by water carriage.

The use of Jointee wood every two or three years would therefore have an excellent effect on the market, and it would cause the wood to be cultivated and looked after; thus giving two sources of supply. The cost is, however, dearer than that of Urhur.

The average of six years' cost of 100 lbs. of pulverised charcoal is 2r. 14a. 1p. Thus explained—

	r.	a.	p.
Wood	1	6	18·6
Fuel	0	10	0·3
Labour	0	0	6·4
Wear and tear	0	3	7·7
	2	14	1·0

As Urhur wood is only procurable after the month of January, necessity causes a supply for the months of November, December, and January to be kept in stock during the rains; and, consequently, there is considerable waste and damage sustained.

Gunpowder made of large or small charred wood appeared nearly equal in strength; and the old Agency proofs show that powder, with 1 lb. extra of charcoal in the proportions, was very superior in range, but not in resisting atmospheric changes. (See Appendix.)

Tests for the Purity of Charcoal.

One hundred grains must be well digested in hot distilled water, when the solution of nitrate of silver and nitrate of barytes will indicate the presence of muriate and sulphate of soda, if any exist. Acids will be rendered apparent by litmus paper. If the solutions contain any alkali, the original blue colour will be wholly or partially restored to the reddened paper.

SULPHUR.

The treatment of this material in the Agency at Ishapore was different according to the quality of the crude sulphur supplied.

In the East much is brought from the Persian Gulf, from Scinde, Sumatra, and Burmah, but all in an exceedingly impure state. There was one standing rule, however, to admit no sulphur into the composition of gunpowder until it had passed once at least through the fusing process.

The prices of sulphur have varied from 4r. 10a. 11p. to 9r. 9a. 2p. per hundred pounds, and the states of purity varying from 92 to 71 per cent., and even less.

The fusing pots are of iron (gun-metal would be better, and is used in England); they are set in proper furnaces, the bottom resting on the masonry, and the flue being carried all round, as this prevents the sulphur at the bottom from being too much heated from being directly exposed to the fire. It is very necessary to attend carefully to the heat in this process, from the following circumstances.*

When sulphur is heated to about 180° Fahr., it begins to give out vapour of a peculiar odour, strong and disagreeable; at 225° it liquifies, and becomes clear, of a bright amber colour; at 350°, or above, it begins to become viscid, and of a deep brown colour; and at 600° it quickly sublimes.

* The proper shape of a pot for fusing sulphur should be rather deep than shallow; the size must be according to the quantity required for consumption. One 2 ft. in diameter, and 2 ft. 6 in. deep, would be enough for a large manufactory, as sulphur is unalterable in store, and may therefore be refined at any season, and supplied for the daily manufacture kept in store. It is better to have two refining pots set in separate furnaces, in case of accidents or repairs; and one of these may be exclusively kept for the first fusing of very impure sulphur.—Editor.

In this process, therefore, the crude sulphur is broken into lumps, and thrown by a ladle in small quantities into the pot, under which the fire is burning ; it must be kept constantly stirred with an iron rod, which should be slightly oiled,* to prevent the sulphur adhering ; and as the first quantity melts more should be added, until the pot is nearly full, and the liquid sulphur looks clear and amber-coloured ; the fire must then be damped, the stirring suspended, and all impurities that rise skimmed off with an iron ladle, and the skimmings put into a vessel by themselves. Small needles of sulphur will in a short time begin to appear on the surface, the fluid sulphur must then be ladled into small wooden tubs of a conical form slightly greased or oiled inside, and then left to cool and crystallise.

These tubs should be narrow at the base and wide at the top, fastened with iron hoops, so as easily to be taken to pieces if necessary ; when the sulphur is cool, by turning the tub upside down, and gently knocking upon it, the contents will come out in a solid cone, having the shape of the interior of the vessel.

This cone will appear of unequal colour, but the pure sulphur will be of a fine pale yellow and equal colour ; and this part must be carefully separated from the rest, and may be considered fit for gunpowder. The impure parts, with the skimmings, may then be mixed with other crude sulphur, to undergo the process of fusing again, or to be carried, if very impure, to the subliming furnace. The impurities will be found chiefly at the small end of the cone, having subsided to the bottom of the tub ; none but the pure, equal, pale yellow colour must be taken.

Sulphur suffers no change in the atmosphere, and is perfectly insoluble in water, so that a small quantity of each sample may be bruised and washed in boiling water, to discover if there are any soluble salts mixed with it, which the loss of weight or testing the water in which it is washed will discover. The following results were ascertained in refining the very best and perhaps the very worst samples of sulphur brought to the Agency.

* Mustard oil is a cheap and useful oil for this purpose in India.

Of 299½ maunds at the price of 3r. 11a. ½p. per maund, about 6 cwt. was melted successively in one of the refining pots as a trial, and produced—

	Cwt.	qrs.	lbs.
Sulphur refined and fit for powder	(None.)		
Sulphur that will require one more fusing	2	0	12
Sulphur that will require two more fusings	0	3	4
Scoria fit only to be sublimed	2	3	24
Loss	0	0	16

The above 299½ maunds were kept entirely separate, and produced 209 maunds of sulphur fit for pulverising, including 80½ maunds obtained by the sublimation of the scoria, and cost as follows:—

	r.	a.
Original cost of the crude sulphur	1105	3
1167 maunds of firewood for subliming, at 17r. 1a. per 100 maunds	204	3
150 maunds of firewood for fusing	26	4
Three men in refining, 45 days, at 4r. per month each	18	0
Two men at subliming, 62 days, at ,, ,,	16	8
Earthern jars, baskets, wear and tear of masonry	15	0
One subliming pot destroyed	178	10
	1563	12

making the cost per factory maund of 7r. 7a. 8p.

The expense of sublimation is 5r. 2a. 4¾p. per factory maund, considering the scoria is of no value. When sulphur is much above this price, the process will pay, but the wear and tear of pots is great.

Another trial was with 298½ factory maunds of very good rock sulphur at 7r. 1a. 8p. the maund as purchased. This produced 290½ maunds fit to pulverise at the following cost:—

	r.	a.
Original cost of sulphur	2123	6
100 maunds of firewood	17	8
Three men in refining, 30 days	12	0
	2152	14

the cost being 7r. 6a. 6p. per maund refined.

Note.—New Mode of refining the Sulphur by Distillation.

As the purity of the sulphur and its freedom from all acids is of great importance in the manufacture of gunpowder, new methods have been introduced of late years in the Government and in the best private manufactories which furnish sulphur of superior purity.

The following description of that used at the Royal mills, Waltham Abbey, will convey full information on the subject :—

A large iron boiler or pot is set in a furnace three feet from the ground; it has a moveable lid fitting well, to be luted with clay when in use. In this lid there is a conical plug which can be removed at pleasure. From the sides of the pot two pipes lead, one to a circular dome, and the other to an iron retort set below the level of the boiler. The last pipe has a casing or jacket round it, which can be filled with cold water : the communication of these pipes with the melting pot are opened or closed by proper valves. About 5 or 6 cwt. of the once refined sulphur is broken up into small pieces, and placed in the melting pot; the plugs in the lid of the pipe leading to the dome are at this time left open, but the pipe to the retort is closed. After from two to three hours, when the heat of the furnace is applied, a pale yellow vapour rises, when the plug in the lid is put in its place, and the vapour is conducted through the pipe to the dome, where it condenses in the form of an impalpable powder, commonly called flowers of sulphur. A small pipe leads from the bottom of the dome, on the opposite side to the furnace, into a reservoir of water, to allow the escape of air, and the sulphuric acid is taken up by the water. In about an hour and a half or two hours after, the vapour becomes of a deep iodine colour, the communication with the dome is then shut off, and that to the retort opened ; a supply of cold water is now kept circulating, from a tank above, in the jacket of the pipe ; the vapour distils over, is condensed as it passes through the pipe, and runs into the retort below in the form of a thick yellow fluid. When nearly all has distilled, which can be known by the jacket getting cold, the communication with the retort is then closed, and the fluid sulphur left an hour to get sufficiently cool to ladle into moulds; the furnace door and the communication with the dome are thrown open again, that the rest of the vapour may pass off into them.

The flowers of sulphur thus obtained are used for fireworks and laboratory purposes, but are unfit for gunpowder, as they contain acids. The crystallised sulphur, after being allowed to cool in the moulds, is taken out and barrelled up for use.

To ascertain its purity, a small portion is burnt by exposing it to heat over a lamp on a piece of porcelain or sheet platina, and no residue should be left, as the sulphur will pass off in the state of vapour into the atmosphere; and if boiled in distilled water, the water should produce no discoloration in litmus paper.

THE FABRICATION OF GUNPOWDER AFTER THE CRUDE MATERIALS ARE REFINED.

The three ingredients to compose the powder are now to be weighed in the proper proportions, dry-mixed, incorporated, compressed, granulated, sifted, glazed, dried, and barrelled.

The sifted ingredients are conveyed to the weighing house in proper quantities, where the man prepares them in the relative proportions of $\frac{75}{100}$ of saltpetre, $\frac{15}{100}$ of charcoal, and $\frac{10}{100}$ of sulphur for a mill charge of 80 lbs.

He uses leaden weights of 30, 12, and 8 lbs., dividing the saltpetre into two proportions, so as to confine the charcoal and sulphur between them.

The whole is slightly intermixed, by hand, in a wooden box, carefully surrounded by a cloth covering to prevent the escape of any of the light particles.

As the entire loss by wastage in the manufacture of the prepared ingredients is about 5 per cent. of the composition, perhaps it would be better if that per-centage was added at first to the mill charge, so as to conclude the process with the full 80 lbs. of powder.

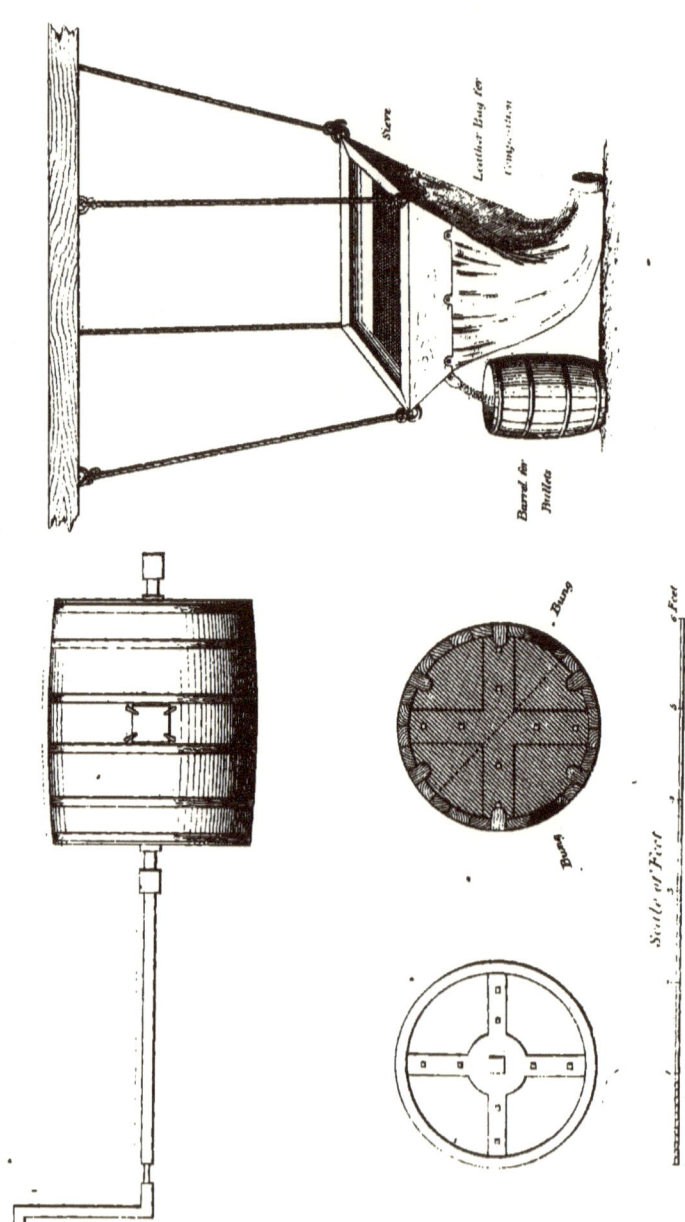

Dry-Mixing.

This is perhaps one of the most important parts of the process, the object being so to intermix the ingredients, that 1 atom by weight of sulphur should be in contact with 1·5 of charcoal and 7·5 of nitre.

In former times it used to be performed upon a wide, flat table, using wooden rollers. In European mills the mixture is made in a large tub, having a pronged wooden stirabout. At Madras, the saltpetre, according to the proper proportion, is put into a wooden box, and undergoes a further pulverisation by a hand roller made of lignum vitæ, which is worked backwards and forwards for one hour and a half; the proportion of sulphur is then added to the nitre, and rolled as before for about half an hour, when the charcoal is added, and the composition of the three ingredients is now well worked together for two hours more, this whole process occupying about four hours.

At Ishapore this process of dry-mixing is carried on in a much improved mode, producing the most perfect intimacy of mixture, and it is thus well described by Colonel Galloway, who introduced it :—

" The composition is put into the mixing or triturating barrels,* together with an equal weight of brass bullets about $\frac{3}{8}$ths of an inch in diameter; each barrel containing a charge for one of the cylinder mills. It is subjected for two hours to the revolutions of the barrels on their axes at the rate of 35 to 40 revolutions per minute; altogether from 4200 to 4800 revolutions; perhaps 4200 may be nearest the truth, it being difficult to keep the people who turn the barrels to the higher rate of working.

" The action of the bullets amongst the composition constantly revolving, tends essentially, not indeed to incorporate, but to intermix closely, and to distribute equally and perfectly, the particles of the different ingredients amongst one another, as well as to increase considerably their tenuity, so that if the process had been faithfully performed at the end of two hours, its

---

* See Plates, mixing barrels.

appearance is that of a dusty homogeneous mass, in which no one ingredient is distinguishable by the naked eye, and to the feel it is perfectly soft, fine, and entirely free from being gritty. Its colour is by no means black, but resembles more the neutral tint of the painters.

"The barrels in use here are 2 feet 9 inches long, and 2 feet 2 inches in diameter; made perfectly cylindrical internally, the outside with a small bulge for the sake of hooping, and with six ledges projecting from the interior of the staves at equal distances $\frac{3}{4}$ of an inch, for the purpose of producing as much irregularity of motion amongst the contents of the barrel as may be.

"They are, in fact, precisely the French tonneaux in which the whole process of manufacturing the powder called Poudre Ronde of Mons. Champy, was performed."

To reduce the labour in working, barrels of a different description were also used here; instead of one barrel of large dimensions longitudinally, four small ones were used—attached round one centre axis; the compositions with their proportions of bullets being thus divided into four, and placed in the four barrels all equidistant from the common axis, each furnished a counterpoise for its opposite weight, and the whole machine was thus not only kept in motion with greater ease, but when moving, like a loaded fly, its motion became accelerated, and might be kept up by the slightest application of power.

But the ingenious inventor forgot the nature of the motion required of the machine; it was not to move easily or to move quickly, but to move so as to produce the greatest possible intestine motion amongst the contents of the barrels, so as to ensure the greatest quantity of trituration of the ingredients by the agitation of the particles and of the bullets amongst them, the bullets being dashed from one ledge to the other on the revolution of the machine.

This degree of motion even in a single barrel, whose diameter is little more than one-third that of the combined set, cannot be preserved if the velocity given exceed 40 to 45 revolutions in a

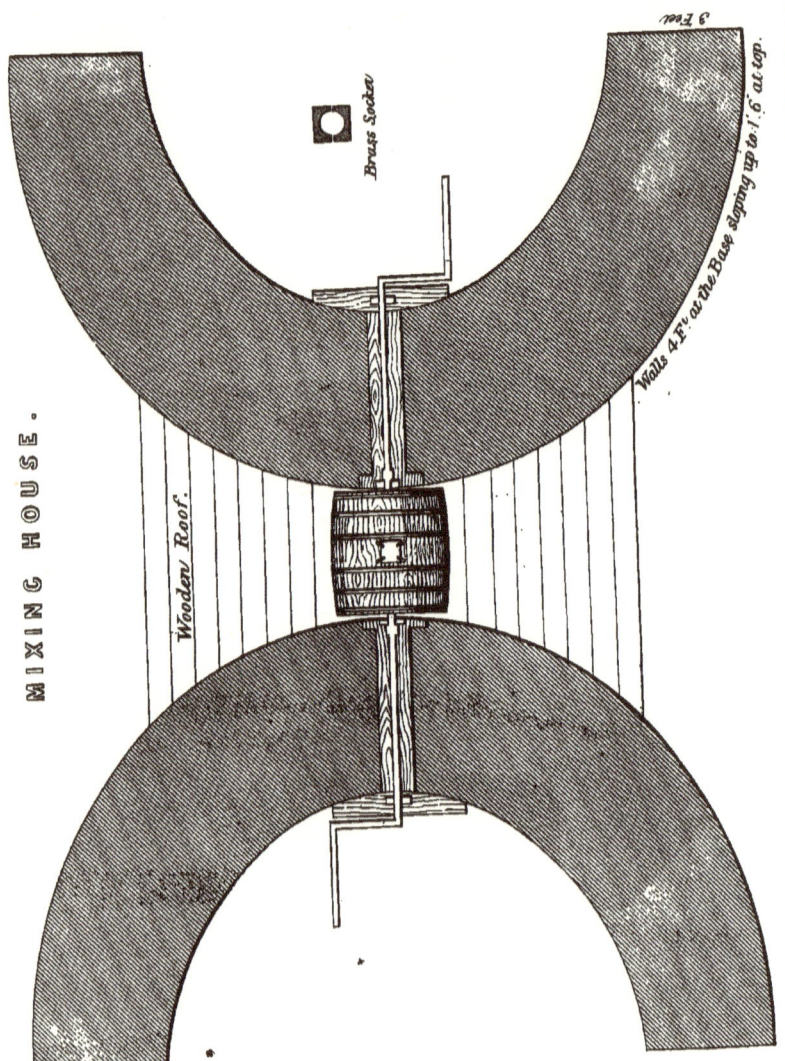

minute, the centrifugal force becoming in excess of the gravitation of the matter moved, which consequently attaches itself to, and remains motionless on, the inner surface of the barrel. We limit the number of revolutions of the single mixing barrel to from 35 to 40 per minute, that being the most efficient rate of motion for the purpose required.

It was found that the composition worked in the combined set for three hours, was not equal to that worked in the single barrel for two, and was often found very inferior. The labourers also soon discovered that the faster they turned the combined barrels, the lighter was their labour; and it was no unusual circumstance to see the barrels moving in perfect silence, instead of hearing the noise of the bullets dashing against the sides.

I had no hesitation, therefore, in recommending that the use of these combined barrels should be abolished, and that the single ones should be used as at first; which was done. Fifteen sets of the combined barrels were then in use, each requiring a spare set of barrels to be filled while the others were working, altogether 120 barrels, worked by sixty men. Their place was supplied by eight single barrels worked by thirty-two men, sufficient to mix composition for the four cylinder mills at Ishapore (see Plate).

The composition is put into the barrel by means of a funnel-shaped bag (of thick cloth or pliable leather; either substance, but to be impervious to the composition), to the mouth of which a copper tube is fixed, which fits into the mouth or door of the barrel, and that of the cloth or leather funnel in unloading is made to embrace the mouth of the budge-barrel, in which the composition is carried to the sifting house for the purpose of separating the balls.

The only alteration since Colonel Galloway's time has been to reduce the number of revolutions from 40 to 20 per minute, and the weight of the bullets to one-half the weight of the composition; there is also a register clock attached to each barrel, which indicates the number of revolutions made.

The ingredients, after this alteration, were found to be as well mixed under the reduced velocity, while the occasional explosions of the barrels which had taken place, were materially reduced in number.

It was found that the quick turning caused the temperature of the composition to rise some degrees above that of the external air. In the slow turning both remained nearly the same—the increased heat of the quicker revolutions no doubt aiding the accidental explosions.

I am of opinion that these explosions may in some measure be accounted for by the direct concussion between two or three of the balls, and perhaps from some impurities of sand, or other metallic particles, in the cast metal of the balls themselves.

The barrels cost 54 rupees each, and last three seasons of manufacture, each furnishing about 1500 barrels of gunpowder. A set of balls will only last one season.

The Ishapore metal of the balls is copper 1, zinc 15; it should not be too hard.

The abrasion of the balls against each other in the barrel imparts to the powder a slight tinge of copper, in some form of a sulphate, as well as adds very minute particles of splintered wood, but these have proved no deterioration to the powder.

Experiments connected with trials of the composition from these barrels will be detailed towards the conclusion of the volume, in the Appendix.

Two men at each barrel work off three charges in twelve hours.

Note.— At Allahabad, when agent for gunpowder and war-rockets, I used mixing barrels made entirely of sheet-copper, which answered perfectly well, and totally secured the mixture from any intermixture of impurities of wood, &c., as with wooden barrels. The brass bullets were cast in iron moulds, and the axles of the barrels were supported on pairs of friction-wheels, running in an oil reservoir well covered from dust, and no explosion ever took place in using them for the five years I was agent.
—Editor.

MIXING BARRELS.

Experiments made by Colonel Anderson with the intention of examining the effect of the Mixing Barrels, Ishapore, 1st July and 1st March, 1848.

	2-oz. Charge, 8-in. Mortar, 68-lb. Ball.		2-oz. Charge, Eprouvette.		Colour.
	Range in Yds.	Average.	Degrees of Arc.	Average.	
Composition simply mixed, but not put in the barrels . . .	{ 5 8 8 }	7	... ...	... ...	Light grey, the different ingredients lying in masses.
Turned in the barrels for half an hour . .	{ 9 15 15 }	13	{ 1° 10' 1° 10' 1° 1' }	1° 7'	Dark grey.
Turned in the barrels for one hour . . .	{ 11 9 8 }	9⅓	{ 1° 5' 1° 15' 1° 8' }	1° 0'	Dark grey, nearly black.
Turned for one hour and a half	{ 24 19 8 }	17	{ 3° 15' 3° 10' 3° 16' }	3° 14'	Black.
Turned two hours,— considered as finished	{ 4 17 17 }	12⅔	{ 13° 10' 13° 15' 13° 17' }	13° 14'	Very black.
Turned for four hours, being two hours extra	{ 21 50 23 }	31	{ 18° 50' 18° 36' 15° 50' }	17° 45'	Very black.

In the above, there is a regular gradation of colour, an increase of range and of arc, but in no correct proportions.

In the old proof books I traced the following trials of February, 1836 :—

	Mortar, 2-oz. Charge.		Eprouvette.		1-lb. Charge, 65½-lb. Ball.	
	Yards.	Average.	Degrees of arc.	Average.	Yards.	Average.
Composition from mixing barrel ready for mills	25	25	21 25			
Ditto, ditto .	{ 30 7 }	18			{ 214 260 }	

Great irregularity of range may be observed with the mortar, but a progressive improvement in the confined tube of the eprouvette.

The molecules of the ingredients may be more reduced and more blended together in the longer period of turning in the barrels.

In England, the mixing-barrels are not used, but compensation for this mode of well mixing is made in the lengthened milling of the charges in the grinding-mills. It may be argued, therefore, that this previous system of dry-mixture would permit of a reduction in the number of revolutions given to the mills.

The strong side-walls, to be observed in the plan, have quite preserved the workmen; in all instances of explosion that have taken place, the barrels and roofing have been blown to pieces and a bit of a copper hoop, in one instance, pierced through a plank at 200 yards distance. The turners are sometimes injured by the iron handles. I think the space between the walls is too confined, and a longer barrel would not be objectionable, were a new set of works to be erected.

In the present arrangement at Ishapore, the barrels being separated from each other, accidental explosion of one does not communicate with another—and though the whole might be turned by one power, either steam, cattle, or water, yet, if closed up, an accident might destroy the whole. By the present separate arrangement the works can be resumed in an hour after an explosion.

Should labourers be scarce, it would be possible to turn the barrels with a few men, by having proper wheels and communications, so to generate the velocity required, and, perhaps, a revolving frame with arms within the barrels might supersede the use of the brass bullets.

At present there are employed two men at each barrel; they work off three charges in twelve hours.

PLAN & ELEVATION
OF MIXING BARRELS & GLAZING REELS. SHEWING THE ADAPTATION OF COG WHEELS TO REDUCE MANUAL LABOUR.

SIDE VIEW
OF GLAZING REELS. PARTLY OPEN.

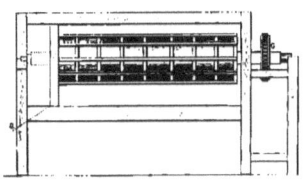

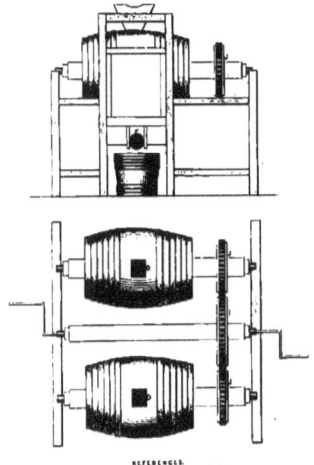

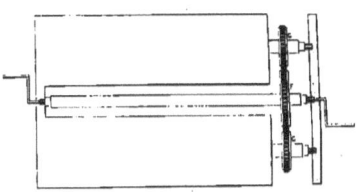

REFERENCES.

REFERENCES.

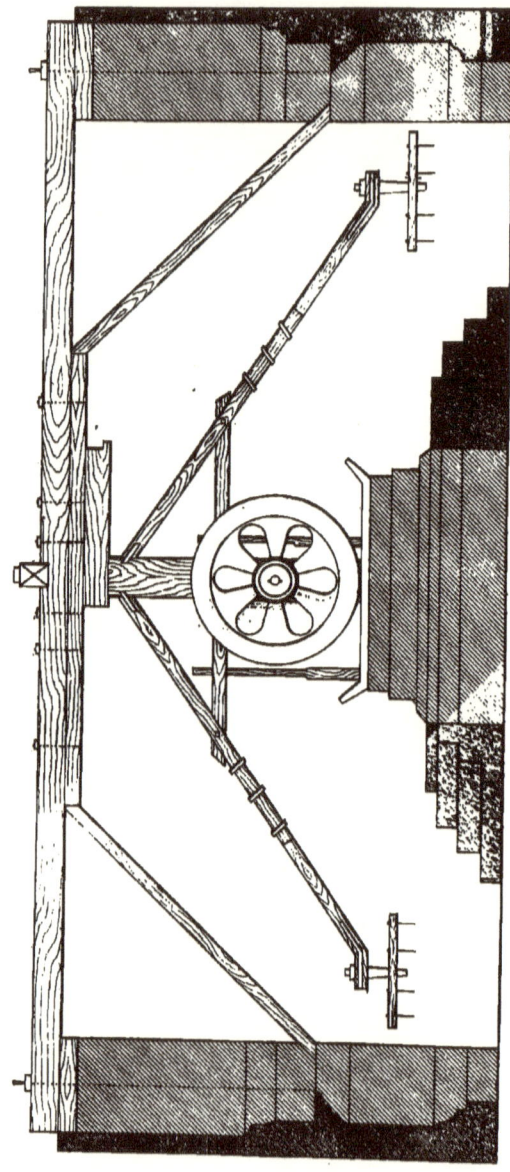

INCORPORATING OR GRINDING MILL USED AT ISHAPORE.

Incorporation of the Ingredients of the Composition.

During the early manufacture of powder, this part of the process was looked upon as the key-stone of the fabrication, on which entirely depended the goodness of the powder, and it was then considered that milling could not be performed for too long a period to any detrimental extent.

In those times the process of milling, long continued, did duty for the dry-mixing just detailed, and for the act of pressing, which will be explained hereafter.

The native mode of incorporating the ingredients was by the simple denkee, or pestle, worked by the foot, and falling into a wooden mortar; such I found to be the case in the wilds of Affghanistan; and such was the mode pursued by which the powder was incorporated in the earlier days of the Ishapore works.

Subsequently an attempt was made to introduce a grand *pilon*-mill, worked by cattle, with several other machines, all of which have been discontinued since the cylinder-mills were introduced.

In the first alteration, these mills were used to grind the crude materials, intermix them with each other, and incorporate the whole into one mass.

The following is Colonel Galloway's description of the mill erected by him. (See Elevation of Mill. See Plate.)

"The construction of the new cylinder mills is extremely simple. The cylinders are 6 ft. in diameter and 18 in. broad on the face; they are of bronze or gun-metal, and their weight is between $5\frac{3}{4}$ tons and 6 tons each. They are termed cylinders because their outline is that of a cylinder, whose axis is 18 in., and diameter 6 ft.; but it will be seen that the weight of a perfect cylinder of these dimensions, of metal, would far exceed 6 tons. To preserve the size whilst we limit the weight, they are consequently made more like a wheel than a cylinder, with a nave 22 in. in diameter, rim 18 in. broad, the space between containing six openings, and the faces are hollowed out to reduce the weight of metal.

"The bed on which they revolve is also of the same metal; the outer rim (or curb of the bed, as it is technically called) is made to slope outwards at an angle of about 35°, and is cast in one piece; and being cast perfectly true, the angle formed by the horizontal and sloping lines thus forms a defined circle, in the centre of which is the box on which the pivot of the upright shafts works, which conveys the motion to the cylinders. The outer plough, which throws the composition inwards under the cylinder, consequently works with the greatest accuracy in the angle of the curb in moving round.

"The cylinders are attached to the upright shafts above mentioned, by a horizontal spindle or axle of iron, $4\frac{1}{8}$ in. in diameter, turned perfectly cylindrical, on which they revolve. This spindle passes through the centre of the vertical shaft and through both of the cylinders, which are keyed up at each end of the spindle, and confined in their proper position by means of washers, which also keep them off the shaft as well as off the keys, and which may be shifted, so as to admit of the cylinders moving either in the same or in different tracks, if required.

"The bed is raised about 6 ft. above the level of the floor of the mill and the bullocks' walk, for the purpose of giving protection to the driver and cattle in case of explosion.

"This great elevation, together with the form of the curb, or outer rim of the bed, which slopes upwards, as above described, gives the blast, already above their heads, a direction still farther upwards, so as to pass over them entirely.

"Even the men who turn the composition, and whose bodies above the middle are on a level with it, by throwing themselves instantaneously down, might possibly find a little shelter from the blast.

"The action of a cylinder mill as a machine for incorporating the ingredients of gunpowder, is perhaps the most perfect of any yet introduced for that purpose. The compound action of grinding and compression seems to be precisely that which is wanted, viz., to pulverise and unite the heterogeneous atoms of the composition.

"The power of these mills is immense, each cylinder weighing nearly 6 tons ; so that with the weight of the spindle, boxes, washers, &c., 12 tons of metal are constantly in motion on the composition. To derive the full advantage of this immense power, it is necessary that the composition be kept well under the cylinders ; this is done by a plough moving on each side of the composition, which is also necessarily stirred up by the men with shovels (whom we call turners), who follow the cylinders, or runners as they are called, taking care at the same time to keep the composition from caking, which it would otherwise do, and drift before the runner.

"These turners are furnished with prongs or shovels made of wood, resembling the human hand with the fingers spread out. I found this preferable to the flat shovel, which laid too much of the bed bare, shoving the composition before it, instead of turning it up, as it ought to be. One man moves round directly opposite the inner plough, and it is here that the principal part of the labour of turning is performed : the side of the plough, offering a perfect resistance to the shovel, admits of the prongs being pushed through the composition, without shoving it on one side of the track of the runners, each prong forcing up its furrow, and thus answering the required purpose in the most perfect manner.

"The turner, who moves before the other runner and outer plough, is merely required to keep patting the composition gently with his shovel, which breaks the incipient cakes, and thus has the effect of entirely preventing the drifting, which, when allowed to form into large sheets or cakes, would fly or " drift," as it is called, before the runner, leaving the bed bare.

"This, it is thought, might be attended with danger. The great weight of the cylinder falling upon the bare bed, it is supposed, might occasion such a degree of percussion and friction as to produce explosion. I doubt this, but still every precaution ought to be observed, and the danger ought to be strongly impressed upon the minds of the people, to ensure their own safety and secure their attention to their duty."

Previous to any disquisition or comparison of the effect of this with that of any other mill, we will carefully examine the facts of the case.

Cylinder weight	6 tons each.
,, diameter	6 feet.
Face of cylinder	18 inches.
Diameter of outside track	6 feet.
,, of inside track	3 feet.

Therefore, $3^2 - 6^2 \times \cdot 7854 = 21 \cdot 105$, say 20 sq. ft., or 2880 sq. in., will be the space covered by the composition.

Allow the line of contact to be $\frac{1}{4}$ in. broad, then $18 \times \cdot 25 = 4 \cdot 5$ sq. in., supporting 6 tons. Hence $4 \cdot 5 : 120$ cwt. :: $1 : 26\frac{1}{2}$ cwt., is the weight per square inch.

Now, the cubic contents of 80 lbs. of composition is 4257 in.; hence the composition would be ·43, or not $\frac{1}{2}$ in. deep.

Again, 80 lbs. $\times 16 = 1288$ oz. in a charge; $2880 : 1288 ::$ $1 : \cdot 41$, say half an ounce to a square inch, as the ratio of composition to surface.

Now what is the action caused by the revolution of this frustum of a cylinder round its axis, while the axis is carried round in a circle? It is a grinding, tearing, mixing, and pressing action combined in one.

For the sake of simplification, let us consider each of these actions in detail, and first the grinding.

It is evident that the grinding action, under the weight of 26 cwt. on each square inch, will be met by the impenetrability and resistance of the composition interposed between the cylinder and the bed; this consists of a stratum of the very finest particles; and as the breadth of the surfaces in contact is not very great at the point where the actual grinding action takes place, I doubt if the particles themselves are reduced to a much finer state than when issued from the sifting-house, though no doubt two or more particles of different ingredients might, under this twisting, grinding action, have their union rendered more complete. The edges and the points of the atoms are abraded, and the contact rendered more facile. These results will be more apparent as the depth of the stratum becomes less.

But we have already ground the ingredients to almost the finest possible state, and the depth of the stratum is considerable.

Next we will glance at the mixing action. Some of this results from the twisting action under and near the line of motion of the cylinder; also from the sinking of the cylinder into and through the mass of the composition, which causes a motion among the particles, a portion of them escaping laterally. Again, we have the two ploughs turning over these raised ridges, separating the mass and altering its form; also two men with wooden forks, who are constantly employed in breaking up the cakes and lumps, and giving the whole a good deal of motion. We have already given to the composition almost all the mixture it can require.

Lastly, we have the pressing of the weight of the cylinders. In many respects this is opposed in result to the grinding and mixing process. The pressing no doubt may, and does force a compact union between the different particles of the various ingredients, and if these have assumed their correct relative position towards perfect amalgamation, then the pressure would confirm the same, and render the arrangement binding.

We do not require the density of mass, because this we seek and subsequently obtain from the continued operation of a powerful press.

Let us pause for a moment on the simple operation of mixing with a pestle and mortar: if we merely press down with the pestle, the matter under it might be broken, but without the twisting round and round and shaking up we should never acquire a perfect mixture; and so it is with our cylinders, the more dense the strata is made, the less easily it is broken up and the matter re-mixed. If the mass of the composition becomes set under the cylinders, their use, since the introduction of presses, is concluded.

Now we have well ground, well mixed, and propose in a subsequent operation to give the composition good pressure: hence there must be some other law or element in action under the mills, and this I take to be the water, which operates to expel the air from between the atoms, to lubricate, damp, and soften the surfaces of the saltpetre, so as to permit the atoms of the other ingredients being pressed into the interstices—a union which the gradual contraction in drying up of the water would render permanent.

Hence the grinding, mixing, and pressing are all of service to cause the water to percolate the mass, bring the particles into close contact, and give tenacity to the whole—constant motion all furthers this end.

A quantity of water holding nitre in solution would, on its evaporation, leave a most minute deposit of nitre on the other particles.

The extremes would be, constant milling continued till all the water was evaporated, when the result would appear in a dry composition such as it left the mixing barrel; or, water holding nitre in suspension to be mixed with the charcoal and sulphur, kept from being precipitated by agitation.

The quantity of water and of mixture under the evaporation are the points to be determined. These I conceive to be various as the attending circumstances, only to be determined by practice.

The conclusion would be—that a certain time is requisite for the cylinder to overcome the elasticity and impenetrability of the damp composition.

That the quicker the cylinder turns on its axle the greater will be the grinding action.

That as regards pressure, 400 revolutions in two hours would be equal to 200 in two hours, although the former would give more pulverisation.

That more tossing about, intermixture, and evaporation, would result from the quicker velocity of the cylinders, but less as regards the work of the turners, who would have diminished time in which to perform their operations.

That the greater the charge, the less it is certainly pressed.

That ploughs, confining the charge under the path of the

runners, render it more thick, and cause it to be less pressed, but enhance the intermixture by extra motion.

That the atmosphere has much influence on the extent of evaporation.

That there may be an essence in the ingredients which escapes in too much handling, as does decidedly the light volatile charcoal.

The following is the remark of Mr. Braddock on this subject :—

" The incorporating mills at Waltham Abbey are turned by water-power. They make six or seven revolutions per minute; the quantity of ingredients laid on a mill at one time is called a charge, it weighs 42 lbs., and is worked for three hours—hence from 1000 to 1200 revolutions of the mill result as the regulated degree of incorporation for 42 lbs. of composition.

" The cylinders are of dark grey limestone, bearing a good polish; not brittle, nor of an easy fracture, and weigh about 3 tons each, and, calculating the weight of the two cylinders at 6 tons, it follows that in three hours, at six revolutions per minute, they subject the ingredients to the action of no less a pressure than 6,480 tons. It is this exceedingly great quantity of manipulative effect, that makes most ample compensation for the imperfect mixture of the ingredients before incorporation.

" The gun metal cylinders at Madras weigh, as nearly as possible, $4\frac{1}{2}$ tons each; the pair of cylinders therefore being 9 tons, and number of revolutions 100, the pressure they exert on the composition is 900 tons—the charge laid on the Madras mill is 60 lbs., about half as much again as at Waltham Abbey—and at the 80th revolution of the mill, gunpowder dust from the corning-house is mingled with the composition, and the whole is then worked and incorporated during 20 more revolutions to complete the established number of 100; so that the Madras powder undergoes, finally, only about one-tenth part of the King's gunpowder.

" There is a certain point beyond which it is unnecessary to carry the process of incorporation, but where that point is gained remains to be fixed. I think it difficult to say, having reason to believe that it differs in different systems of manufacture.

"To determine the maximum effect of the cylinders at Madras, 60 lbs. of composition were milled from the rising to the setting of the sun; it was made into powder, proved, and found greatly inferior to that which had been only milled with 100 rounds. The powder so made was kept apart some years after it was proved, and as often found of the same inferiority. Similar quantities were milled with 1000, 500, 400, and 200 rounds, and found still in corresponding proportion inferior.

"In the 'Aide Mémoire,' p. 707, ed. 1819, may be seen the results of some experiments made in France in 1816, on the incorporation of powder in Pilon mills, whereby it appears that 17 hours' stamping produced a powder no stronger than 8 hours' stamping. The following were the ranges in metres :—

8 hours	260·6
11 hours	261·5
14 hours	262·6
17 hours	258·4

"These experiments plainly show that there is a certain point at which the process of incorporation has attained its maximum, and beyond which the powder derives from it no increase of strength.

"The practice of mingling the dust of gunpowder with the fresh composition is not in use in England.

"The gunpowder made from reworked dust or mill-powder gains no additional strength by its additional incorporation; on the contrary, it is not so strong nor so regular in its effects as the powder which is made from fresh ingredients."

From a manuscript memorandum the following is given as the Madras mode of procedure :—

"The composition having been brought from the mixing-room, one charge of 60 lbs. is placed on the bed of the mill, and sprinkled with 4 pints of distilled water; the mill is then put in motion, and at the 17th revolution 20 lbs. of gunpowder dust, received from the corning-room, is added to the above quantity

MODE OF MANUFACTURING GUNPOWDER. 77

of composition without stopping the mill, which continues revolving till it has completed 100 revolutions, which number is denoted by a tell-tale or dial plate ; the time occupied with one charge is 35 minutes.

" The composition is pressed into hard cakes by the weight of the cylinders, which weigh 6 tons."

In the following Tables we have some results worthy of notice :

	Weight of 2 cylinders.	Time of working charge.	Revolutions per hour.	Charge of the mill.	Water.	Average temperature.	Remarks.
	Tons.	Hrs.		lbs.	Qts.		Revolutions.
England	6	3	{360 / 180}	42	1	50°	{360 by water. / 180 by horses.}
Bengal	12	2	150	80	3	} 80°	
Madras (Bradock) .	9	½	200	60	...		
MSS. Mem. . .	12	½	200	60	2		

TABLE I.
Ratio of weight and time, to charge.

						Ratio, England being 1.
England	.	42 :	18 :: 1 :	·42	.	1·
Bengal	.	80 :	24 :: 1 :	·3	.	·392
Madras (Bradock)	70 :	4·5 :: 1 :	·075	.	·170
MSS. Memo .	.	60 :	6 :: 1 :	·1	.	·238

TABLE II.
Ratio of revolutions, weight, and time, to charge.

England	.	.	42 : {6480 / 3240} :: 1 : {154 / 77}	.	1·
Bengal	.	80 :	3600 :: 1 :	45	.	·292
Madras	.	60 :	900 :: 1 :	15	.	·097
Ditto, MSS. .	.	60 :	1200 :: 1 :	20	.	·129

In addition to which, at the 70th revolution, 20 lbs. of dust is added to the Madras charge, further reducing the ratio of water to the composition :

England . 1· }
Bengal . . 1·6 } in fair proportion to the heat of climate.
Madras . 1·4 }

The evaporation of the atmosphere in India is so much greater that a much shorter time, or less numbers of revolutions, will be required to reduce a mixed damp mass of composition to an equal degree of tenacity, than in Europe. The whole process is in its results very analogous to kneading of bread, mixing of mortar, or making clay for bricks : a certain quantity of mixture reduces all these articles to the required tenacity, beyond which few manufacturers would think it necessary to carry on the labour ; indeed, extra labour would vitiate the process.

If water equal to the evaporated quantity was added to every 100 revolutions, I believe the composition would retain the same tenacity up to 10,000 revolutions ; but, if water was not added, that after a time it would deteriorate into dust from which the lighter particles would escape.

I consider the Madras powder to be nearly equal to the Bengal, and neither to be greatly inferior to the English ; yet by Table I. we find the products for mixture to vary from 1 to ·238, and by Table II. from 1 to ·129—variations in no way commensurate with the trifling difference in quality of the powders. Hence I argue that a very large amount of labour has been, and is, thrown away, and that double the quantity of composition might be milled at the Ishapore works in the same period ; that much lighter cylinders would answer equally well, especially since the introduction of presses, which now entirely supersede one of the former chief objects of milling.

The question has been much argued and variously treated and tried, but never, I think, in its simple bearing.

Mixing barrels and presses have been superadded, and yet no reduction made in the quantity of milling. Can there be any reason given why the Madras powder of 100 revolutions should be equal to the Bengal of 240 ?

Colonel Galloway considered that the power of 28 lbs. would keep the cylinders in motion over the empty bed, and that 200 lbs. would continue the motion over 60 lbs. of composition.

I find it requires full work for five good bullocks to move the mills for four hours in every twelve, and to keep up 120 revolutions per hour.

MODE OF MANUFACTURING GUNPOWDER.

Each of the mills is provided with a register clock to record its revolutions.

Much argument was entered upon to determine the number of revolutions, and many experiments made ; at last a final trial was ordered. Barrels of powder were made from 100 to 600 revolutions. These were distributed to various stations, and ordered to be regularly tried.

This powder was made in 1836, after the mills had been reset up, and cylinders newly faced ; and would therefore be a superior specimen of the manufacture.

The agency proof of these samples is given in the following page.

TABLE OF AGENCY PROOF.

Description of Powder.	8 inch mortar, 2 oz. charge, ball 68lb.					8 inch mortar, 1 lb charge, ball 65¼ lb.					Eprouvette, 2 oz. charge.				
	Mortar No. 5 or 22, 1836.	Mortar No. 20, 1837.	Mortar No. 20, 1838.	Mortar No. 20, 1840.	Mortar No. 8, 1843.	Average.	Mortar No. 5 or 22, 1836.	1837.	1838.	1840.	Mortar No. 20, 1843.	Average.	1836.	1837.	1838.	1840.	1843.	Average.
Musketry.	Yds.	Yds.	Yds.	Yds.	Yds.	Yds.	Yds.				Yds.	Yds.						
100 revolutions of mills · · Made in April, 1836.	72	76	78	67	71	364·72	727	...	...	...	650	1377·688	22 23	...	21 6	20 50	21 30	85 59 21 37
200 ditto · · ·	79	76	72	67	64	358·71	721	...	...	...	633	1354·677	22 52	...	21 6	20 50	21 32	86 20 21 35
300 ditto · · ·	79	84	94	80	87	424·84	753	...	...	...	757	1510·755	22 53	...	21 44	21 9	22 4	87 50 21 57
400 ditto · · ·	75	79	81	71	70	376·75	735	...	...	...	592	1327·663	22 23	...	21 51	21 6	21 37	86 67 21 44
500 ditto · · ·	81	77	81	68	65	372·74	768	...	...	...	651	1419·709	22 56	...	21 31	21 5	21 22	86 54 21 43
600 ditto · · ·	79	83	81	85	74	409·81	756	...	...	...	653	1409·704	22 47	...	21 54	21 11	21 21	87 13 21 48
Bombay powder, 1835—36	88	84	...	...	86	258·86	790	...	...	...	721	1511·755	21 49	...	...	...	22 9	43 58 21 59
Totals, including Bombay	553	559	494	438	517	...	525	...	...	...	4657	...	158 13	...	129 12	126 11	151 35	...
Deduct Bombay	88	84	...	...	86	...	79	...	...	...	721	...	21 49	...	...	...	22 9	...
	465	475	...	...	431	...	444				3936		136 24		129 12	126 11	129 26	
Ordnance.																		
100 revolutions · · Made in April, 1836.	80	76	86	71	73	386·77	611	...	...	...	504	1115·557	20 27	...	19 3	18 48	19 20	77 38 19 20
200 ditto · · ·	89	78	89	81	74	411·82	585	...	...	...	492	1077·638	20 48	...	19 23	19	19 31	78 42 19 40
300 ditto · · ·	89	84	93	81	87	437·87	592	...	...	...	605	1197·598	20 52	...	19 51	18 57	19 45	79 25 19 51
400 ditto · · ·	88	74	86	83	75	406·81	586	...	...	...	485	1071·635	21 10	...	19 28	19 8	19 28	79 14 19 48
500 ditto · · ·	87	79	92	83	78	419·83	584	...	...	...	492	1076·538	20 50	...	19 40	19 11	18 28	78 17 19 34
600 ditto · · ·	90	85	92	86	78	431·86	602	...	...	...	492	1094·547	20 57	...	19 55	19 15	19 16	79 23 19 50
Bombay powder, 1835—36	80	85	...	...	81	...	592	...	...	...	528	1122·561	19 39	...	...	...	19 17	38 56 19 28
Totals, including Bombay	603	561	538	488	546	...	415	...	...	...	3598	...	144 51	...	117 20	114 19	135 5	...
Deduct Bombay	80	85	...	...	81	...	59	...	...	...	528	...	19 39	...	...	...	19 17	...
	523	476	538	488	465	...	356				3070		125 12		117 20	114 19	115 48	

Note.—Mortars No. 5 and 22 were returned in 1836 as deteriorated, after two years' use. No. 20 was used at the short range till 1842, and having become deteriorated was sent to the long range, and is inferior. No. 8, used but little for long range, was in 1843 brought to the short range.

To determine the best quantity for mill charge, Colonel Galloway records the following experiments :—

8-INCH BRASS MORTAR, SHELL 50 LBS., CHARGE 3 OZ.

	Mill charge 60 lb.		Mill charge 80 lb.	
	Musketry.	Ordnance.	Musketry.	Ordnance.
	Yards.	Yards.	Yards.	Yards.
100 revolutions	128	129	128	119
200 ditto	150	144	149	131
300 ditto	172	172	167	158
400 ditto	165	158	155	141
Totals	615	603	599	549
	Eprouvette.			
	Degrees.	Degrees.	Degrees.	Degrees.
100 revolutions	24	21	23 1/4	21 1/4
200 ditto	24 3/4	21 1/4	24 2/4	22 1/4
300 ditto	25 3/4	23 2/4	25 1/4	23 1/4
400 ditto	25 2/4	22 3/4	24 3/4	22 1/4
Totals	100	88 2/4	97 3/4	89

These trials exhibit but trifling difference.

Again, we have the following remarkable experiment on the subject of mill charge :—

	8-inch Mortar, 68 lb. ball, 2 oz. charge.	Eprouvette.
	Yards.	Degrees.
Mill charge 40 lbs., 300 revolutions musketry.	95	22 3/8
„ 50 lbs., „ „	95 1/4	22 1/8
„ 60 lbs., „ „	96 1/5	22 3/8

and to this last charge 14 lbs. of dust were added, making the charge 80 lbs. at the taking out. Here we do not find any of the difference we were prepared to expect; in fact, as each of these had early attained its maximum effect, so they remained stationary.

In the matter of the velocity of the cylinders, I find recorded in the old books of the Agency the following experiment, made by horses, giving 300 revolutions in one and a-half hour :—

	Date.	Musketry.			Ordnance.		
		8-inch Mortar, 65¼ lb. ball, 1 lb. charge.	8-inch Mortar, 68 lb. ball, 2 oz. charge.	Eprouvette.	8-inch Mortar, 65¼ lb. ball, 1 lb. charge.	8-inch Mortar, 68 lb. ball, 2 oz. charge.	Eprouvette.
Powder milled by horses, 300 revolutions in 1½ hour.	6 Dec. 1834	Yards. 725	Yards. 88	° ′ 22·17	Yards. 554	Yards. 94	° ′ 20·5
	19 Dec. 1834	753	75	23·5	593	79	20·40
	12 Jan. 1835	688	75	22·50	511	76	20·30
	Total .	2166	238	68·12	1658	249	61·15
	Average .	722	79	22·44	552	83	20·25

This is probably the quickest rate of revolution ever given to cylinders in India.

The slowest rate which I can find recorded is, that of the commencement of the season, 1848; the bullocks being all new were extremely slow, and required two hours and forty minutes to work off the charge.

Powder milled by bullocks: 240 revolutions in 2 hours and 40 min. October, 1847.	Average of five trials made on the 1st of every month to April.	Musketry.			Ordnance.		
		8-in. Mortar, 68-lb. Ball, 1-lb. Charge.	8-in. Mortar, 68-lb. Ball, 2-oz. Charge.	Eprouvette.	8-in. Mortar, 68-lb. Ball, 1-lb. Charge.	8-in. Mortar, 68-lb. Ball, 2-oz. Charge.	Eprouvette.
		Yds. 784	Yds. 102	° ′ 23·9	Yds. 630	Yds. 101	° ′ 20·49

The 1-lb. charge was here with a 68-lb. ball. We may affirm that no great gain is apparent from the difference of 300 revolutions in one and a half hour, and 240 revolutions in two hours and forty minutes, the first being, in fact, a double velocity.

We have thus seen that there appears no great appreciable difference between a double ratio of mill charge of velocity or of revolutions. It must be noticed that we have no measure for the quantity of tossing about, the amount of evaporation of the moisture, or any very precise mention of the quantity of water ; whether, for instance, in the 600 revolutions in four hours only the three quarts of water was given, as settled for the 300 revolutions in two hours, or whether double water was afforded, which would require, of course, double the work to reduce the composition to the same state of tenacity and adhesion.

Density of mass is not sought for, because this operation is now obtained by the subsequent operation of pressing. All, then, we seek in the operation of milling is, to overcome the natural repulsion between the particles, to expel the internal air from between the atoms, and thus engender a strong tenacity and adhesion amongst them : a point more to be judged of by touch and experience, than reached by measure.

Extremely dry dust, without being remilled and watered, cannot be pressed into a cake, on the one hand ; while, on the other, a very small addition to the three quarts of water would cause a liquid state, in comparison with the usual damp composition ; and between these extremes lies the answer to the inquiry.

Hence the heat of the atmosphere, quantity of water, amount of tossing about and being pressed to cause the water to percolate the mass, must all be considered—and these will hardly be the same in any two charges ; but for practical work, a proper medium quantity of each is soon found.

In the native manufactories of gunpowder in India, the composition is made much more damp, and in this state is forced to drop or distil through the catgut sieves they use to form their grains.

My opinion is, that a little less water, and a reduced number of revolutions, would fabricate equally good powder ; and in the event of a sudden demand of powder for war, a greater supply might be furnished in a shorter time.

The following record, in regard to the weight of cylinders, may well find a place here :—

Description of Gunpowder.	8-in. Mortar, 68-lb. Ball, 2-oz. Charge.	Pendulum Eprouvette.	
	Feet.	Deg.	Min.
Cannon.			
Heavy Bengal double cylinder mill	313¼	23	36⅜
Light Bombay ,, ,,	310⅝	23	31¾
Light Bombay single ,,	306⅝	22	30
Musketry.			
Heavy Bengal double cylinder mill	314¾	25	45
Light Bombay ,, ,,	320½	25	40
Light Bombay single ,,	292½	25	36⅓

All circumstances, so necessary to any comparison of gunpowder, are not recorded, but the ranges indicate very little inferiority in the single light cylinder.

The single cylinder would allow the turners much more time and space in which to turn over the composition, and break up the lumps; in short, to give the desired intermixture and motion.

The state of the mills, as to the level surfaces of the bed and cylinders, is of much consequence. In this point, I believe, consists the reduction of the revolutions; for I am convinced that 100 revolutions in a good mill are equal—nay, superior—to 200 in one out of order; and that after a year's work in a mill, it will require a compensation of at least twenty revolutions to keep it up to its proper work.

We are not told in the above record the breadth of the faces or the distance of the cylinders from their working centre, and hence the area of the ring of the bed over which the composition is spread and worked; elements affecting the thickness of the composition, the velocities, and hence the milling obtained.

In England, in consequence of the danger from explosions, the mill charge is regulated by law to 42 lbs. of composition, which is well damped.

The revolutions are variously stated; by some authors as 480 in the hour from water power; the time of working the charge being from three to six hours, according to the state of the atmosphere.

Ploughs are used; but I strongly suspect that the turners are not, as with us, constantly employed *over* the powder, but now and then visit the mills to lay the composition even; having previously stopped the machinery. Many of the cylinders are of stone; and cast-iron beds are mentioned by Mr. Wilkinson.

It requires one chuprassee, two turners, six bullocks, and three drivers to work off four charges in twenty-four hours at Ishapore.

The cost of the present mills may be resolved into—

	r.	a.	p.
Two gun-metal cylinders, about 5 tons each, at 1r. 3a. 4p. per lb.	27,057	1	8
One bed of ditto, at 1r. 1a. 8p. per lb.	8,546	13	10·4
Machinery	2,500	0	0
House and foundation	3,625	10	2
Total	41,729	9	1·2

The necessary weight may be obtained by cast-iron wheels inserted into a brass rim, should new cylinders ever be required.

Stone beds might be obtained at a less cost than the above-mentioned articles of brass, which are soft, and soon rubbed into hollows.

Colonel Tennant, Bengal Artillery, writes to me that he considered powder made by the pilon mills to be superior to that fabricated by the cylinder mills, for this reason:—that the sulphur played a certain part in the composition of binding into one molecule the other particles, whether by the plastic adhesive tenacity inherent in the sulphur, or by its electricity. If the former be taken as the active cause, a certain degree of heat and friction is requisite to generate this adhesive attraction and soften the sulphur; while, if electricity be considered as the combining and binding cause, then also was friction and heat requisite.

The nature of the pilon mill was such, that by the fall of the pestle much motion was given to the composition as it escaped sidewards and upwards from under the pestle; while, by the movement of the trough longitudinarily, these side heaps were in turn brought under a second pestle; and in their turn the composition of these side heaps was forced down, much escaping laterally and upwards; that thus there resulted a constant motion and friction, and intermixture of the particles, which raised the sulphur into the adhesive state, or excited its electricity. That, taking either cause as the active one, a particle of sulphur required heat and friction to generate the required state; and then a certain freedom of motion in space, as it were, to permit the particle of sulphur to wander about until it had drawn into itself its proper coating of charcoal and saltpetre; which obtained, it then lost its power of attraction and adhesion, or even electricity. Now the pilon mills had all the required elements of motion, friction, and intermixture, while the very essence of the cylinder mills is pressing, which in its nature represses both mixture and motion, and movement of the particles, except as much as may result from the ploughs and the forks in the hands of the turners.

The longer the milling is continued, the harder and denser becomes the cake; and thus there is less motion of the particles. Convex-faced cylinders cause something of this lateral play, and when moving in different tracks, they afforded more mixing by the second breaking up the cake formed under the preceding cylinder.

Thus convex-faced cylinders, not following each other in the same track, are superior to flat-faced cylinders following each other at the same distance from the centre of motion.

The necessary heat may be obtained in this country (India) with a less velocity than is requisite for the colder climate of England; hence the mills may require to be worked with far greater quickness in Europe.

To the absence of motion, want of mixture, and of agitation, may be attributed an inferiority, perhaps, of cylinder to pilon mills.

The pilon mills used in India were generally of two batteries of 12 pilons each. The theoretic weight was about 80 lbs., falling from a height of 10 ft. at 50 times in a minute, on a charge of 22 lbs., for a period of from seven to eleven hours; thus an enormous quantity of pounding was given to a small charge.

Bruising.

The next step in the process of the manufacture conveys the

composition from the mill to the bruising-house. Here men, seated in a large vat, pick out any very hard bits of mill-cake, as fit for corning ; and rub down between a roller and a plate of zinc all smaller lumps, till the mass is of one uniform consistency.

Hence there is an apparent undoing of the work of the mills in this operation.

The reduction to one consistency is necessary, to enable the composition to run into the interstices between the sheets of copper of the press-box.

There is perhaps no fitter place to introduce a question, often raised, how best to re-work up the dust which is obtained at every stage of the manufacture.

It has been mixed up with the fresh composition under the cylinders, in the bruising-house, before reaching the press, and in several other modes ; which have all ended, at Ishapore, in a mill being appropriated to the dust, at 40 revolutions to the charge, with one quart of water. Some particles of the dust, in its working and re-working, must receive many thousands of revolutions.

It is by many manufacturers considered that the dust consists of a greater portion of charcoal, which has separated in the course of manufacture, being the lightest of the component particles ; but, on analysis, I did not find this to be the case.

I do not believe the dust to require more incorporation than it has already received ; but it may become too dry for the press, especially in India, hence the propriety of a little water and a few turns under the cylinders; forty revolutions is the utmost that is required.

This point is of importance, as to finish 100 barrels of powder, requires 140 barrels of new composition, 40 being returned in dust from the various stages.

Several trials were made on this subject, which are here given.

The operations of the bruising-house require one man for each mill.

EFFECTS OF NUMBER OF REVOLUTIONS.

No. 1.—ISHAPORE, APRIL 22, 1834.

Description of Powder.	Musketry.		Ordnance.	
	8-in. Mortar, 1-lb. Charge, 65½-lb. Ball.	Pendulum Eprouvette.	8-in. Mortar, 1-lb. Charge, 65½-lb. Ball.	Pendulum Eprouvette.
	Yds.	Deg. Min.	Yds.	Deg. Min.
Powder with only 50 revolutions in the mills	729	22 25	590	20 45
Powder with only 100 revolutions in the mills	754	23 7½	602	21 2½
Powder from dust, but not re-milled, dry, pressed as usual .	791	23 20	619	21 25
Powder from dust re-milled with 50 revolutions	758	23 25	605	21 20
Powder from dust re-milled with 100 revolutions . . .	747	22 25	602	21 35
Powder from dust re-milled with 150 revolutions	766	23 10	618	21 35

No. 2.—ISHAPORE, MAY 1, 1834.

Description of Powder.	Musketry.			Ordnance.			Remarks.
	8-in. Mortar, 1-lb. Charge, 65½-lb. Ball.	8-in. Mortar, 2-oz. Charge, 80-lb. Ball.	Pendulum Eprouvette.	8-in. Mortar, 1-lb. Charge, 65½-lb. Ball.	8-in. Mortar, 2-oz. Charge, 80-lb. Ball.	Pendulum Eprouvette.	
	Yds.	Yds.	Deg. Min.	Yds.	Yds.	Deg. Min.	
Powder from composition receiving 300 revolutions in the cylinder mills, not mixed with dust, of common manufacture	747	94	22 10	549	98	19 50	Very equal.
Powder made solely from dust of the common manufacture, re-milled with 50 revolutions in the cylinder mills, corned, glazed, &c., as the above	731	94	22 30	554	101	19 50	

No. 3.—ISHAPORE, JUNE 2, 1834.

Description of Powder.	Musketry.			Ordnance.			Remarks.
	8-in. Mortar, 1-lb. Charge, 65¼-lb. Ball.	8-in. Mortar, 2-oz. Charge, 80-lb. Ball.	Pendulum Eprouvette.	8-in. Mortar, 1-lb. Charge, 65¾-lb. Ball.	8-in. Mortar, 2-oz. Charge, 80-lb. Ball.	Pendulum Eprouvette.	
	Yds.	Yds.	Deg. Min.	Yds.	Yds.	Deg. Min.	
Powder made from fresh composition and dust incorporated together in the mills; 15 lb. of dust being added to the charge of fresh composition at 260 revolutions	755	95	22 45	591	91	21 2½	
Powder from fresh composition and dust, incorporated in the bruising-house as usual with all common manufacture	744	95	23 30	598	94	20 55	
Ishapore common manufacture delivery, No. 63	762	97	23 7½	587	96	20 45	About one month old.
Ditto, ditto, No. 64	754	100	22 50	583	104	20 47	
Ditto, ditto, No. 65	739	98	22 55	603	102	20 55	

I believe all these powders to be of one age—about a month. It is certainly strange how very little difference is to be discovered between them. There exists an indication that the 50 revolutions fresh powder is slightly inferior; that of 100 revolutions proving the best, even superior to that of 300.

The dust-powder of 50 revolutions is equal to any, even to the dust of 150 revolutions.

Dust-powder, being already dampish, would probably reach the amount of tenacity of fresh composition of 100 revolutions in about half the time. There appears no difference, whether the dust was mixed up in the bruising-house or under the cylinders.

In the 300 revolutions, fresh composition, as probably the most dense, we trace the worst range in the ordnance-powder, and in the dust not milled at all, the very best range. I have no doubt this last powder was very porous and light, hence in the larger charges it ranged most high, but how this powder would have stood travelling and keeping was not ascertained.

Much depends on the state of the dryness of the dust; when very dry, I could hardly force it into a rotten porous light cake, which would not have borne graining.

Much depends, as stated before, on the state of the beds and cylinders; when these are perfect, I suspect the best powder is reached at 150 revolutions, and that all above is labour lost, whether with dust or fresh composition.

Pressing.

The next step carries the bruised composition to the press.

In earlier days of the manufacture, this operation was not performed; but the composition was pressed into cake, more or less thick, under the cylinders.

This mode was, in the first instance, superseded by a press, in which the whole mass was formed into a dense block, to be subsequently broken up.

A great improvement next resulted from the introduction of copper sheets between strata of composition. This plan has been attended with the best success.

The presses are thus described by Colonel Galloway :—

"We now introduce, horizontally, sheets of copper, at regular intervals of three-quarters of an inch, among the composition; so that, when the whole is pressed, the composition is taken out in separate cakes, of a superficies equal to the horizontal section of the press-box, and half an inch in thickness.

"These cakes are perfectly smooth and well defined on both sides, resembling so many slabs of black marble, and almost equally hard when dry; and when broken still more closely resembling in fracture that of marble, having all that closeness of grain and gloss which is seen in that substance when recently fractured.

"For the convenience of loading the press, the composition-containing box is made to fold backwards, instead of being loaded with composition, as it stands within the cheeks of the press; the front moves on hinges, and is made to lift up.

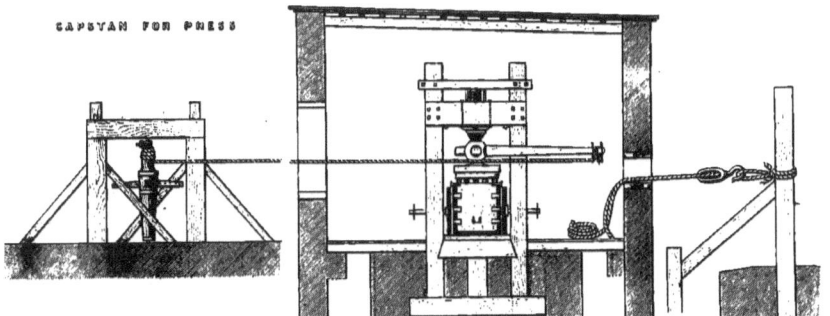

Plate 7.

PLAN SECTION AND ELEVATION OF NEW PRESS HOUSE ISHAPORE.

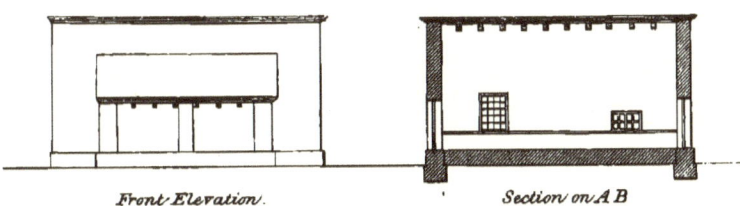

Front Elevation.   Section on A B

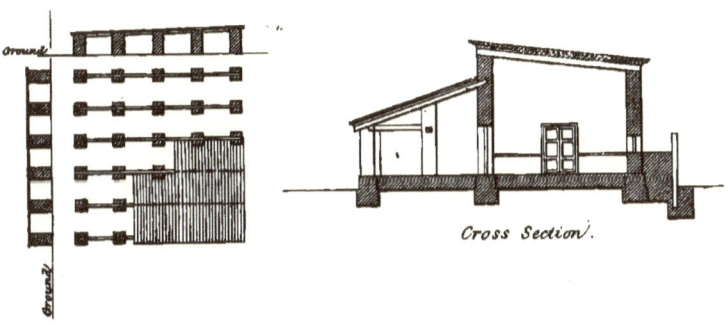

Cross Section.

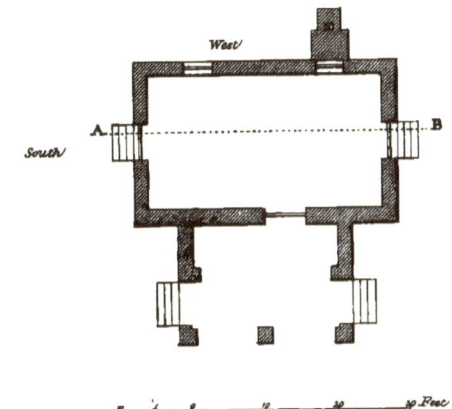

Published by John Weale London.

"The whole box, thus folded backwards, takes its position behind the press, with its front now become, as it were, the lid or top ; so that the sheets of copper, horizontal when the box was in the press, are now vertical, and the composition is put in between them with great ease and all at once, which shortens the labour of loading the press exceedingly : for without this contrivance, each layer of composition must have been put in separately, beginning with the lowermost ; it is, in fact, an improvement on the French mode of pressing in plateaux.

"When loaded, the front is shut down and bolted, and the box is raised up, and being attached to the bottom of the press by hinges, is folded up into its position between the cheeks of the press. The blocks are now placed over the lid or top of the box, and the power of the screw is applied.

"These blocks are of hard wood; and as well as the lid of the box, are made small enough to go down within the box, as the pressure is exerted.

"The quantity of composition put into the press is regularly measured by a measure. Our presses hold 500 lbs., and are worked by eight men, with a lever and capstan, the arms of which should be 6 ft. instead of 4, as at present, which would save labour. In order to secure as much as can be done the essential point of equality of composition, besides the test of exhaustion of the power in the men, we have the presses gauged and a mark made, so that the volume of composition being always the same, when the stamp of the press reaches that mark, we know that a sufficient quantity of compression has been given.

"If sufficiently pressed, the quantity of moisture being correct, as I have before said, the cake on being broken presents a clean, smooth, shining fracture; otherwise the fracture is coarse, rough, and dull, without any gloss, an appearance so easily discriminated that it is unnecessary to be more minute in describing it."

There are small rods $\frac{3}{4}$ in. square, used to keep the copper sheets separate when loading.

From Mr. Braddock we gather only a few remarks on the art of pressing, because it was not in use at Madras. He says :—

"At Waltham Abbey each 500 lbs. of composition received pressure considered to be equal to 600 tons."

The following is a fair description of the press in use at Ishapore. (See plates.)

The upright posts are 22 in. broad. The screw beam is 2 ft. 2 in. broad. The thicknesses are shown in the plate.

A tenon of 9 in. passes through the foundation timber, and is bolted through with an $1\frac{1}{4}$ in. bolt. Of the screw-box beam, two tenons $4\frac{1}{4}$ in. thick, pass through each post; and two of 4 in. thick slip across the front and rear edge of the posts; and two bolts, $1\frac{1}{4}$ in. thick, secure each end. The head is composed of two pieces, about 10 in. broad, let upon the post half their breadth, and let 1 in. into the posts, so that they project 4 in. front and rear. The space between, at the outer end, is filled up with a small block, and bolted with inch bolts.

Above the beam, under the press-box, is a platform rabbeted, $1\frac{1}{2}$ in. into the faces of the posts, and extending 8 in. beyond the cheeks of the press in front and rear.

In front and rear of the press-box, a rabbet, $\frac{1}{2}$ in. deep, is made across; into these rabbets the low edges of the front and rear planks rest. These planks are 3 in. thick, chamfered off at each end to 2 in. The false cheeks of the press are 3 in. thick, and so long as to extend $3\frac{1}{2}$ in. beyond the outside of these planks; and across each end a piece of hard wood is riveted $3\frac{1}{2}$ in. broad, and 1 in. thick. When the press-box is filled and set in its place, the front and rear planks are set into the rabbets in the platform, and pressing against the press-box; then the false cheeks are screwed home, so that they likewise touch the press-box, and the ends of the front and rear planks are laid hold of by the piece of hard wood riveted across the ends of the false cheeks. Thus forming another and stronger box, closely embracing the press-box on all sides, so that it is enabled to sustain the lateral pressure, which is very considerable.

The press-box is made of Sisoo planks, 1½ in. thick, and strongly clamped with copper clamps, riveted on the inside; it is 11 ft. 5½ in. wide, 2 ft. 3½ in. long, and 2 ft. 7½ in. deep. The screw, inclusive of the head, is 2 ft. 10 in. long; diameter over the threads 7½ in., thickness of the head ⅜ of an inch, depth of the thread ⁵⁄₁₆ths, thickness of the thread ⅜ of an inch; diameter of the head of the screw 14 in.; length of the head 13½ in., diameter of the hole in the head, 7 in.

Taking into consideration the loss of the time by constant shifting of the lever, this machine (though not costly in itself) is expensive in its result on the powder.

After the press-box is charged, 8 press blocks are put in, at which point there are 3·5 threads of the screw exposed; after which, the operation is as follows :—

Layer of Press blocks.	Quarter Revolutions of Screw.	Revolutions of Screw.
2	20 by hand of 4 men	5·
	7 by 2 handspikes, 1 man each . . .	1·75
1	24 with small lever, by 3 men	6·
1	8 small lever	2·
	22 large lever and windlass, with 6 men .	5·5
4	81	20·25

Now, as it requires four quarter movements, or four quarter revolutions, of the lever, to one revolution of the screw, the levers have to be shifted eighty times, and the screw to be screwed back twice, to admit the blocks.

The windlass makes 3½ revolutions to 1 quarter revolution of the lever.

There remains 1 foot 3 inches of mass in the box when finished. The loss of time and loss of impulse is very great. The present screws might be improved if second or third threads were added to them;[*] or, if they were fitted with a crown wheel,

---

[*] After this was written, there was one awful explosion at the press-house; five men were killed, and not a vestige was left of the building. The lighted bits

and some machinery admitting of their being worked by bullocks, with no stoppage for shifting the lever, or addition of press-blocks: a division of labour among the men, and a succession of boxes, one being emptied, the second being pressed, and the third being filled by different parties, would enable one press to work off the composition of four or five mills with greater facility. The only disadvantage I can discover being the larger quantity of powder assembled in one spot, and the danger of explosion when hurry and velocity are given to operations on gunpowder.

Great care is requisite that the composition be uniformly and evenly worked into the intervals between the copper sheets, in loading the press, with the wooden slices.

The present press-boxes at Ishapore contain about 320 lbs. of composition, being the charges of four mills. It takes about one and a-half hour to work one box clear.

The cake, on being taken out of the box, has a dampish appearance; but on being exposed to the sun, becomes quite as hard and even very similar to slate.

If the great force used in compression be borne in mind, some idea may be formed of the force again requisite to separate the cake from the sheets of copper, or indeed to re-open the box.

To make an accurate calculation of the power of the screw moved under the many modes just described, with the consideration of the resistance of the sheets of copper, and of the composition, and of the friction of the screw and ropes, would be no easy matter.

I am induced to write off all the turns by hand and handspikes to the above; to consider the windlass as merely sufficient to bring into operations the full powers of six men, and to estimate the pressure as that attained by the six last turns of the screw. Then—

of wood were scattered over the whole enclosure, and the results might have been terrible. The press-houses at Ishapore are all too small, and hardly placed at sufficient distances from each other: no accident had before taken place.

Diameter of the circle of leverage . . 16 ft. 8 in.
Distance between the threads . . . ⅜ of an inch.
Power of a man . . . 150 lbs.
Number of men . . 6
Revolutions of the screw . 6

Therefore, $16.8 \times 3.1416 \times \frac{3}{8} = 1407$, say 1400; $1400 \times 6 \times 150 \times \frac{1}{2240} = 562$ tons per revolution of the screw.

$17.5 \times 27.5 = 481$ square inches in the superficies of the box.

$\frac{562}{481} = 1.17$ tons, or 23 cwt. per square inch.

375 lbs. of composition = 6000 ounces.

$\frac{562}{6000} = .093$ tons, or 1·86 cwt. of pressure per ounce of composition.

Mr. Braddock says "that every 500 lbs. of cake was at Waltham Abbey submitted to a mean theoretic pressure of 600 tons."

It is difficult to estimate the result of an increased number of turns of the screw. I pressed some composition with both eleven and with twenty-two turns of the lever; but the cake from the latter did not indicate any greater density. The fact is, after a certain point, I suspect the strain fell on the various parts of the machine, on the bottom of the box, tenons, cross heads, and side-posts, but did not increase the density of the composition.

Composition fit to press is too damp to run into our density measure. Fresh dry composition from the mixing barrels will so run, and gives a density of 145 drams, while dry much-handled dust gives 240; our density measure holds 307 drams of distilled water $\frac{240}{307} = .78$, as the specific gravity of dust. We press the composition into half its bulk: therefore $.78 \times 2 = 1.56$, will be about the specific gravity of cake. I made many experiments by taking the specific gravity of cake in distilled water. Common press cake runs between 1·6 and 1·8, while mill cake varies between 1·5 and 1·7; the average is about 1·75. Of course this result depends on many circumstances, as the bit selected being from the centre of the box under the screw, or from the sides. There was an indication that thicker pieces gave a greater density; perhaps in the thinner pieces all the water was evaporated, while in the thicker bits the interstices may have been occupied by water and not air; for, on the evaporation of the damp, the interstices would not close up, but remain as honeycombs filled with air. I thus make solid gunpowder to have a specific gravity of 1·75. Allow our ordnance powder to give by our measure of 33·25 cubic inches, 280 drams, its specific gravity is ·912.

Hutton gives solid gunpowder 1·74, and gunpowder in grains close shaken ·937; a proof that my calculations are not very far wrong. Probably the average of our cake is 1·8, or higher than the English.

The advantages and disadvantages of pressing and glazing powder are fairly laid down by Mr. Braddock in the following memorandums, which in some measure anticipate the question of glazing. He says:—

"The susceptibility that even the best powder possesses to absorb moisture from the hygrometric property of the charcoal, renders pressing and glazing always desirable, and in some cases indispensable.

"It is essential that gunpowder should not only possess great impellent force, when newly made, but that it retain its force to remote periods. No other modes of effecting this are known at present, than by imparting density to the powder, and a gloss or polish to the surface of the grain.

"The operations of pressing and glazing preserve the powder; they make it competent to withstand the shaking and friction of carriage; and render it less liable to deteriorate if kept long in store, or if subjected to the influence of humid atmospheres."

This cannot be better illustrated than by an extract from the report of experiments made on Marlbro' Downs in 1811.

"Mill cake gunpowder cannot retain its strength because the grains are too soft and porous, and, in consequence, attract moisture like a sponge. Mill cake gunpowder made in the year 1789, ranged this year 3628 yards.

"Gunpowder manufactured from hard-pressed cake has a firm close grain; and, consequently, is not liable to attract moisture. A charge of this powder similar to the charges which were used with unpressed cake powder, ranged 4193 yards, although it had been made five years longer than the former.

"Moderately glazed powder is more durable than unglazed powder, because the grains are rendered firmer, and less liable to attract moisture.

"The benefits of pressing and glazing are absolute; the disadvantage (if so it may be termed) is rather imaginary than real, unless the powder be of inferior quality.

"These operations interrupt the rapidity of combustion, and therefore, in all ordinary cases, they impair the propellant force of the powder. This deterioration has been estimated as high as from $\frac{1}{5}$ to $\frac{1}{4}$ of the range: that is, if a given charge of mill cake powder ranges 1000 yards, the same charge of the same powder when pressed and glazed will range but 750 or 800 yards. This refers to the powder only when newly made; we have just shown that it does not apply when it is 20 or 30 years old, for then pressed powder will range further than unpressed.

"It is a well-known fact that pressed and glazed powder does not range so far as mill cake gunpowder.

"The Hon. Mr. Napier, while superintendent of the Royal Laboratory at Woolwich, found, from a mean of 600 experiments, that pressing and glazing gunpowder reduced its strength, about one-fifth if the powder is good, and nearly one-fourth if it is of inferior quality. This ratio of deterioration corresponds exactly with experiments I made on gunpowder fabricated at Madras in 1813, according to the English system of manufacture. The loss of range was a little more than one-fifth, but less than one-fourth; but the degree of density, as well as size of the grain, will very much modify the result of experiments made to ascertain the quantity of loss.

"It does not appear necessary to investigate the causes why dense powder ranges short of lighter powder of the same manufacture; it is sufficient that such is the fact; but if it be thought a question of curiosity worth examining into, we think it attributable not to loss of inherent strength, or the less copious extrication of the elastic fluids, but simply to the delay in their due development. We think that the gunpowder of light specific gravity ranges further than powder of greater density, only because it explodes with greater facility; for the same reason that fir will burn quicker than oak, the one is more solid than the other. Time, however, reverses this action; the porousness of the light powder makes it more susceptible of injury, it imbibes more humidity than the dense powders, and what it gains in immediate effect, it loses by long keeping."

Thus dense powder, in large charges, does not display its full impellent power before the act of impulsion is over—from its slower ignition. Suppose we were to make a column of solid cake one foot long, just fitting a musket, it would not explode, but burn vividly and quietly to the end. The fluid disengaged would force the column of solid composition up the bore; the portion unburnt would be shot forth into the air, but to no useful purpose; the unburnt portion would be greater as the density of the solid column of composition was greater. The same takes place in long narrow charges of power; much is exploded to no purpose as the density of the powder is increased. There exists a ratio of inflammation to the elasticity of the fluid, could we hit upon it, but then such ratio varies with every change of circumstance.

In small charges, exposed over a large space, and hence not deep, density is an object, as it concentrates the fire and fluid, otherwise left too free and unconfined; but this soon disappears with increase of charge. On the other hand, density is of the greatest effect in preserving powder through time, carriage, and change of climate. Hence we sacrifice a portion of the impelling power to the necessity of durability, and perhaps in some measure also to the desire of pleasing the eye of inspectors, who require a hard uniform grain, free from dust.

Again, each year's keeping, and every mile of transit, combine by the abrasion of angles to form a dust, and thus to counteract this fault of too hard a grain. The greater the density of the cake, the less may be the size of the grains.

VARIETIES OF DENSITY.

The following statement of densities are from my own experiments :—

Mill cake, fresh, ⅜-inch thick, 4 or 5 days old . . .	1·76	
,, 1 day, thick and well cleaned, a selected bit	2·09	Average.
,, 50 revolutions, 25 days old, unpicked, rough	1·54	1·73
,, 100 ,, ,, .	1·70	
,, 150 ,, ,, .	1·58	
Press cake, thin fine pieces, selected, ¼-inch thick, 5 days old	1·65	
,, not cleaned, rough, 6 months	1·86	
,, ,, 7 days, 22 turns . . .	1·83	
,, ,, ,, 11 ,, ...	2·02	Average.
,, dry dust, 14 days old	1·80	1·79
,, best that could be selected, ¼-inch thick, 22 turns	1·66	
·, ,, ,, ⅛-inch thick	1·85	
,, cylinder mill, very thin and clean . . .	1·69	

The following facts were ascertained :—1280 drams of fresh press-cake, placed in a house of the mill-yard during the month of November, parted with 14 drs. of weight by evaporation of the moisture in seven days = ·019. Exposed for six months in a like situation, from April to November, 5 lbs. lost 14 drs. in the first seven days, and then continued nearly at the same weight during six months ; 5 lbs. of cake, well dried on exposure to the sun, absorbed 8 drs. of moisture in three days, and the same quantity of very damp cake parted with 15 oz. 6 drs. of water in the same period. The press-cake requires two or three days in the sun ere it is fit to corn. The total quantity of water given to composition is about ·075. In England, the best Bramah's hydrostatic press is used for pressing, at a cost of some 1200*l.* each. In time these will no doubt be introduced into India. The present presses in use cost about 3000 rupees each, of which the screws, male and female, will require nearly 1000 rupees.

The complement of men for each press is one mate and six men to work off cake for twenty barrels of powder in twelve hours.

The copper sheets should be changed by degrees, some new ones being given every month, as much depends on the perfect condition of these sheets; the drying-terraces attached to each press should be covered with copper, to increase the heat, and thus more quickly dry the cake. The cake being now well dried in the sun, is advanced to the next stage of the process.

Granulation.

The old process of corning, or of breaking up the solid cake into grains, is described by Colonel Galloway as follows :—

"The process of corning, that is, of forming the powder into grains, was formerly performed at this manufactory as described in several books, viz., by breaking the large block of composition above described, of 500 or 600 lbs. weight perhaps, first with heavy wooden mallets, and then with light ones, till it was reduced to small pieces from the size of a cubic inch downwards; these were put in small quantities into sieves of parchment with holes in them, just sufficiently large to admit the largest grains of the powder required. Everything smaller went through of course. These sieves were placed on a frame horizontally supported (some frames contained 24 sieves) from the four corners, and revolving by the motion of a crank in the centre, so that a violent horizontal and circular motion might be given to the frame. Over the composition in the sieves a flat but circular, rounded piece of lignum vitæ, or other hard wood, was put, so that when the frames revolved this disc moved round within the sieves, dashing against the rims with considerable force, and breaking the bits of composition that might intervene; this action of the disc, and motion of the powder under it, broke the larger lumps of composition to a size equal to admit of their passing through the holes of the sieves; and also rounded them into spherical grains, more or less perfect in proportion to the hardness of the composition.

"But this season, since the cylinder-mills have been in use, and I have endeavoured to attain the utmost possible density of grain in our powder, I have not only found that the corning-sieves, as such, have been perfectly useless, but that in breaking down the cakes to granulate the powder, the wooden slabs and

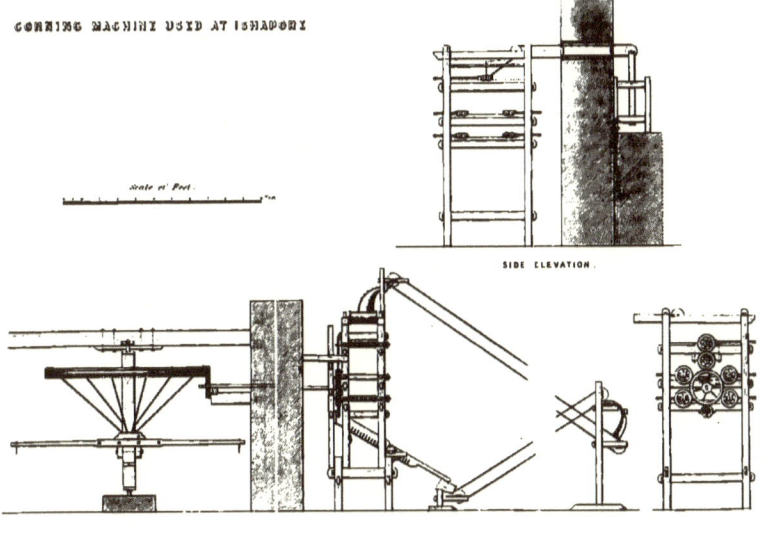
CORNING MACHINE USED AT ISHAPORE

mallets used before were chopped up by the sharp edges of the hard grains, like so much chaff; these chopped fibres of wood were necessarily mixed with the composition and the dust of the powder, from which it was impossible wholly or even nearly to extract them; millions of particles, being of the same gravity with the dust, fell along with it in winnowing, and being of the same size, went through the same meshes of the sieves.

"They were consequently carried back to the mill and worked up with the fresh composition, forming a most extensive impurity in it, equal perhaps to that of which I had hoped we had got rid by the introduction of metallic cylinders and beds, in the room of the wooden troughs in which the incorporation was formerly carried on here.

"I have been able to obviate this great evil entirely by introducing slabs of metal instead of wood, and using mallets of lignum vitæ, so that no foreign substance can now find its way into the powder; these slabs are 3 ft. 10 in. long, 15 in. broad, and $\frac{3}{4}$ in. thick, and are cast out of the old beds of the cylinder mills made here by Mr. Farquhar many years ago, composed of a kind of pewter, Banca tin, with an alloy of zinc."

This mode, with trifling alteration, appears to have been continued until 1834, when the modern granulating machine was introduced.

At present the press-cake, after being exposed to the sun and air for about 48 hours, is, when quite cool, sent to be corned : which is done as follows :—

The corning machine consists of a frame of strong tough wood, in which are placed five pairs of brass rollers (toothed), with several brass wheels to work them. The cake is passed between these rollers which reduce it to grain and a portion of dust.

There is a large sieve under the machine, kept in motion by the same power that works the machine, one pair of bullocks. All cake that is broken up fine enough for the grain of powder passes through this sieve and is received into small barrels underneath it, while the parts that are not broken fine enough are carried back, on elevating bands worked by the machinery, to be passed again through the rollers. (See plate.)

As the small barrels under the sieve are filled they are carried to the sifting house.

The runs from the different corning machines in various-sized grains are about as follows :

	Ordnance.	Musket.	Dust.	Loss.
Bengal cake, three days in store	·334	·329	·312	·023
,, ,, one month ,,	·360	·348	·285	·005
England, Waltham Abbey	·555	·277	·16	·006
Madras	·38	·22	·40	...
Bombay	·37	·31	·29	·03

The large sieve fixed to the corning house frame is composed of brass wire of 13×13 meshes; all that passes through this sieve is fit for powder of some one of the three sorts—Ordnance (O.) ; Musketry (M.) ; and Rifle (R.) ; below which are Fine (F.), and Dust (D.). These two last are hardly to be called powder. All that will not pass through the sieve in the corning house is returned to the rollers to be broken up smaller.

The machinery of the corning house is of a very rough description, all cast and finished in the Agency. The metal is made purposely soft, to avoid any chance of concussion. All parts exposed to friction are kept well oiled. The wear and tear of the wheels and rollers is very great ; a set of wheels would probably last five seasons, but a set of rollers hardly two seasons; the latter are 3 ft. $2\frac{1}{2}$ in. long and $3\frac{4}{10}$ in. in diameter—perhaps too light, as they often bend or break when the cake is very hard.

Rollers of increased strength would be an improvement, but, if too large, the velocity might be dangerously augmented, a result to be avoided in powder works.

In England the rollers are large drums, similar to those of an organ barrel, into which are screwed the teeth of brass ; these are thus replaced when broken or worn.

A pair of Ishapore rollers will cost . . 150 rupees.
The entire machine about . . 3000 ,,

In 12 hours' constant work it could corn about 100 barrels of powder, but at the end of the month would require very extensive repairs.

The present establishment is three mates and six men. This house was once destroyed by explosion, with great loss of life. I consider the great absence of rigidity from all our very rough machinery to be an advantage, as the giving way of the parts prevents concussion, and saves explosion.*

Sifting.

From the corning house the entire run is carried to the sifting houses, where it is separated into sizes by hand, men working common sieves suspended from the roof of the house.

Were labour dear I have no doubt that a machine might be made which would save much of the time and trouble now undergone in passing the powder through several sieves in succession; but it is a question whether the result would be cheaper or less dangerous.

The sieves in use at Ishapore are—

Number.	Holds.	Meshes in square inch	With 2-oz. Charge.	With 1-lb. Charge.	Eprouvette.		Density of Ishapore.	Density of English.	Marks.
			Yds.	Yds.	°	′			
5 ...	Kunkur . .	13	77	453	...		296	298	K
4 ...	Ordnance .	17	90	618	20	41	281	279	O
3 ...	Musketry .	24	94	793	22	57	270	269	M
2 ...	Rifle . . .	34	95	827	22	35	256	254	R
1 ...	Fine . . .	54	89	437	23	36	248	244	F
0 ...	Dust . .	...	...	...	...		...	...	D

* I believe one of the great causes of explosions in gunpowder manufactories to arise where there is machinery in quick motion, from the accumulation of the dust of powder round the axles of the parts of the machinery; and wherever these are, the supporting them on double friction rollers, with reservoirs of oil, well covered, as I used with my mixing barrels at Allahabad, is a great preservative against these disastrous accidents. I had only one trifling explosion, which was in the grinding mills, during the five years I was agent at Allahabad.—EDITOR.

Further details of experiments as to sizes of grain will be given in the Appendix.

Glazing.

The various kinds of separated grains are next advanced to the process of glazing.

Much importance is attached to this portion of the process, which I am not quite prepared to argue the value of.

From inspection, and from various memoranda, I am convinced that the large grained ordnance powder of the English service is not submitted to this operation.

It probably adds a little to the durability of the powder, and to the uniformity of the range, as reducing the grains to nearly the same size, and thus equalising the combustion of the charge.

The following is the description of the glazing process :—The powder is sent to the glazing house, where the whole is glazed by putting 100 lbs. of powder into a skeleton rib-barrelled frame, covered with coarse but equal-fibred canvas.

These barrels are turned on their axis for three hours, which gives a slight polish to the grains, and at the same time clears them from all dust.

The glazing reel or barrel is 3 ft. 10 in. long and 14 in. in diameter inside. It is formed by 8 longitudinal ribs of wood, with short stays from rib to rib to strengthen the frame, and with heads at each end into which the ends of the long ribs are morticed. The canvas is lashed to the heads besides being sewed the whole length of the side.

Two of these glazing barrels work in one large box or plank covering, on brass axes fixed to the heads of the box, and brass sockets to receive them in the supporting frame of the box ; one man turns each by a copper crank handle attached to the projecting end of the axes. There are 10 or 11 of these used every day in the working season.

As the harder surface will take a better polish than a softer one, I consider that this operation should follow the drying of the powder, and not precede it, as is the present mode. Glazing should

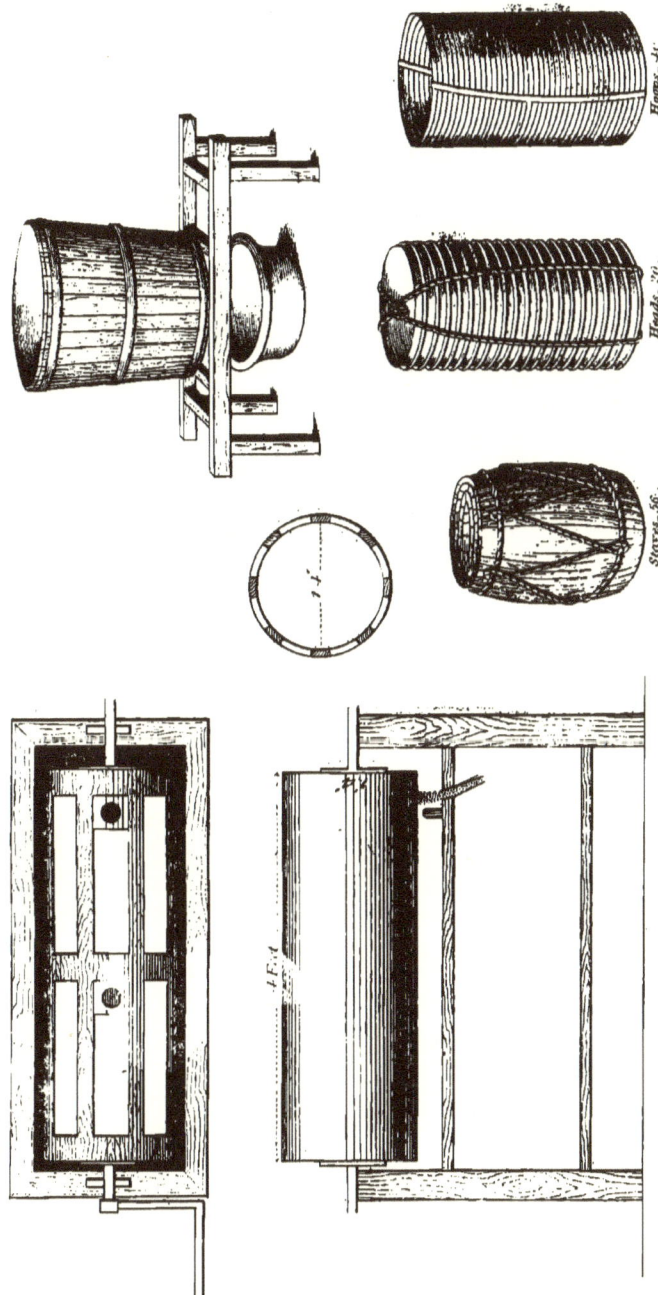

be the finishing act of the manufacture, ere the powder be passed through the final sieve before being barrelled for despatch to the magazine.

There are ten men working at these reels in a very confined space; were any accident to take place there would result a distressing loss of life. It would be an advantage if these reels were turned by a simple mechanical power, to turn the whole at once, which might easily be constructed, and the workmen would thus be comparatively secured from danger.

It is probable that under the term of glazing very different operations are included. In the Indian process glazing takes place when the grains are dry and hard, but in Europe the powder is probably glazed in a damp state, ere the powder is dried, and then no doubt alteration of shape, roundness of form, would result, all ending in the increase of density in a certain measure of capacity.

The English reels are much as those at Ishapore, but are made with cross rods to increase the friction, which serve also to strengthen the frame; and, for the convenience of unloading, the frame is so constructed as to be capable of being lowered to an incline, with an opening for this purpose at that end.

Drying.

In the variable climate of Europe it has been found necessary to resort to artificial means for drying the large quantities of powder at the manufactories.

This is accomplished by gloom stoves, or in rooms heated by steam-pipes to the required temperature, rising by degrees from 66° to perhaps 140°, and then sinking back to 66°, by the same regular degrees in 24 hours.

But in India, with an ample command of solar heat, and a continued season of dryness without rain, there can exist no reason for resorting to artificial means.

English powder being considered as usually superior to the Indian, the use of solar desiccation has been considered by some as a cause of the inferiority.[*]

[*] See Appendix in "Allahabad Experimental Powder."—EDITOR.

It is well known that solar rays have an effect in dissipating certain substances—hence their use in bleaching; but it is not proved that any bad effects are produced on the simple elements, or the compounded substance, of gunpowder. Indeed the powder is nearly as strong when fresh from the corning house and before exposure, as after lying for three days in the sun on the terraces in use at Ishapore.

The object in drying gunpowder is, by evaporation, to get rid of the water or dampness caused by the use of water in the milling, which then amounts to about $7\frac{1}{2}$ per cent.

This water is in a constant state of passing off during the different processes subsequent to the milling. In the presses it is forced out in a great degree, while in all the subsequent various handlings, as in corning, sifting, &c., a further portion is evaporated. Still a small quantity of moisture remains, and it is the object of drying to dissipate this.

The fear that is usually entertained is that under too great a heat some of the ingredients may alter their form.

Thus, sulphur is said to evaporate at 170° Fahr., but this is a temperature not to be reached from simple exposure to the solar rays in India. I find that in the register of three years, at 11 a.m., the temperature in the heaps of gunpowder but once exceeded 139° Fahr.

The following is the description of the Ishapore terrace :—It is raised 18 in. above the ground by masonry, into which wooden sleepers are laid, and over them platforms of wood, four in number, 94 by $21\frac{1}{2}$ ft. each, with passages between them. These platforms are covered with sheet copper.

Over this drying cloths, or sheets of canvas, are laid, and on these the powder is spread about $1\frac{1}{2}$ in. deep in the thickness of stratum.

The powder is brought out about 9 a.m. and taken in about 3·30 p.m., a little later or earlier according to the season of the year. During this interval of time it is repeatedly raked and turned. The whole platform is enclosed with a wall 6 ft. high, in which there are two openings on every side, with shutters, how-

DRYING TERRACES.

ever, to close them up, so as to regulate the temperature, which is somewhat raised by this enclosure of the area.

This platform is sufficiently extensive to dry for a manufacture of 32 barrels daily.

The chief faults are, the sheet-copper being far too light, and nailed on the platform in sheets by copper nails, rather than consisting of long rolls soldered together. A good slope would also assist in draining off dew and rain, while the wall to the east should be very low, to avoid the shadow cast by the sun when at a low altitude in the winter season, and the days are comparatively shortened; perhaps the walls are too high, and there should be a shed close at hand to receive the powder cloths.

The process is as follows : The day promising well, about eight o'clock, when the dew of the night has disappeared, the powder-cloths are spread over the terraces, and the powder, emptied from barrels, spread over them—one, two, and three days dried, being kept separate; the whole is then spread evenly out by rakes of wood, to about an inch in thickness; these fields of powder are constantly being raked and turned over.

Towards evening the powder is gathered up in heaps, which are tossed up and shaken in the air if there is any wind, and thus winnowed and dusted ; this done, the whole is returned to the barrels, and carried for the night to the magazine. This process is continued for three days.

The powder leaves the terraces heated to about 110° Fahr.; during the night it sinks a little towards the uniform temperature of the air of the magazine, which seldom varies much from 80° at this season. Tables of the trials of temperature are given in the Appendix.

The gunpowder thus exposed for three days to the sun, on the second day became rather greyish in colour, and during the third assumed a very pale grey; but after being removed to the shade returned to its original colour, black.

New and improved terraces, with thicker copper, with a slope to the south, and only one division, thus forming two platforms, were afterwards sanctioned, sufficiently large to dry 300 to 400 barrels of powder at once. The expense of them probably 40,000r., but they will last for many years, and prove a saving ultimately.

When the third day's drying is completed, the powder is carried to the weighing magazine; there it is weighed into quantities of 100 lbs., and filled into barrels.

The barrels are then conveyed to the magazine. At the close of the month, the powder being proved, and found up to the established range, the bungs of the barrels are well closed down with wax cloth, and covered with a piece of leather. The heads are then marked:—

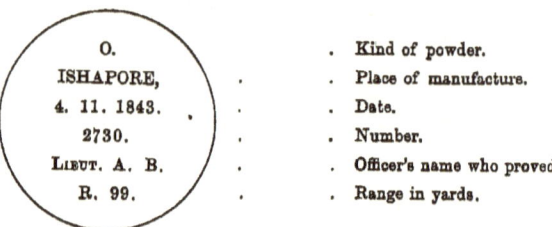

. Kind of powder.
. Place of manufacture.
. Date.
. Number.
. Officer's name who proved.
. Range in yards.

The barrels are then delivered to the Ordnance Department.

Packing, Transporting, Storing.

Before the powder is carried to any distance, the barrels are done up in wax cloth and in gunny (a coarse canvas), also well lashed with rope. This packing probably costs per barrel 2r., but is admirably done, and never to my knowledge during all our long and distant campaigns was the gunpowder found to be injured.

The transport of the powder depends of course on the mode of carriage peculiar to the country through which it is passing.

Thus, from Calcutta to Delhi may be performed by water at a cost of 2r. 8a. per barrel. If we suppose carts to be used from Delhi to Loodianah, the charge will perhaps be 12a. To reach the frontier, say, Peeshawur, the barrels will be loaded on camels, and the expense incurred reach 3r. If to the actual outlay for carriage be added all the contingent expenditure for guards,

·attendants, loss, and minor charges, perhaps from 70 to 80 per cent. may be added to the original cost of the powder, and thus when the interest of block and capital are included, the price of the powder is doubled from first cost at the manufactory.

In magazines it is ordered that the barrels be constantly rolled over. I believe a great improvement would be effected if now and then, during the hottest season of the year, the barrels were taken out a few at a time in some secure place, and well heated in the sun. This exposure would drive off much of the dampness which attends all magazines. The staves also, from shrinking under the heat, would admit of the copper hoops being well set up at such a time.

In England, all powder that has been at sea or on any campaign is *re-stoved* on return. This operation drives off any contracted damp, but exposure to the Indian sun produces much the same heat as that to which stoves in Europe are raised.

A small pucka terrace attached to, but at a proper distance from, a magazine, would be very advantageous when any powder is found to have contracted dampness, as the powder might be passed through a sieve, and the dust extracted; and from this dust, and other damaged powder, saluting cartridges might be formed, or the saltpetre extracted for magazine purposes at a trifling expense.

Cost of the Powder.

Secondary, and only secondary, to the quality of the powder is the cost. Good powder made with a small outlay is the point required from the agent by the Government; but much of the cost depends entirely on causes beyond the control of the agent, as on the price of the crude materials.

This assertion will be better understood when it is added that the cost of the nitre alone is one-half of the expense of powder.

All the ingredients and necessary articles vary with the rates of the day.

The cost of the powder of 1848, per 100 lbs., may be resolved into the following items :—

COST OF ISHAPORE POWDER.

Ingredients.

	r.	a.	p.	r.	a.	p.
97 lbs. 14 oz. crude saltpetre, for 75 lbs. of pure nitre, at 7r. 9a. 4·357p. per 100 lbs.				7	6	9·4
10 lbs. 9 oz. of crude sulphur for 10 lbs. of pure, at 5r. 1a. 9·35p. per 100 lbs.				0	8	7·59
91 lbs. of urhur and jointee wood for 15 lbs. charcoal, at 2a. 5·4p. for 80 lbs.				0	3	1·4
				8	2	6·39
Tools, stores, materials, and firewood used up, viz.,						
Firewood	0	14	0			
European stores	0	12	0·68			
Country stores	0	2	0			
				1	12	0·68
Labour, including all establishments				3	0	9
Bullocks for motive power { Feeding				1	1	6·81
{ Death				0	1	8·9
Interest on fixed capital in block				1	8	6·27
				15	11	2·05

Many of the items of charge depend on the quantity made during the year.

The average price from 1841 to 1848 is, per barrel of 100 lbs.—

	r.	a.	p.
Maximum	20	7	9
Medium	18	0	11
Minimum	15	11	2

But in an article of such great national importance, price should ever be a secondary consideration compared with quality.

The English service powders cost 5*l.* upwards for the 100 lbs., say 50 rupees.

The best sporting powders sell in London about 2*s.* to 3*s.* per lb.—10*l.* to 15*l.* the 100 lbs.

Blasting powder is sold by dealers at from 50*s.* to 75*s.* per 100 lbs.

Previous to 1814 Mr. Farquhar made the powder on a contract of 32*r.* per barrel, of 100 lbs.

Ishapore, Colonel Galloway's powder of 1825-26, cost only 18*r.* 15*a.* 3*p.* per barrel. The Bombay powder of 1846-47, cost 27*r.* 11*a.*; the Madras powder of 1846-47, cost 29*r.* 11*a.* 8*p.* per 100 lb. barrel. (See Appendix.)

On the Motive Power used for making Gunpowder.

Every species of power has been used in powder mills.

Running water is a most excellent agent where available, costing little, requiring no great attendance, and hence, on explosions, less danger to life exists.

Steam is now much used, but is obnoxious to this fault, that it assembles together in a space too small so much of the explosive matter. When accidents have taken place the loss of life and destruction of property have been excessive.

At Ishapore the entire motive power is of bullocks, which enables all the houses to be entirely independent of each other, and so distant that the explosion in one house has hardly ever communicated to the next.

Each of the Ishapore mills requires three changes of six bullocks each, or, with an allowance for sick or lame, at least 24 bullocks for each mill.

The work of these cattle is extremely heavy, being the circular movement of twelve tons of metal on a damp substance for four hours in every twelve, at the rate of three miles the hour, covering a full distance of twelve miles, with hardly a single moment of rest in the whole period. Such is probably the very maximum effect obtainable from a first-rate young bullock, and far above the aged and infirm; indeed, the work tells exceedingly on all the cattle, they being much reduced in condition when the season for manufacture closes, in spite of the utmost care and attention bestowed upon them.

The average complement of eleven years has for five mills been 204 head of cattle, with an average casualty of 26, giving about eight years effective work in each animal; but this average is too favourable.

Under the present large quantity of powder required, not less than 280 head should be kept up, with an annual supply of at least 35 fresh young beasts. The cattle should be yearly sent of the same age (say, four years), that a regular and constant influx of youth and strength may take place. When the regularity of the supply has been interrupted, or the admitted cattle have been aged, or even of one age, ultimate compensation in after years will be demanded and must be paid.

The bullocks cost from 30r. to 40r. each. During the working season, one driver with a small proportion of Sirdars is allowed to each pair; but not so during the rains, when the manufacture ceases; then one man is allowed to four bullocks. This is perhaps a bad policy, as the men, knowing they will be discharged at the close of the season, take less interest in their cattle than is proper. Sirdars receive 10r. monthly pay, and drivers 4r.

In the working season each bullock receives three seers of grain and as much straw as can be eaten, but only two seers of grain, four seers of straw (boosie), and one seer of oil-cake in the resting season. The total expense of the motive force by bullocks cannot be less than 2r. on each barrel of gunpowder.

The food given to these bullocks should be of the best description. The pace at which they are driven requires they should receive the largest possible nourishment in the smallest volume, and such as can be easily consumed and digested.

The bullocks of the present day are not so powerful as they were twenty years ago. The breed of large cattle is rapidly disappearing.

The average expense on this head for the years 1834, 1836, expense of feeding and servants, per bullock, 6r. 9a. 4½p. per month, and the charge per barrel of powder on this head, 2r. 8a. 9p., varying, of course, with the quantity of powder made and the prices of food.

A separate hospital and good cattle doctor are much required.

Hygrometric Proof.

To ascertain the quantity of damp absorbed by gunpowder has ever been a subject of inquiry.

Various modes have been adopted; many of them extending over an exposure of nearly a month, but powder is so extremely susceptive under change of atmosphere, that one trial under a well-defined variation of atmosphere exhibiting marked results, is ample.

I used 500 drams of powder highly dried in the sun, and then exposed for one night, spread over a sheet of paper 19 in. by 13 in. in area.

It was laid in a small room of wood, about 10 feet from the ground, by this the powder is merely subject to the variations in the superincumbent strata of the atmosphere. I then take its weight and density, and, if necessary, try it in the mortar or eprouvette ; next night, the same quantity on the same paper is laid upon the pucka floor of the drying terràce. It now receives the damp of the lowest strata, and also imbibes some of the damp existing in the bricks of this floor.

This second night's exposure tells powerfully on the powder, which always exhibits a marked increase of weight, decrease of density, and other appearances of damp.

It is again tried in the mortar and eprouvette, and compared with the range of its original state.

When any new class of powder is to be tried under this process, some well-known powder should be also tried with it, to afford a standard of comparison.

From this experiment has resulted the following Report:—

HYGROMETRIC REPORT.

Description of Powder.	Boarded Floor.		Pucka Floor.		Remarks.
	Weight.	Density.	Weight.	Density.	
Common manufacture. O.	+ 3	+ 2	+ 14	0	Colour and grain as usual, $\frac{1}{100}$ = ·028 of damp taken up.

Proof.

	Mortar.	Difference.	Eprouvette.	Difference.	Remarks.
Before exposure			21° 0′	° ′	
After the boarded floor	not tried.		20 56	0 4	Total 1° 49′
After the pucka terrace			19 11	1 45	

The actual results depend much on the state of the weather.

The following Report made on this subject to the French Minister of War, on the powder manufactured at the establishment of Bouchet, in 1824, is extracted from the British Indian Military Repository:—

The quantity of powder operated upon was 100 grammes of French, and 100 grammes of English powder. The two powders were spread upon two pieces of glass of equal surfaces, and placed by the side of each other, in a cavern of no great depth, but very damp, from 15th of February to 10th of March. During the time the centigrade thermometer was between $5\frac{1}{2}$ and 6 degrees, and the hygrometer between 96 and 99 degrees.

On the 10th of March, that is to say, after having been exposed to the damp air for 24 days, the powder was weighed as follows: The French powder 101·30 grammes, and the English 101·80 grammes. This had thus increased 1-56th of its weight, and the other 1-76th.

Submitted afterwards in the same state, and immediately after weighing, to the hand eprouvette, the powders yielded, upon an average of 5 trials, the French, 19° 95′ and the English 18° 38′, which in my form would stand—

		Weight.	
French powder	. .	+·0131	
English powder	. .	+·0178	

		Hand Eprouvette.	
French { Before exposure .		21 76	° ′
{ After exposure .		19 95	−1 81
English { Before exposure .		20 24	
{ After exposure .		18 38	−1 86

These results are not very dissimilar to mine acquired in two nights' exposure. The great object should be to obtain decided and well-marked differences under similar circumstances with a standard powder for comparison.

Proof of Powder at the Agency.

The manufacturing part of the powder being finished, it is requisite that some standard of strength be established; and some mode settled as to measuring it. Moreover, if the powder did not continue of one uniform strength, or in some known ratio of a conserved standard, all the science, experience, and practice of the Artillery would be useless. It is also necessary that the powder should retain its established strength, and be able to bear transport.

Many modes have been adopted, in various times and in different places, to obtain a correct measure of the strength of powder, all more or less good in their plan. Every species of ordnance, with every possible charge, have been tried, and several machines have been invented and made for this express purpose. The great desideratum being, that the trial should be made with as much uniformity of proceeding as possible, every variation tending to lead to error: a comparison of proofs of powder made under varying circumstances is very perplexing and uncertain.

With the same machine I believe the results of the proofs of equal powder to be nearly uniform, and that provided the same instrument be used, that it little matters what description is adopted.

The present authorised mode is a Gomer Mortar of 8 in. diameter, 8 cwt. 1 qr. in weight, 1 ft. $4\frac{3}{10}$ in. length of bore. The shot a ball of solid iron of 68 lbs. in weight, 7·85 in. in diameter. Charge of powder, 2 oz.; elevation, 45°; proof distance for the shot to be thrown, 63 yards; if below this range the powder is rejected.

A decrease of half a tenth of an inch in the diameter of the ball, or an increase of the same quantity in the diameter of the mortar, will render both unserviceable for proof, as will also an enlargement of the vent of half a tenth of an inch.

In former days it was the custom to try separately each barrel of powder; but now the officer selected for the proof duty, takes a quantity from as many barrels as he pleases of the previous month's manufacture ; these he mixes, and from the mass weighs out 25 charges of Ordnance and 25 of Musketry powder.

He carefully tries each of these charges in the mortar, with regular and careful uniformity in loading. The average of the ranges constitutes the proof range of the month's produce.

As the instruments are far less used by this than the old system, the abrasion of the metals is small, and as the circumstances are nearly equal, the results are in proportion identical.

As a short barrel is favourable to a quickly igniting powder, while a long barrel is more advantageous to a slowly burning powder, that both cases may be brought into examination, it has lately been ordered that the average arc of the pendulum gun eprouvette be also given for each powder under trial with a charge of 2 oz.

The monthly results of the trials as given in the annexed Table show little variation in the powder of different years, when one month old.

PROOF AVERAGES. 117

ISHAPORE AGENCY PROOF AVERAGES, 1846, 1847, 1848.

		Mortar 2 oz. Charge. Range in yards.							Eprouvette 2 oz. Charge.							Average.	
		Dec.	Jan.	Feb.	Mar.	Apr.	May	June	Dec.	Jan.	Feb.	Mar.	Apr.	May	June	Mortar. Yards	Eprouvette.
1846	{M / O}	98 / 94	94 / 94	90 / 94	89 / 92	93 / 93	97 / 96	89 / 97	23 25 / ,,	22 32 / 21 21	23 10 / 21 12	22 57 / 21	22 34 / 20 38	23 26 / 20 56	23 21 / 21 35	92 / 94	23 6 / 21 7
1847	{M / O}	99 / 102	98 / 99	99 / 98	96 / 98	92 / 93	94 / 96	90 / 97	23 25 / 21 18	23 20 / 20 59	23 / 21 6	23 / 20 5	22 46 / 20 53	22 47 / 20 47	23 2 / 20 39	95 / 97	23 3 / 20 49
1848	{M / O}	105 / 107	95 / 100	100 / 97	107 / 100	106 / 103	107 / 105	105 / 101	24 / 21 17	23 4 / 20 17	23 8 / 20 1	23 35 / 20 33	23 35 / 20 35	23 8 / 20 4	22 53 / 20 38	104 / 101	23 20 / 10 37
Average	{M / O}	100 / 103	96 / 97	96 / 98	97 / 96	97 / 96	99 / 99	94 / 98	23 2 / 21 17	22 58 / 20 52	23 / 20 46	23 12 / 20 34	22 58 / 20 42	23 / 20 55	23 / 21		

Proof for the Commandant of Artillery.

To ascertain that the powder does not deteriorate by keeping, at the close of the practice season of the next following year, the Commandant of Artillery sends to the Arsenal for any barrels at hand of the last year's manufacture. These are taken indiscriminately from the number in store, and from these barrels a trial is made with every available piece of ordnance. Hence this proof exhibits excellent service ranges of what may be expected from Bengal powder with the common description of ordnance in use, great and small.

The occasional falling off of the 68-lb. ball proof in this annual report from that of the first proof at the Agency, has often attracted the notice of the authorities and of Government.

But the variation may, I believe, be satisfactorily accounted for in several ways.

    1. From any deviation in shape or windage of the mortar and shot compared with those first used at the Agency.
    2. From the temporary accession of damp from the magazines on the river.
    3. From the acclimating of the powder itself from its fresh state at the manufactory to its average state with reference to the atmosphere.
    4. From the difference in the mode of setting home the ball.

The deviations of range in different mortars have often reached 18 yards.

The powder in passing from its highly-finished and well-dried state at the Agency through all the variations of one year's mutable climate in Bengal, will lose about one-tenth of its original range in small charges, and from that estimate will improve or deteriorate a trifle with reference to the atmosphere in which it is immediately exposed.

If the contact between the ball and the converging sides of the Gomer Mortar is not complete, so that there is considerable windage, the range of a shot with the 2-oz. charge will be reduced one-half nearly.

It will also be noticed that the ranges from all the pieces of ordnance do not follow the first, or 68-lb. ball proof, but often the reverse, and that a good range from the 2-oz. charge is often followed by a proportionable decrease of range from larger charges in longer-barreled pieces than the mortar. This has reference to the length of the bore and the inflammability and expansion of the powder.

The general average will be found to correspond admirably with the various range-tables formed from practice at the different artillery stations.

The totals exhibit a uniformity not to have been expected, and in the numerous and varied pieces of artillery used the errors of one have counterbalanced the errors of a second, producing a general equality.

AVERAGES OF RANGES FROM THE COMMANDANT'S PROOF, TAKEN WHEN THE GUNPOWDER WAS ONE YEAR OLD.

		Elevation.	Charge.	1838.	1839.	1840.	Average.	1841.	1842.	1843.	Average.	1844.	1845.	1846.	Average.	General Average.	1847.	1848.
8-in. mortar, 68-lb. ball proof . .	M	45°	2 oz.	60*	69†	71†	$66\frac{2}{3}$	72·1†	$68\frac{1}{4}$†	$64\frac{3}{4}$	68	61*	67	71†	$66\frac{1}{3}$	67	$59\frac{3}{4}$	78
,, ,, ,,	O	,,		62·5*	64*	72†	66	68·4†	$70\frac{1}{4}$†	$61\frac{1}{2}$	66	64*	64*	71	66	66	71	75
13-in. mortar . .		45	2 lbs.	550	573	484	$535\frac{2}{3}$	550	587	592	576	569	575	568	$570\frac{2}{3}$	560	445	551
10-in. ,, . .		45	1 8	739	804	808	$783\frac{2}{3}$	729	771	719	$739\frac{2}{3}$	573	790	742	$701\frac{2}{3}$	741	590	693
8-in. ,, . .		45	1 0	886	887	792*	855	811*	928†	966†	901	880	903†	908†	897	884	740	803
$5\frac{1}{2}$-in. ,, . .		45	0 8	1240	1167	1119	1175	1077	1196	1134	1135	1220	1179	1093	1164	1158	890	1154
24-pounder, iron .		1	8 0	729	935	775	813	684	872	915	823	977	751	801	843	826	691	866
18-pounder, ,, . .		1	6 0	720*	927†	738*	795	704*	745	854†	767	992†	789*	737†	839	800	648	970
12-pounder, ,, .		1	4 0	693	1020	776	$823\frac{2}{3}$	730	$1002\frac{1}{2}$	$872\frac{1}{2}$	868	889	810	759	$819\frac{1}{3}$	837	731	906
10-in. iron howitzer .		5	3 0	533†	523†	461	$505\frac{2}{3}$	495*	526†	475	498	549†	639†	464	$550\frac{2}{3}$	518	529	525
8-in. ,, .		5	2 0	552	509	520	527	566	605	475	538	543	665	516	574	546	583	749
24-pndr. brass howitzer		5	2 0	1163	970	961	1031	941	$1054\frac{4}{5}$	$1164\frac{2}{5}$	1053	1271	993	952	1072	1052	1115	1069
9-pounder brass gun .		1	2 4	674*	694†	660	673	605*	674*	736†	671	786†	697†	639	707	683	760	708
6-pounder brass gun .		1	1 8	638	737	638	671	672	$611\frac{1}{5}$	$716\frac{3}{5}$	666	738	676	621	678	671	644	648
Common musket .			6 drs.	156*	139*	147*	147	161*	220†	183*	188	228†	239†	266†	244	193	220	201
Light Infantry			6 do.	176	127	155	152	142	248	311	233	178	239	181	199	194	180	133
Artillery fusil . .			4 do.	155	106	148	136	103	193	225	173	213	226	167	203	170	164	122
Pistol . . .			4 do.	59	89	94	80	85	111	230	142	239	191	167	199	140	106	167
Pistol			3 do.	64*	94*	85	81	91*	79*	143†	104	129†	213†	101*	147	110	83	92
Totals . .				9·849	10·434	9·504	$9{\cdot}917\frac{1}{3}$	9·286	10·560	10·825	10·209	11·099	10·706	9·824	$10{\cdot}540\frac{2}{3}$	10·216	$9{\cdot}249\frac{3}{4}$	10·510

Note—* Less than average. † More than average.

The Court of Directors' Proof.

The last and most minute Report is that called the "Court of Directors' Proof." It is carried on at each of the Presidencies, Bengal, Bombay, and Madras, on the powders of the several Agencies, by a committee of artillery officers, and is as full and particular as could be desired.

I have abstracted the results of the Reports of 1845 from each Presidency. The average must be the most fair value of the Indian Agency powders.

The size of the grain is not determined with the precision that might be desired. It would, perhaps, be an improvement were five pounds of powder passed through each sieve (five in number composing a set), and the quantity of grains retained on each noted.

The hardness is that of the cake whence the powder is cut, and is in some degree a measure of the quantity of milling and pressing given to the composition. The density is that of the mixed grains, or of the powder, and is directly as the size of the grain and the hardness of the cake.

The state of the atmosphere at the period of trial will affect all these quantities, as will the mode in which the results are taken.

From the ranges we may notice the great differences in the mortars, or in the mode of loading.

Total from report of
- Bengal . . . . . 421 yards.
- Madras . . . . . 478 + 57
- Bombay . . . . . 578 + 100

This is greatly in favour of the Madras and Bombay powders. The powders being all acclimated to the same atmosphere, the range is almost identical from the 2-oz. charge.

Experiment No. 3 entirely depends on the materials—dry mixture and proportions, perhaps, on the charcoal, more than any other of the materials. Now, as I believe the Madras powder to contain one pound and ten ounces less of charcoal, and one pound and ten ounces more of sulphur, I do not understand its being, when pulverized, the most quick of ignition, and hence forming a more quick burning fuze composition, unless this may be attributed to the cake being less hard, from the diminished milling at Madras.

In the percussion musket experiments we may remark that, as the Madras powder, being the most dense, gives the best mortar range with the 2-oz. charge, so it gives the lowest musket range.

The Bombay powder, with the lowest mortar range, exhibits the best musket result, being less dense and less hard.

The time of the train burning will be influenced by the quickness of the ignition of the composition, varied by the size and combination of the grains. Hence the Madras is the quickest.

In the wet weather report we may notice the result of an accession of damp to the powder, from the state of the atmosphere at the time.

Bengal	Dry weather	421
	Wet	398—23
Madras	Dry weather	478
	Wet	427—51
Bombay	Dry weather	578
	Wet	564—14

The boards in the musket proof do not appear to have been of the same wood; hence they afford no comparison between the two seasons.

I suspect all the small-grained powder will have reached the same degree of dampness.

The result of the 60-lb. exposure depends entirely on the previous state of the powder, on the atmosphere of the day, and on the size of the grain. Small grain is more liable to injury from damp than larger.

All the powders must have been damp, and thus lost weight by exposure to the sun.

Powder exposed is so quickly affected by the atmosphere, that without minute data on all the atmospheric phenomena it is impossible to explain the results.

I was not prepared to find that the decreased quantity of charcoal in the Madras powder did render it more susceptible under atmospheric changes.

Does the diminution of the charcoal account for the less

TRIENNIAL REPORT ON POWDER. 123

smoke and fiercer burning of the powder, or is the last due to the diminished milling? Powder standing so many tests of such various kinds may be fairly depended upon for regularity of strength.

RESULT OF THE TRIENNIAL REPORT ON POWDER FROM THE THREE PRESIDENCIES—
BENGAL, MADRAS, AND BOMBAY.
Hot Weather.

Powders of 1845, one year old.	Bengal Report. May, 1846.	Madras Report. July, 1846.	Bombay Report. June, 1846.	Result.		
				Total.	Average.	
Colour.						
Bengal . .	Black	Grey black	{ Bluish black			
Madras {	Bluish black	Bluish black	Bluish black			
Bombay . .	Black	Black	{ Lighter than Madras			
Size of Grain.						
Bengal {	492	492	500	1484	494	Remained of 512 drs. on a sieve of 576 meshes to the square inch.
Madras } O	506	507	508	1521	507	
Bombay {	500	492	506	1498	499	
Bengal {	174	244	202	620	206	
Madras } M	54	28	125	207	69	
Bombay {	154	154	218	526	176	
Hardness.						
Bengal . .	32	4	19	55	18	Remained of 128 drs. on a lawn sieve after being mealed.
Madras . .	42	4	16	62	20	
Bombay . .	46	14	23	83	27	
Density.						
Bengal { M	264	272	306	842	280	Drs. in a measure base inches, height 3·5.
{ O	274	280	328	882	294	
Madras { M	266	263	317	846	282	
{ O	272	280	334	886	295	
Bombay { M	256	252	302	810	270	
{ O	278	272	333	883	294	
				M	O	
	4th May. Thermom. 93. Barometer 29·8. Hygrometer, 85·5.	17th June 7 a.m. Thermom. 85·5. Barometer 29·9. Hygrometer, 85·5.	2nd April. 7 a.m. Thermom. 76. Barometer 29·8. Hygrometer, 74.	Bengal. Madras. Bombay.	842 883 846 886 810 882	Total densities. ,, ,, ,, ,,

Ranges.

		Bengal.			Madras.			Bombay.					
		2-oz. charge.		Charge 1 lb. Mortar.	2-oz. charge.		Charge 1 lb. Mortar.	2-oz. charge.		Charge ½ lb. Mortar.	Total.		Average.	
		Mortar.	Eprouvette.		Mortar.	Eprouvette.		Mortar.	Eprouvette.		2 oz.	1 lb.	2 oz.	1 lb.
Bengal	M	71	24° 34′	838	80	23° 5′	828	100	24° 75′	382	251	2048	83⅝	819
	O	76	22 14	665	77	21 5	649	97	21 1	309	250	1623	83⅓	649
Madras	M	74	23 50	783	82	24 9	813	98	24 85	257	254	1953	84⅔	781
	O	71	21 38	590	81	21 4	567	93	21 75	279	245	1436	81⅔	574
Bombay	M	63	23 24	763	82	24 6	814	98	25 75	352	233	1929	81	771
	O	66	20 56	551	76	21 5	659	92	21 45	298	234	1508	78	603
Total .	.	421		4190	478		4330	578		1977	1477	10497	402⅓	

Experiment No. 3.

Time of burning 8 inches of a 13-inch fuze.

Sulphur 9, Mealed Powder 17, Saltpetre 15 — Composition.

Bengal . .	33⅕	19 Only	26⅓	78	26
Madras .	35⅗	18 5 inches	23	76	25⅓
Bombay .	30	22 long.	26	87	29
	Percussion Musket.		Charge, 4½ drams.	Boards ½ in. thick.	
Bengal .	17⅚	19	22·6	59	19⅔
Madras . .	15	19⅚	22·	56	18⅔
Bombay .	16⅗	21	24·4	62	20⅔

Time of burning 50lbs. length of train, 87 ft. long, 2 in. broad, in seconds.

						O	M
Bengal	M	17	21	17	Bengal	60½	55
	O	21½	24	15			
Madras	M	17½	19	14	Madras	56	50½
	O	18	23	15			
Bombay	M	14½	21	13	Bombay	62	53
	O	21	24	17			

WET WEATHER PROOF.

		Bengal, September.		Madras, December.		Bombay, July.			
				No. 2. 2 oz. charge. 8-inch mortar and eprouvette.					
		2 oz. charge.		2 oz. charge.		2 oz. charge.			
		8-inch Mortar.	Eprou- vette.	8-inch Mortar.	Eprou- vette.	8-inch Mortar.	Eprou- vette.	Total.	Average.
Bengal	M	69	23 18	75	22 24	96	24 50	240	80
	O	72	20 41	70	21 2	96	21 50	238	79¼
Madras	M	66	23 10	74	23 24	87	24 40	227	75⅔
	O	71	20 34	74	21 2	94	22 0	239	79⅔
Bombay	M	57	22 40	64	23 0	94	25 41	215	71⅔
	O	63	20 32	70	21 0	97	21 0	233	77⅔
Total		398		427		564			

		Percussion Musket, charge 4½ drams. Boards ¼ of an inch thick.				
Bengal		15¾	25	23	65	21⅔
Madras		16½	24⅔	23	63	21
Bombay		14	25	25	64	21⅓

		60 lbs. exposed for 1¼ hours in the sun, from 1·45 p.m., and then weighed after exposure.		
Bengal	M	− 2 drs.	−39	−160
	O	+14	−38	−144
Madras	M	− 4	−32	−128
	O	+ 0	−34	−176
Bombay	M	+10	−38	−192
	O	+ 2	−30	−128
		Thermometer, 86½°	Thermometer, 79½°	Thermometer, 86°

Exposure for 12 days, in different quantities, on trays,—the powder 1 inch deep.

	Bengal, September.	Madras, December.	Bombay, July.
	Nearly all the small trays lost a trifle, and the 20-lb. trays gained very little.	All gained. The 20-lb. trays gained 1 oz. 10 drs.	In all instances the 20-lb. trays lost 4 to 5 oz. The smaller trays gained.
	Remarks.		
Bengal . . Madras . . . Bombay . {	Very slightly caked. Much caked. Rather more than Bengal.	Slightly caked. Much caked. Rather more than Bengal.	No Remarks.
	Musketry more than ordnance.	All the musketry more than ordnance.	
	Thermometer, 87° to 88°.	Thermometer, 79° to 82°.	Thermometer, 81° to 89°.

Madras Observations on Flashing.

Bengal Powder. { No residuum, no beads, no sparks observable in the ordnance, and but few in the musket powder; clear, bright light; the smoke-marks extended from 6 to 12 inches on each side the train. The musket powder slightly caked, the lumps breaking when pressed by the hand.

Madras Powder. { Left no residuum or beads; a few sparks observable in both M and O powders; the flame clear and bright; the marks of the smoke not so great as the Bengal powder, but extended as far on each side the train. The M powder burnt fiercer and made more noise than any of the other powders. The Madras M powder slightly caked, but not so much as the Bengal M.

Bombay Powder. { Left no residuum or beads; a few sparks observed in both O and M powders; the flame clear, but not so bright as the Bengal; the smoke-marks extend from 8 to 15 inches on each side of the train; the powder not caked in the least.

Extra Glazing.

Circumstances induced me to make an extended trial of the effects of glazing. The following table gives the results at each period, as the operation on a single charge proceeded.

First. Let us examine the process of glazing in India. One hundred pounds of well dried powder are enclosed in a reel covered with coarse canvas, length 3 ft. 8 in., diameter 1 ft. 4 in., solid capacity 8844 cubic inches. One hundred pounds of powder will occupy 2743 cubic inches; hence there is a space for movement of 6101 cubic inches. The reel is turned for two hours at the rate of 1500 revolutions per hour.

This motion will cause the removal of all the dust from the surface of the grains, the truncating of the angles, and the abrasion of the sharp edges, from which facts may be expected the following results :—

A general diminution in the size of the grain, with a mixture of grain ; a reduction of the density of the powder ; an increased liability to be affected by the atmosphere as the grains become reduced in size ; a decrease of quickness of inflammation by the polish and absence of dust, counterbalanced by an increase of inflammation by the reduction of size and mixture of grains. The result will be variable as either effect may preponderate.

Let us examine what inferences may be drawn from the table of experiment.

An increase of density of 10 drs. in the 36-hour glazed, when taken fresh from the reel, the damp being driven off by the friction ; but a decrease of 3 drs. when exposed in the usual manner to the atmosphere.

The diminution of density results from the permanently reduced size of the grain. The large grain of sieve No. 4 is reduced in quantity from 404 to 330 drs., by which difference the quantity of sieve No. 3 is increased from 82 to 162 drs.

The single size of the original ordnance has resolved itself into three sizes.

In the 2-oz. mortar range there was a slight improvement

of 3½ yards, and in the eprouvette an increase in the arc of recoil of 0° 11′.

In the pure ordnance unmixed grain of this powder there appeared a gain of density of 10 drs. before drying, but of only 2 after that process.

To appearance the 36-hour glazed powder shows a very trifling advantage. The colour, previously a deep black, did not alter ; but the grain, on exposure, remained a little harder than the grain of the less glazed.

The slight improvement in the small charges is hardly to be considered much in favour of the long glazed ; while, in the larger charges, the unglazed powder, both from mortar and cannon, will give longer ranges.

Glazing will probably cause powder well preserved to last a little longer without becoming dusty.

When the expense is taken into consideration, I can see no gain whatever by the operation being continued longer than two hours. Indeed, was a sudden demand for powder made for immediate service, I believe the whole operation of glazing might be neglected, or very materially reduced in time. All that is necessary is to free the grain from dust. Glazing continued beyond this point can only end in a reduction of the size of grain with a rounding of the grains, and slight, but very slight polish.

Mr. Braddock, and the generality of writers upon gunpowder, consider pressed and glazed powder will not range so far as mill cake powder. These statements relate to mere density, and are attributable rather to the first operation of pressing, than to the subsequent one of glazing, for press cake is more dense than mill cake.

I am not aware that the simple question of glazing has been considered alone, and I much doubt if the ordnance powder manufactured in England, is submitted to this operation ; its grain being a mixture of many sizes, and less hard than the Indian powder, it also contains very large amounts of dust.

Results from Prolonged Glazing of Ordnance Powder at Ishapore.

Time in glazing reel.	Thermometer in the glazed powder.	Density. Before drying	Density. After drying	Weight used in sifting.	Retained on No. 4 sieve.	Retained on No. 3 sieve.	Retained on No. 2 sieve.	Lost in sifting.	Mortar. Average.	Eprouvette. Average.	Remarks.
				drs.	drs.	drs.	drs.	drs.			
3 hours, the usual time	82	278	284	500	404	82	10	4	102	21	Colour slate; grain as usual
6 hours	83	282	286	500	408	83	4	5	103¾	21 18	Dark slate; grain good.
9 hours	85	284	282	...	370	122	4	4	103¾	21 11	Colour black; grain hard.
12 hours	86	288	284	...	364	128	4	4	106	21 9	Colour bright black.
15 hours	84	288	284	...	366	122	4	8	105¾	22 42	Colour deep black.
18 hours	87	288	286	...	364	126	4	6	106	22 19	
24 hours	85	288	286	...	362	132	2	4	105	21 21	
27 hours	82	288	284	...	352	140	4	4	108¾	21 24	
30 hours	83	288	282	...	336	160	1	3	107¾	21 42	
33 hours	81	288	282	...	332	164	1	3	104¾	21 19	
36 hours	78	288	281	...	330	162	4	4	105¾	21 11	
Average	83	287	283	...	...	...	...	...	105	21 30	

Hygrometric Report.

	Boarded floor.		Pucka floor.		Remarks.
	Weight.	Density.	Weight.	Density.	
The regular 3 hours glazed	+ 3	+ 2	+ 14	− 0	Colour and grain as usual.
36 hours glazed	+ 4	+ 1	+ 13	− 8	{ Colour black, grain harder than the above.

		Mortar.	Eprouvette.
Proof.			
The regular 3 hours	{ Before exposure	102	21
	{ After boarded floor	89	20 56
	{ After pucka floor	80	19 11
36 hours glazed	{ Before exposure	105¼	21 11
	{ After boarded floor	96	20 40
	{ After pucka floor	82	19 28

On the receipt of the above Reports, the Military Board was pleased to order one barrel of musketry powder, to be made of 3, 6, 12, and 24 hours' glazing. This was done, the common manufacture of the season standing for the three hours glazed. Previously to sending this powder to Dum-Dum, I made the experiment recorded in the following Tables.

Very little difference can be traced in the various densities or ranges, as exhibited in Table No. 1.

Again, in the exposure, Table No. 2, very little variation is seen; the 24-hour glazed appears to have absorbed less damp, although the grains were reduced in size by the operation of glazing.

The Hygrometric Table No. 3 shows no great superiority in the 24-hour glazed powder. On the 24th of October, or nearly one month after the last trial, I examined these powders, which had continued to lie exposed in the magazine. All proved good, nor could I distinguish one from the other in appearance.

No. I.
PROOF REPORT OF 1849.

		Density.			8 In. Mortar, 2 oz. charge.				Eprouvette.			
	1st June, 1848.	27th and 31st October, 1848.	1st and 2nd November.	Average.	1st June, 1848.	27th and 31st October, 1848.	1st and 2nd November.	Average.	1st June, 1848.	27th and 31st October, 1848.	1st and 2nd November.	Average.
Unglazed.	258	260	260	259	104	95	95	98	23 6	21 53	22 16	22 25
Regular 3 hours.	262	266	262	263	105	97	92	98	23 4	21 55	—	22 29
6 hours.	264	260	264	262	104	95	97	98	22 48	21 56	22 18	22 20
12 hours.	262	260	262	261	105	96	97	99	23 11	21 45	22 10	22 22
24 hours.	266	262	260	262	106	95	97	99	23 8	21 43	22 26	22 25

(Musketry)

No. II.

EXPOSURE REPORT OF POWDER HUNG UP IN THE AIR IN GUZEE* BAGS, DAY AND NIGHT, FROM THE 1ST OF JUNE TILL THE 1ST OF OCTOBER, 1848.

Description of powder.	Weight on the 1st of June.			Density on the 1st of June.	Weight on the 1st of October.			Density on the 1st of October.	Remarks.
	lb.	oz.	drs.		lb.	oz.	drs.		
Unglazed	2	...	...	258	2	...	6	256	Bright black, hard, no dust.
6 hours glazed	2	...	...	264	2	...	4	260	Bright black, hard, one friable lump, no dust.
12 hours glazed	2	...	...	262	2	...	4	258	Bright black, hard, no dust or lumps.
24 hours glazed	2	...	...	266	2	...	3	259	Dull brown, hard, several friable lumps.

(Musketry)

* Coarse cotton.

No. III.

HYGROMETRIC PROOF OF POWDER ON THE PUCKA TERRACE, 19TH AND 20TH SEPTEMBER, 1849.

Description of Powder.		Weight at			Density at			Remarks.
		6 P.M.	6 A.M.		6 P.M.	6 A.M.		
		drs.	drs.		drs.	drs.		
Unglazed .	Musketry	500	508	+ 8	258	256	− 2	Clodded and set together, colour black, grain very soft, a little dust.
6 hours glazed .		500	517	+17	262	258	− 4	Slightly clodded, a little set together, grain softer, colour deep and black, no dust.
12 hours glazed .		500	510	+10	262	254	− 8	Slightly clodded, colour deep, no dust, grain soft.
24 hours glazed .		500	512	+12	260	253	− 7	Slightly clodded, colour deep black, grain soft, no dust.

On the Density of Powder in regard to Range.

Captain Bishop truly remarks, "That it is of the utmost importance to attend to the quantity of water. If the cake be very moist the water in the composition occupies certain interstices, which itself occasions, and which in the process of drying are left as receptacles, which inclose particles of air that introduce themselves as the water escapes. This powder will always be light, pulverable, susceptible to every change in the atmosphere, and be improper for keeping. A cubic foot of this light powder weighs 48lbs., while that of the denser powder weighs 53lbs."

Dr. Scott, at Bombay, maintained, "That fine powder is stronger than coarse, and that allowing a quantity of fine grain to remain with the coarse improves the strength."

Captain Bishop considered that fine powder is *not so strong* as coarse, which result he considered to be proved by the *one* ounce charge experiment. Assertions diametrically opposed, and yet,

EFFECT OF DENSITY ON RANGE.   133

to a certain extent, both true! Captain Bishop considered, "That large grains were denser than small, as cut from the densest and strongest places in the cake."

Mr. Braddock says, "We think that gunpowder of light specific gravity ranges further than powder of greater density, only because it explodes with greater facility ; for the same reason that fir will burn faster than oak." This, I have no doubt, is the truth.

Suppose the composition from which the powder is made to be perfect in its elements and manipulation, that is to say, suppose the matter of the powder to be merely the solid state of the elastic fluid to be generated, only waiting the required heat to cause explosion ; then a charge of moderate size, in a single block, will not explode, but burn away steadily but fiercely, when ignited from the exposed surface, there being no passage for the fire to the centre of the mass. Hence, sufficient heat is not concentrated at one instant to create and expand the fluid. As the number of pieces are increased, so is the passage for the fire, and so is the surface exposed to the action of the fire, and so is the quantity of air between the pieces ; so that the whole is exploded with greater facility. All things being the same, the facility of inflammation will be inversely as the density of the powder.

Now the moment the fire touches any part of a charge, that part inflames and expands ; this fluid drives before itself, in confined tubes, the distant unexploded portion of the charge.

It would appear that the flame or fire has no power in itself to proceed or go before the expansion of the fluid ; hence there is a ratio between the velocity given to the unexploded portion of the charge, which is the velocity of the ball, and the rate of passage of the fire through the charge :—If T be the time of passage of the ball up the tube, t the time of passage of the flame through the charge, then t should not be more than T, if greater, then a portion of the charge will be fired beyond the tube to no effect. If the density of the powder is such as to increase the time, t to $2\,t$, it is clear, one half of the power of the charge will be lost.

In very small charges unconfined by any tube, as one ounce

in the 8 in. mortar, the reverse is experienced, because the powder is spread over a large space, and, without any depth, occupies an extended surface. Here the fire is less opposed, the large grains are less quickly separated by the fluid, also being of a greater density, two ounces occupy less space than the same weight of smaller grained powder, hence the heat and the fluid are more concentrated.

In this ratio of the inflammation of powder to the ratio of ball's velocity, we may trace the resulting decreased effect from a very minute accession of damp ; for all have witnessed the difficulty of inflaming damp powder. This will also account for a fact recorded by Mr. Braddock:

" Humidity and dryness are well known to exert a great and opposite influence on gunpowder, and when it is heated by artificial means, and fired while it possesses a high temperature, the ranges of shot are amazingly increased." As it may sometimes occur in practice that a longer range may be required, while any addition to the charge might not be made effectual to promote it, it may be useful to state an experiment which seems to point out that the same weight of powder will produce this result, if it be only allowed to acquire an increase of temperature before it be used.

One ounce troy of powder fired in a $4\frac{1}{2}$ inch mortar, shell 8lbs., gave a medium range of . . . . . . 141 yards.

One ounce of the same powder was heated in a copper pan to about 400° of Fahrenheit, and then fired as before, gave a medium range of . . . . . . 242 yards.

The following trials were made with a 24-pounder brass gun, at the same degree of elevation specified. The range is taken to the first graze of the shot.

		Yards.		Yards.
Point blank,	6lbs. of powder	480	10lbs. of powder	480
2° elevation	,,	1100	,,	1100
$2\frac{1}{4}$,,	,,	1155	,,	1158
$2\frac{1}{2}$,,	,,	1210	,,	1216
$3\frac{3}{4}$,,	,,	1496	,,	1497
4 ,,	,,	1552	,,	1552
$4\frac{1}{4}$,,	,,	1599	,,	1599
$4\frac{1}{2}$,,	,,	1646	,,	1646
$4\frac{3}{4}$,,	,,	1690	,,	1693
5 ,,	,,	1746	,,	1740

Here are too many coincidences to be the effect of accident, and therefore we may conclude, that in every case 4 lbs. were blown out of the gun unconsumed.

The accession of a quantity of damp cannot alter the proportions of the ingredients, or abstract from their amounts: but it delays the progress of combustion, and retards the concentration of the fluid.

We hear of cannon being loaded with 40 or 50 lbs. of powder, and the mind is at once deceived into the idea of the great tenacity of the metal of the gun; but the fact is, that probably after 1 lbs. that it would have made no difference on the metal were the rest of the 40 or 50 lbs. composed of sand or sawdust. Of a drier powder 12 lbs., and of a damper powder 8 lbs., would, probably, only be burnt to any useful effect.

The ratio of the length of the charge to its diameter will vary with the humidity of the powder, but still is almost a fixed quantity, which cannot be exceeded to any good purpose.

In the Court of Directors' proof, we find the difference of twenty seconds in the time of the total burning of the three trains of 87 ft., between the ordnance and the musketry powder; but there is no difference between the composition of the two powders except in the size of the grains.

If the initial velocity of the ball from a musket 3 ft. 5 in. length of barrel, is 1,700 ft. in a second, we have $\frac{9}{1700}$ for T as this maximum of inflammation. Now the difference in the inflammation of dampish powder is perceptible, while $\frac{4}{1700}$ of a second will hardly be appreciated. How much more will this effect of damp be experienced in the very short tube of a mortar.

In the old proof books, I find the following experiment taken to ascertain the general results of hard and medium pressed cake:—

Description of Powder.		Density.	Charge, 1lb. 65lb. ball. 8-inch. mortar.
			yards.
Soft mill cake	M	237	955
	O	240	940
Hard mill cake	M	262	875
	O	280	699
Medium pressed cake	M	259	835
	O	272	674
Hard pressed cake	M	266	786
	O	288	620

These, tabulated according to densities, will prove, in a wonderful mode, the value of density in ranges.

Density.	Range.	
237	955	Hardly one of these ranges is misplaced in an inverse ratio of density. Hence a difference of 51 drams in the Ishapore measure gives a loss range by 335 yards, or 6 yards for each dram.
240	940	
259	835	
262	875	
266	786	
272	674	
280	699	
288	620	

According to the report for the French Minister, the density of the French powder was to the litre 905 grammes, while the English powder was 857.

According to the Ishapore measure, this would give the former 276, and the latter 261 drams.

Sir John Burgoyne estimates the specific gravity of powder at ·9200 which gives, by the Ishapore measure, 281 drams.

Mode of ascertaining the Density.

The density of the powder is a useful index of the mode in which the work is being performed in the various parts of the manufactory.

The slightest change is instantly betrayed by alteration in the density.

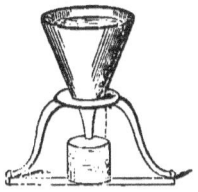

The measurements of the cup and stand are as follows :—

Cup, interior dimensions	Diameter of base	3·5	inches.
	Height	3·5	,,
Funnel	Diameter at top	7·75	,,
	Height	9·	,,
Diameter of tube		·05	,,
Distance from the bottom of tube to the top of the cup		2·5	,,

One and a quarter pounds of ordnance powder, or one and a half of musketry, is thrown into the funnel descending by the tube to the cup; the level of the grains at the top of the cup is struck off by a piece of copper, and the weight taken in drams, say 262, which constitutes Ishapore density. This divided by 307·2 will give the specific gravity of the powder.

The size, height, and pressure must always be the same.

ON THE BARREL DEPARTMENT.

POWDER barrels should be well made of perfectly dry well-seasoned wood—so close that no dust can escape, so strong that they should be secure against the common accidents of transport. They should, indeed, be water and air tight. The barrels used in Bengal are serviceable, as is proved by the excellent state in which the agency powder is found after it has been carried from one end of India to the other; but the packing is very heavy and costly. Still, when the nature of gunpowder is taken into consideration—its cost, and the labour to produce it—and the necessity that it should not deteriorate in store, thus rendering the acquired skill and practice of the artillery useless, surely it is of the utmost importance to use every means of preserving it securely.

Mr. Walker's patent barrels have been introduced, lined with a thin case of copper, or rather, a copper cylinder is cased over and protected by an outward covering of wood.

These are, no doubt, more protective of the powder, but they are expensive and heavy, and always occupy the same room, full or empty. Three common barrels, taken to pieces and packed up for store or carriage, only occupy the same space as one of the patent barrels.

The native mode of packing gunpowder in dubbahs, or vessels of raw hide, is most excellent. These dubbahs are air and water tight, very elastic, and seldom break open as do the wooden barrels with a fall. Covered with a casing of wicker work, they would prove a most superior vessel for holding gunpowder or transporting it from one magazine to another. Perhaps they would be liable to injury from atmosphere, or from those destructive insects, the white ants. But if each magazine were supplied with a complement of patent barrels, the powder might be carried to them in these dubbahs, and exterior varnish or other chemical suitable composition might be applied to them to secure them from the evils above mentioned.

Several kinds of wood have been tried in India for powder barrels. Common refuse oak is soon destroyed by the ants and other insects. Gomer wood was for a long period the material used, but it proved heavy, hard to work up, and very brittle. At present all the barrels are made of teak.

The regulated interior dimensions for powder barrels are—

Diameter of bulge	16 inches.
,, head	14 ,,
Length of staves	21 ,,
Thickness of staves at head	1 inch.
,, ,, bulge	$\frac{5}{8}$,,
Diameter of bung hole	1·5
Weight	34lbs.
Contents	100 to 112lbs. of powder.
Contents in cubic inches	3180

There are four copper hoops to each barrel of the following measurements :—

Length . . . 4·7ft.	Breadth .	. 1·25 in.
Weight. . . . 2lbs. 2oz.	Thickness .	. . 0·1 in.

The weight of a new barrel complete is from 35lbs. to 40lbs.; that of a patent barrel 45lbs. These are considered to measure 4·08 cubic feet each for tonnage.

The rivets of the hoops range from 43 to 60 in the pound.

Repaired barrels are allowed to have the staves reduced to $\frac{3}{8}$ in the bulge, and $\frac{5}{8}$ at the head; the weight being thus reduced to 25lbs.

The staves, or wooden casing, of the patent barrels are thinner than in common barrels.

There is great loss in resetting-up old barrels. Many of the edges being broken in transit, require to be recut to enable them to join correctly. Hence the heads have to be reduced in size, while the openings for the heads are enlarged by the trimming of the staves, whereas the old heads, as such, are useless, and require to be enlarged by a new centre bit. Even then the job is not very satisfactory.

The mode at present adopted is, that the half wrought heads and staves are supplied by contract at the average rate detailed in the table of prices.

The master cooper sets them up at the contract rate for workmanship.

First the fresh staves are set up with iron former hoops over the fire to give them the required bend and curve. In this half wrought state they are retained as long as possible for the wood to dry. In this first operation many staves are broken.

The next year these half-wrought barrels are finished. The staves, now well set, are cut, trimmed, pared down correctly, and the edges fitted with the utmost exactness. The heads are also sloped off, cut carefully to a perfect circle, and fixed in the groove, when the copper hoops are well driven home. The barrel being finished, is retained as long as possible in the magazine.

The great advantage of this plan is, that by occasionally setting home the hoops, any seams caused by the shrinking or drying of the wood are immediately closed. The new staves had never sufficient space given them in the storing sheds for the circulation of air. In England steam machines are used for the manufacture of barrels : these, in time, will doubtless reach India.

When filled, these barrels will bear very great direct pressure.

Some barrels, made with extraordinary care, were left under water for a few days, and admitted no fluid inside to spoil the contents ; but the common run of barrels will not long resist the action of the fluid on its seams. To ascertain this fact, I made the following experiment :

April 23*rd.*—A.M, 8h. 25m.—Placed a barrel on a copper cooling-pan, so that merely a small section of the bulge was touched by the water, which did not reach the crown.

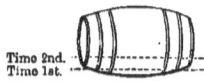

Time 2nd.
Time 1st.

At 4 p.m. a little water had entered between the staves, and a few small clods of powder existed. The water had not penetrated the wood.

In twelve hours more, the powder would have been all damp.

At 5 p.m. placed a second barrel so that the water reached $2\frac{1}{2}$ inches up the head over the crown.

April 24*th.*—At 8 a.m. opened the barrel ; $1\frac{1}{2}$ inch of the water was absorbed, the powder was half dissolved and much clogged.

From a bung-hole of diameter 1·5 inches one of these barrels will empty itself, if inverted, in about five minutes.

The following is the minimum value of a barrel, with no charge for tools or establishment.

		R.	A.	P.		R.	A.	P.
4 Half heads	at	0	3	7·6	=	0	14	6·4
18 Staves of teak	,,	0	1	10·0	=	2	1	0·0
4 Copper hoops	,,	1	3	3·0	=	4	13	0·0
4 Rivets	,,	0	¼	0·0	=	0	1	0·0
Making in work	,,	0	6	9·0	=	0	6	9·0
Total						8	4	3·4

The barrels are divided into a class with 4, and a class with 6, copper hoops each. The latter were required for the lower tier of barrels on shipboard, but are now seldom called for.

My experience in Affghanistan led me to suggest to the Military Board, in March, 1845, some alterations in the powder barrels, as set forth in the following extract.

As the matter stands at present it is usual to consider four 100 lb. barrels as the load for a camel, that is—

Powder	400 lbs.
4 Barrels	140 ,,
Ropes gearing—tarpaulings	20 ,,
Total	560 lbs.

Four barrels also involve extra ropes. Now, 560 lbs. is soon found to be above the average load of even one of our best camels at the pace we force them to proceed.

It becomes necessary to reduce the load, one barrel is taken away, one is then slung on each side of the animal, and one is piled on the top of the saddle; a difficulty arises in fixing this single one securely; from frequently rolling down it is constantly injured.

I therefore conceive that barrels capable of containing 150 lbs. of powder of the length of the saddle of a camel, and not increased in diameter, would be very useful, and enable a convoy to start with a medium load, which it would continue to carry per camel. This arrangement would be attended with much less trouble in loading and unloading, with some saving of expense in ropes and slings.

The load will thus stand—

Powder	300 lbs.
2 Barrels	90 ,,
Rope, &c.	15 ,,
Total	405 lbs.

which I think is a better medium weight. The heads remain the same as at present, only the staves are to be made longer; perhaps six hoops will be more secure than four.

There will be a trifling saving in the barrelling expense of the 100 lbs., but the chief object has reference to facility of transport. I do believe such barrels will be found most convenient at stations depending on camel carriage.

The dimensions proposed are as follows:—

Interior diameter at bulge	16 inches.
,, ,, head	14 ,,
Depth between heads	28 ,,
Weight	45 lbs.
Contents—powder	100 ,,

It is not beyond the strength of a single man to carry this barrel, and it rolls equally easy. I cannot anticipate any increased danger in the mass of 150 over 100 lbs. of powder.

Hoops and Staves.

I was directed to make certain experiments towards ascertaining the strength of zinc hoops, with a view to their employment in the construction of powder barrels.

It consequently became necessary to ascertain in some mode the actual strength or resistance in powder barrels, towards establishing a scale of comparison.

I determined to try the experiment mentioned in philosophical works, of the power of a column of water, if sufficiently high, to burst any barrel; and thus, in the height of the column, to obtain the required measure.

I consequently selected 12 ft. of a leaden pipe, 1 in. in diameter; this when filled with water, had no effect on the barrels.

The pipe was then increased to 24 ft. With a new barrel, the water was forced through the pores of the end of the staves, but the barrel was unaltered.

With a good repaired barrel the result was much the same.

With a very thin staved and hooped barrel, such as would not be sent out of the agency, the staves bent a little, the seams opened, and the water escaped.

A still thinner staved barrel, with iron hoops of the thickness of $\frac{1}{20}$ of an inch, allowed the water to escape at all the seams, the hoops appeared quite unaltered.

Having thus reached no satisfactory results, I proposed to try the strength of the various component parts. I made a scale of rod iron, and suspended the hoop between the hook of the scale and the hook of the gin, which last was loaded until the hoop broke, the results being—

A.
Hoops.

Dimensions—Length, 4 ft. 8. in. Breadth, 1¼ in.

	Weight given. lbs.	
Hoop from 12 oz. copper	344	Torn in half at hook.
,, ,, 16 oz. copper.	430	{ Torn at upper, broke at lower hook.
,, ,, 40 oz. copper	2236	Broke at hook.
Hoops of common powder barrel about 60 oz	4859	{ Cut ¼ across at the hook end. Rivet dragged through the hole.
Ditto ditto soldered, and no rivet	5461	{ Broke below soldering, where it may have been a little weakened by the fire.
Hoop of ditto cut up centre, being half breadth	2365	Gave at rivet hole.
Ditto ditto ditto	1333	Gave at rivet hole.
Ditto ditto ditto without rivets soldered	1935	Broke in middle of side.
Hoop ½ breadth of 12 oz. copper	86	} Broke at rivet.
,, ,, 16 oz. ditto.	86	
Hoops iron, from sulphur cask, breadth 1¼ in., thickness $\frac{1}{20}$ in.	3053	Torn at lower hook.

I then added side bars to the scale rods, placed between them a stave, and suspending the scale by a ring to the staves added weight till the stave broke. The result was as follows :

B.

Staves.	Measures.	Thickness.	Weight required to break.	
	Inches. Length. Breadth.	Inches.	lbs.	
An old stave, three times set up, very dry	21 by 2·7	$\frac{3}{4}$	258	The staves all broke readily in the centre at the weight mentioned, some of the wood was very dry from the action of the fire in giving the bend.
An old stave once set up, returned from Bombay dry	21 by 3	$\frac{3}{4}$	645	
A new stave cut down and ready for setting up, good		$\frac{7}{8}$	817	
A fresh half-wrought stave untrimmed	22 by $3\frac{3}{4}$	$1\frac{1}{8}$	1892	
A ditto ditto divided in half } average of each half.		$1\frac{1}{8}$	1118	

Barrels.

I next loaded weights on a barrel full of saltpetre, when the weights reached about 6,628 lbs. a stave broke, and three others were flattened down and separated, the mass of weight had then reached the resistance of the saltpetre.

A new empty barrel stood 7,000 lbs. when the head slipped in being so forced by the staves becoming straight, two of the staves were split, hence new barrels will stand a direct external pressure of three tons.

To Analyse Powder.

To 100 grains, add 600 grains more or less of distilled water, then filter the solution through clean filtering paper. The water is then to be evaporated over a spirit lamp, the dried residue will be the proportion of saltpetre. The mass collected on the filtering paper consists of the sulphur and charcoal combined. If this residue be placed in a copper dish and heated to above 240°, the sulphur will disengage itself in fumes, and leave the charcoal.

If the saltpetre of any quantity of gunpowder to be examined is not pure, by dropping a few drops of the solution of nitrate of silver into the clear solution that has drained through the paper filter, any impurity of chloride salts will be indicated by the clear solution becoming cloudy : the proportion of impurity may be detected by chemical tests.

Sekh Gunpowder.

In passing Peishawur on the return from Kabul, in December, 1842, I purchased from the Tooshuk Khanah a beautiful matchlock and appointments, which had been presented to Sir George Pollock, G.C.B., by the young Prince.

Every article was of the best description, and the powder-horn contained about one pound of Sekh powder.

Considering the rank of the donor, I have no doubt that it was powder of their first quality.

This powder remained until 1849 ; on opening the horn then, to my astonishment I found it perfectly good.

I had also taken at the battle of Tazee, from an Afghan chief, an excellent Sekh matchlock, with the barrels of which I made the trials recorded under the head " Long Lahoor Matchlock."

With 5 drams of English powder the initial velocity of the small ball of the matchlock is superior to that of the large ball of the English musket, which with 5 drams would only penetrate 6 boards, while the matchlock, with 5 drams, penetrated $8\frac{1}{2}$ boards.

From the matchlock, $3\frac{1}{2}$ drams from the wretched powder of the ship " Trident " gave an initial velocity equal to that from $3\frac{1}{4}$ drams of our own fine musketry powder—a fact requiring attention and consideration.

The strength of this " Trident's " powder may be seen in a subsequent Table, headed " Various Proofs."

After the battles of the Sutlege, the common Sekh powder was submitted to proof and comparison with Bengal powder, of which the following is the result :—

PROOF TAKEN AT KUSSOOR ON THE 16TH JULY, 1846.

8-in. mortar.   Shell filled with sand, 45 lbs.   Charge, 2 oz.

1.	Bengal P. 78	Sekh powder	14
2.	,, 80	,,	31
3.	,, 65	,,	13
4.	,, 75	,,	18
5.	,, 75	,,	20
6.	,, 80	,,	19
	Average 75½	Average	19·16

In 1849 I turned attention to the powder in the horn given with the matchlock: the result was, that in an 8-inch mortar, with 2 oz. charge, and 67 lb. ball, it ranged 53 yards, to the Bengal powder 94, under the same circumstances, and with the éprouvette gave an arc of 16° 52′ against the Bengal musketry powder arc of 23° 5′. The density of the Sekh powder was 272 to the Bengal powder 262. The appearance of the Sekh powder may be thus described—grain mixed, round as if cast, and not very hard, not much dust; colour, bluish black; apparently contained a large proportion of sulphur.

To analysis, this powder gave—

Saltpetre $\begin{cases} \text{Better than 1 boiled} & 50 \\ \text{Inferior} & 19 \end{cases}$ . . 60·

Sulphur . . . . 12·5
Charcoal . . . . 12·5
Loss . . . . 6·

Total . . . . . . 100·0

In 1844-45 one of the cleverest of the Sekh Sirdars, who resided some time at Benares, when passing down the country, exhibited to Colonel Brooke, C.B., the projection of a small shell without either gun or mortar.

This was done by excavating a hole in the ground at an angle of about 45°, with a small chamber like the contraction of the bore of a piece of ordnance. Tent pins were driven so as to cover the bottom of the bore, and a piece of quickmatch was inserted at the mouth. The shell was then prepared with fusee, and fired. The shell was projected about 300 yards, and exploded in falling to the ground; the charge was small, but no weights or measure recorded. The excavation was very little injured in firing two rounds.

Buildings.

The distance between buildings containing powder should be beyond the range of the quantity contained in each house. The range of powder forced by resistance into one direction is as the quantity, but, when left unconfined, will perhaps be as the square root of the quantity. The distance between the Ishapore Mills, say 60 yards, is proved by experience to be well calculated for about 80 to 100 lbs. of powder, and may be assumed as the unit; hence for the press houses and corning houses, containing upwards of 400 lbs. of powder, the interval should be double at least.

All the houses should be as large as possible, for the purposes of room in which to work, and for free circulation to the fluid in case of explosion; they should also be as high as possible, to remove all beams and rafters from the flame; these should also be as heavy as possible, with due regard to economy and convenience, that they may be carried by the explosion to as little distance as possible.

From the flight of burning beams or splinters lies the great secondary danger from explosion.

Perhaps the better form of walls would be strong corners or plinths in any position from which it is desirable to turn the blast, with fillings-up of very weak masonry, to give way before the fluid in any more safe direction.

As few door or window frames as possible should be inserted, with as little wood-work as is compatible with convenience.

EXPERIMENTS ON MORTARS.

To arrive at any certainty in the matter of the proof of powder, it becomes necessary to well understand the instruments of proof in all their circumstances. To this end I instituted a long series of experiments on each. My great aim was to have only one circumstance in variation, and the remainder constant; the utmost care was given to obtain this end.

First, in regard to the mortar; with all other circumstances identical, the range was taken from 1 to 64 drams, and from one ounce to a pound.

Next, to ascertain the value of weight, a brass ball was fired off, placed on the lathe, and reduced internally each time by 5 lbs. of metal. It is true the centre of gravity was not always the same, but this could not be avoided.

To determine the effect of windage, Colonel Wilson,* then in the Cossipoor foundry, after each trial reduced the shot externally by one-tenth of an inch in diameter.

This was done with the precision for which the Cossipoor foundry is celebrated.

Elevation was tried by a progressive advance on the quadrant.

Recoil by the mode and means indicated in the Table.

After this, an attempt was made to ascertain the value of the circumstances of charge and size of grain as operating on the gun pendulum. The results are mentioned under that instrument.

Lastly, the musket was used.

The experiments on this head were made in the usual mode, by fixing the barrel in the rest, and firing at planks secured in a

---

* Now Sir Archdale Wilson, K.C.B.

stand placed at the regular distance. But it was soon found that half-inch planks, with an inch interval, were destroyed after a few rounds; to obviate this difficulty, the interval between the planks was omitted; then one-inch planks, with one-inch interval; and lastly one-inch, with no interval, was adopted, which proved the best arrangement.

The equation between these modes is recorded, so that the result under one mode may be reduced and compared with that of any other. Captain Bazely, the Principal Commissary of Ordnance, kindly furnished the muskets. Every possible care was taken in keeping all the circumstances as nearly identical as possible. The observations are faithfully recorded, and may be depended upon, though the deductions drawn from them are crude, and may be erroneous. Still these recorded facts may be useful to others.

I have added a table of musketry results on planks, compared with the ranges obtained from the average of the Commandant's proof at Dum-Dum.

Also a table of trials of various powders obtained from time to time.

The powders from the ships "Trident," "Good Hope," "Perseverance," and "Mysoor," had laid in. the Myapoor magazine from the dates mentioned until sold by auction, in 1847.

The results are curious, and show that powder inferior in mortars and broader tubes is not so inferior in narrower tubes.

As much interest has been raised on the subject of Sekh powder and Sekh matchlocks, I have added a separate paper on this head.

Also a tabulated statement, tracing the effect of powder as far back into past years as I could obtain for it authentic and undoubted authority.

Charge.

COMPARATIVE PROOF BY A PROGRESSIVE INCREASE OF DRAMS OF ORDNANCE POWDER OF 1844-45.

Weight of ball, 68 lbs.
Diameter of ball, 7·92 in.
Diameter of mortar, 8·02 in.
Windage, ·10 in.

Ranges in feet.

A	B	C	$\dfrac{B}{A}$	$\dfrac{B^2}{B^1}$	$\dfrac{B^N}{B^1}$	A	B	C	$\dfrac{B}{A}$	$\dfrac{B^2}{B^1}$	$\dfrac{B^N}{B^1}$
Charge in drams.	Range in feet.	First difference.	Range for each dram.	Ratio of increase of one.	Ratio of increase.	Charge in drams.	Range in feet.	First difference.	Range for each dram.	Ratio of increase of one.	Ratio of increase.
1	10	—	10	—	—	33	307	+ 8	9·3	1·	—
2	17	+ 7	8· 5	1·70	1·7	34	315	+ 8	9·26	1·02	—
3	31	+ 14	10·33	1·82	3·1	35	321	+ 6	9·17	1·01	—
4	35	+ 4	8·75	1·12	3·5	36	330	+ 9	9·16	1·02	—
5	45	+ 10	9·	1·28	4·5	37	342	+ 12	9·24	1·03	—
6	58	+ 13	9·66	1·28	4·5	38	351	+ 9	9·23	1·02	—
7	67	+ 9	9·57	1·45	6·7	39	357	+ 6	9·15	1·01	—
8	71	+ 4	8·87	1·05	7·1	40	369	+ 12	9·32	1·03	—
9	83	+ 12	9·22	1·16	8·3	41	378	+ 9	9·21	1·02	—
10	110	+ 27	11·	1·32	11·	42	384	+ 6	9·14	1·01	—
11	114	+ 4	10·36	1·03	11·4	43	387	+ 3	9· 0	1·00	—
12	119	+ 5	9·91	1·04	11·9	44	405	+ 18	9· 2	1·04	—
13	127	+ 8	9·76	1·06	12·7	45	414	+ 9	9· 2	1·02	—
14	135	+ 8	9·64	1·06	13·5	46	423	+ 9	9·19	1·02	—
15	144	+ 9	9· 6	1·06	14·4	47	435	+ 12	9·25	1·02	—
16	166	+ 22	10·37	1·15	16·6	48	459	+ 24	9·56	1·05	45·9
17	167	+ 1	9·82	1·	16·7	49	456	+ 3	9· 3	1·01	—
18	183	+ 16	10·16	1·09	18·3	50	465	+ 9	9· 3	1·01	—
19	189	+ 6	9·94	1·03	18·9	51	477	+ 12	9·35	1·02	—
20	204	+ 15	10· 2	1·07	20·4	52	489	+ 12	9· 4	1·02	—
21	228	+ 24	10·85	1·11	22·8	53	489		9·22	1· 0	—
22	237	+ 9	10·77	1·03	—	54	495	+ 6	9·16	1·01	—
23	240	+ 3	10·43	1·01	—	55	510	+ 15	9·27	1·03	—
24	252	+ 12	10· 5	1·05	—	56	513	+ 3	9·16	1·00	—
25	258	+ 6	10·32	1·02	—	57	525	+ 12	9·21	1·02	—
26	261	+ 3	10·03	1·01	—	58	534	+ 9	9· 2	1·01	—
27	273	+ 12	10·11	1·04	—	59	558	+ 24	9·45	1·04	—
28	274	+ 1	9·78	1·00	—	60	567	+ 9	9·45	1·01	—
29	285	+ 11	9·83	1·04	—	61	573	+ 6	9·30	1·01	—
30	292	+ 7	9·73	1·02	—	62	576	+ 3	9·20	1·00	—
31	294	+ 2	9·48	1·00	—	63	585	+ 9	9·28	1·01	—
32	307	+ 13	9·59	1·04	30·7	64	582	+ 3	9·09	0·99	58·2

EXPERIMENTS WITH CHARGES.

	Total.
Of A . . .	2,080
B . .	19,647 = average loss per dram.
C . . .	572
$\frac{B}{A}$ . . .	612·08
$\frac{B^2}{B^1}$ . . .	67·61

$$\frac{B}{A} \times \frac{1}{64} = \frac{612\cdot8}{64} = 9\cdot56$$

1 dram = 10

$$\frac{15\cdot16\cdot17 \text{ drs.}}{3} = 9\cdot93 \;—\;\cdot07$$

$$\frac{31\cdot32\cdot33}{3} = 9\cdot45 \;—\;\cdot48$$

$$\frac{47\cdot48\cdot49}{3} = 9\cdot37 \;—\;\cdot08$$

$$\frac{63\cdot64}{2} = 9\cdot18 \;—\;\cdot19$$

$$\text{Total} \;\frac{\cdot82}{4} \;\cdot205$$

$$\frac{82}{63} = \cdot013 \text{ loss of range per dram.} \quad \frac{\cdot013}{10} = \cdot0013 \text{ per foot.}$$

$$\frac{10 + 909}{2} \;.\; 9\cdot54 \text{ mean of extremes per dram.}$$

Total B = 19,647 ⎫
Total A = 2,080 ⎬ 9·44 average of extremes per dram.
⎭

COMPARATIVE PROOF BY A PROGRESSIVE INCREASE OF OUNCES.

Diameter of mortar	. . .	8·04 inches.
,, of ball	. . .	7·92 ,,
Windage	. . .	0·12 ,,

A	B	C	$\frac{B}{A}$	$\frac{B^N}{B^i}$	$\frac{B^2}{B^1}$
Charge in ounces.	Range in yards.	1st difference.	Range for each ounce.	Ratio of increase of one.	Ratio of increase.
1	47	—	47	—	—
2	87	40	43	1·851	1·851
3	130	43	43·3	2·765	1·494
4	168	38	42	3·574	1·292
5	213	45	42·6	4·531	1·268
6	245	32	40·8	5·212	1·150
7	287	42	41	6·106	1·171
8	328	41	41	6·978	1·142
9	369	41	41	7·851	1·124
10	419	50	41·9	8·914	1·136
11	455	36	41·3	9·680	1·085
12	516	61	43	10·979	1·134
13	563	47	43·3	11·970	1·091
14	614	51	43·8	12·970	1·197
15	674	60	44·9	14·340	1·097
16	723	49	45	15·360	1·072

152   CHARGES AND RANGES.

	Total.		
Of A	136	$\begin{cases} \text{Total B} = \\ \text{Total A} = \end{cases}$	$\left.\dfrac{5838}{136}\right\} = 43 \cdot 6$ yards per oz.
B	5838		
C	676	Total $\dfrac{C}{A-1} =$	$\left.\dfrac{676}{15}\right\} = 45$ average difference.
$\dfrac{B}{A}$	684·9	Total $\dfrac{\frac{B}{A}}{16}$	$\left.\dfrac{684 \cdot 9}{16}\right\} = 42 \cdot 75$
$\dfrac{B^N}{B^1}$	123·081		
$\dfrac{B^2}{B^1}$	18·304		$\left.\dfrac{47+45}{2}\right\} = 46$ mean range per ounce.

On inspection of column B, we notice an approach to an arithmetical progression, of which the common difference decreases as the number of drams increases. Taken in periods of sixteen drams—

$$\begin{array}{lll}
\text{1st period of 16 drs.} & \text{common difference} & 10\cdot 4 \\
\text{2nd} \quad ,, & ,, \quad ,, & 9\cdot 3 \\
\text{3rd} \quad ,, & ,, \quad ,, & 10\cdot 1 \\
\text{4th} \quad ,, & ,, \quad ,, & 8\cdot 4
\end{array} \Bigg\} \text{Average, } 9\cdot 55$$

Assume the column B to be a regular arithmetical progression, then the common difference $= 9 \cdot 07$. Sum of the series 18944, only 703 less than the sum exhibited in the table. Or, if we take the column $\dfrac{B}{A}$, the value in range of each dram, then $10 - 9 \cdot 09 = \cdot 91 \div 63 = \cdot 0144$, the average decreases in value of each added dram.

This column might be treated as a geometric progression where the common ratio $\left(\dfrac{z}{a} = d^{n-1}\right)$ would be ·998. Hence $\overline{\cdot 998}^{15} \times 10$ is the value of each dram in a charge of 16 drams. But this ratio of ·998 must be limited to a few terms, and it will probably answer best to sixteen.

9·78 ft. or 3·26 yards may be taken as the average range of a 68 lb. ball, with a dram of powder, from an 8-in. mortar, as described.

If the range be inversely as the weight, then one dram should convey one pound of weight in the shape of a ball 7·92 diameter, with a windage of 0·1, from an 8-in. mortar, 221 yards;

CHARGES AND RANGES.

to be decreased in the ratio of $\overline{\cdot 998}\,^{n-1}$ for each increase of the terms of the charge.

221 yards × 1 ÷ 1 lb. of ball = for a dram.
221 yards × $\overline{\cdot 998)}^{15}$ × 16 ÷ 68 = 50·3 for the ounce charge } with a 68 lb. ball.
50·3 × $\overline{\cdot 998)}^{15}$ × 16 ÷ 1 =   777 for the 1 lb. charge .}

In fact, in the large tubes of mortars, within reasonable limits, the range is nearly as the charge, for a larger addition of weight of powder makes but a small increase to the depth of the charge, and hence the total ignition is not delayed as in narrow tubes.

A table of ranges might be better constructed from the first, second, and third differences, if necessary, according to the formula of the Summation of Series,* where the sum of the series would be $a + x\,d' + x \cdot \dfrac{x-1}{2}\,d'' + x \cdot \dfrac{x-1}{2} \cdot \dfrac{x-2}{3}\,d''',$ &c. the value in range for each increase of charge being considered as a diminishing series, by reason of the delayed ignition, and the quantity of the resistance of the air being increased with augmented velocity.

Worked out from the recorded ranges of 1, 6, 11, and 16 ozs. the following is a range table for Bengal musketry powder from an 8-in. mortar :—

Powder. Ounces.	Range. Yards.	Powder. Ounces.	Range. Yards.
1	47	9	374
2	83	10	428
3	121	11	470
4	160	12	518
5	200	13	567
6	242	14	617
7	285	15	668
8	329	16	720

According to a rough conclusion by Sir John Burgoyne, two inches of powder in a—

Hole 1 in. in diameter will blow out 7 in. of clay.
,, 2   ,,   ,,   18 ,,
,, 3   ,,   ,,   20 ,,

The friction at the circumference will be as the diameters;

* See Baker's and Dowling's "Rules and Formulæ." 1862.

the areas and the weight of the clay will be as the square of the diameters. If the latter, or weight of clay, measure the result, the 3 in. hole is the more effective size for two ounces of powder. This is a question which should be determined.

If these facts are correct, they prove how much depends on the form, or rather on the thickness of the charge.

Diameter of bore. Inches.	Area of bore.	Depth of powder. Inches.	Quantity of powder. Oz.	Quantity of clay. Cubic ins.
1	·7854	4·4	2	5
2	3·1416	1·1	2	56
3	7·	·48	2	140

Note.—In my remarks on the effect of *reverberation* in large charges of powder, with a heavy shot before it (see Appendix, on the paper on "War Rockets"), it will appear that great consideration in calculating the force of gunpowder should be given to this cause, a subject hardly noticed before, I believe, by any writer.—EDITOR.

Weight.

Comparative Proof taken at Ishapore, with a Brass Ball, Diameter 7·91 in., by Reducing the Ball Internally to the following Weights.

Weight of the ball				Charge, 2 ozs. Diameter of mortar, 8·02. Windage, 0·11.				E		C	Charge, 1 lb. Diameter of mortar, 8·04. Windage, ·13.						C	B lb / B oz	Ratio
lbs. A	D A¹/Aˣ	Difference	N	Yards B	Difference	Flight of ball	Depth in the ground	Bˣ/B¹	Bᴺ/B¹	B/A	Yards B	Difference	Flight of ball	Depth in the ground	Bˣ/B¹	Bᴺ/B¹	B/A		
60	1·09	5	10	95	10			1·10	1	1·58									
55	1·2	5	15	105	10			1·09	1·10	1·90									
50	1·3	5	20	115	7			1·06	1·21	2·3									
45	1·5	5	25	122	10			1·08	1·28	2·7									
40	1·7	5	30	132	15			1·11	1·38	3·4	793	60		1·4	1·075	1·075	132	8·3	·075
35	2	5	35	147	18	5"	in 5	1·11	1·54	4·2	853	23	13"	1·3	1·026	1·10	155	8·1	·938
30	2·4	5	40	165	20	5½"	4	1·12	1·73	5·3	876	26		1·2	1·039	1·13	175	7·6	·960
25	3	5	45	185	21		3	1·11	1·94	7·4	903	20	15	1	1·022	1·16	204	7·3	·945
20	4	5	50	206	17			1·11	2·14	10·3	922	25	18		1·026	1·19	230	6·9	·927
15	6	5	55	223	22			1·1	2·35		947						270	6·4	
10	12	5	60	245	23		3	1·1	2·58		1058	111		1·5	1·116	1·33	351	6·4	1
5	60	4		268	21			1·1	2·83		1123	65			1·061	1·41	448	6	·937
1	0	1		289	6			1·08	3·05										
0				295					3·11										

EFFECTS OF REDUCING WEIGHT OF BALL.

Total to 20 lbs., 2 oz. charge.		Total to 20 lbs., 1 lb. charge.	
A	360	B	7474
D			
B	1272	$\dfrac{B^2}{B^1}$	7·365
$\dfrac{B^2}{B^1}$	8·78	$\dfrac{B^N}{B^1}$	9·007
$\dfrac{B^N}{B^1}$	13·32		
$\dfrac{B}{A}$	36·74	$\dfrac{B}{A}$	19·65

At the reduction of the 40 lbs., the ball contained $5\tfrac{1}{2}$ lbs. of powder, which is about the ratio of the specific gravity—powder 1, metal 8 $\dfrac{40}{8} = 5$.

Now, as far as the reduction of weight to 20 lbs., we have actual experienced results.

The object is to complete the Table.

The column $\dfrac{2 \text{ B}}{1 \text{ B}}$ offers results so nearly similar, that we cannot be far wrong in assuming them as identical, and taking the average of 1·1 as the uniform ratio of the range for a reduction of 5 lbs. of metal, all other circumstances being constant, and the velocity low.

40 lbs. $- 5 = 35$ lbs. $132 \times 1\cdot1 = 147$.   The Table shows 147.

Next $\dfrac{n \text{ B}}{1 \text{ B}}$ is almost a continued geometrical progression of this common ratio 1·1. Hence for a reduction of 40 lbs. or $5 \times 8 = 40$ $\overline{1\cdot1}^8 = \log. \cdot 041393 \times 8 = \cdot 331144 \, nn = 2\cdot 14$.

$$\dfrac{8 \text{ B}}{1 \text{ B}} = \dfrac{206}{95} = 2\cdot14 \therefore 8 \text{ R} = 1 \text{ R} \times \overline{r}^{,8}.$$

If we extract the 5th root of this 1·1, we have a ratio for a decrease of 1 lb.

Log. of $1\cdot1 = 041393 \div 5 = 008278 = nn = 1\cdot019$, say 1·02 for a reduction of 1 lb.

What would be the range for a reduction of 59 lbs., or at 1 lb. ?

Log. of $1\cdot02 = 008278 \times 59 = \cdot 488402 \, nn = 3\cdot079 \times 95 = 291$ for the range of 1 lb. of metal in shape of a ball 7·91 in. diameter, with a windage of ·11 and charge of 2 ozs. of powder.

EFFECTS OF REDUCING WEIGHT OF BALL. 157

What would be the range at 59 lbs., or with a decrease of one pound?

$95 \times 1.02 = 96.8$, range of a 59 lb. ball in the above shape.

By Table $\dfrac{95\cdot}{\text{diff. }1\cdot8 \times 5} = 9$ yards, while for a difference of 5 lbs, is the range of a 60 lb. ball the Table shows 10 yards.

For an increase of weight, we have only to inverse the ratio.

$$\text{For 65 lbs. } \frac{95}{1\cdot1} = 86$$

$$70 \text{ lbs. } \frac{95}{1\cdot21} = 79$$

In the pound charge the results are nearly the same, 1·052 being the average ratio.

Log. $1.052 = 022116 \times 7 = 154812\ nn = 142$. Table at 25 lbs. $= 1.41$.

$793 \times 1.42 = 1131$. Table as above for 25 lbs. $= 1123$.

The regular progressive decrease in ratio $\dfrac{\text{B lb.}}{\text{B oz.}}$ indicates new laws resulting from alteration in the momentum and velocity.

The full force of the powder, in the large charge, may not have time to operate on the lighter body, which has left the tube ere the whole of the fluid has been evolved from the powder.

The records of the flight and penetration are too few to establish any rule.

These facts tend to the advantage of hollow projectiles, in the decreased weight of the shells to be carried, and the probably greater destruction from the larger quantity of exploding powder within the hollow of the shell.

Whether these advantages would counterbalance the loss of momentum in the falling ball remains to be seen.

An interesting experiment might be made in progressively hollowing out an 18 or 24-pounder brass shot.

Now, if we consider the action of the powder to be a momentary force, then the velocity generated at the issue from the mortar is $V = \frac{m}{b}$. When $b = 0$, then $V = m = f$, the force of the powder ; which could be measured by the range.

This may be diminished for the weight of the ball by the ratio 1·02, raised to the power of the number of pounds.

f of 2 oz. of powder = 295. Table at weight 0.

$\overline{1·02)}^{60} = 3·13 \cdot \cdot \frac{295}{3·13} = 94$. The Table gives 95 for a 60 lb. ball.

Now, in the former experiment (Table 1) we found the range of a 68 lb. ball, with 1 oz. of powder, to be 50 yards : $\overline{1·02}^{68} = 3·65 \times 50 = 182$ for the simple force of 1 oz.

This multiplied by ·909, or ratio for increase of charge from 1 to 2, gives $164 \times 2 = 328$ for the f of 2 ozs.

In the Table on elevation it is established, that half the range at 45° is equal to the altitude due to the velocity. Hence $\frac{295}{2} = 147$, is the altitude due to the simple unloaded charge.

The same experiment gives the altitude due to a 68 lb. ball as 44 yards. $44 \times \overline{1·02}^{68} = 44 \times 3·65 = 160$, the altitude due to a charge of 2 ozs. unloaded.

It would appear that these reductions in the weight b augment the initial velocity in the direction of the curve, by increasing it directly in a ratio of the reduction of weight.

The form of the curve would hence be different, and the height greater ; consequently the velocity attained on reaching the ground may be increased ; the momentum at this point will depend on the difference between increased velocity and diminished weight.

The resistance of the air will be increased by the augmented velocity, and by the size of the ball being greater in proportion to its solid contents.

The thickness of metal for the shell necessary to resist the impelling charge, and the falling momentum, requires to be ascertained.

In many instances more is not required, as I believe greater damage would often result from the explosion of an increased quantity of powder, than from the effect of the large splinters from the thick sides of the heavier shell.

In destroying gates, we find powder in a leather bag almost as destructive as from a petard.*

Windage.

COMPARATIVE PROOF BY REDUCING THE BALL EXTERNALLY TO THE FOLLOWING DIAMETERS.

Ball.		Diameter of mortar, 8·02. Charge, 2 oz.				Diameter of mortar, 8·04.			
						Charge, 2 oz.		Charge, 1 lb.	
Diameter of ball.	Difference.	Weight of ball.		Yards range.	Difference.	Depth in the ground.	Yards range.	Difference.	Depth in ground.
		1 lb. oz.				ft.			ft.
7·92		67 12		100		·4	780		1·6
7·78	·14	62 11		51	49		646	134	1·11
7·67	·11	60 2		34	17	30	566	80	1·5
7·59	·08	58		24	10	·4	20	487	79	2·8
7·47	·12	55		12	12	·6	13	426	61	
7·37	·10	52 7		19	+7		17	462	+36	

To deduce any practical results from this Table is a matter of extreme difficulty, because there are two items in constant variation, both the weight and the diameter of the ball. Also in some cases a third, in the difference of diameters of the two mortars.

---

* The surrounding atmosphere offering its resistance to the expansion of the gaseous volume of the fired powder. Hence, that powder which is quickest of ignition is the best for this purpose; but quick fulminating powder would not be so destructive in extent as good gunpowder.—EDITOR.

IN THE DIFFERENCE OF THE TWO MORTARS.

Mortar $\begin{Bmatrix} \text{Long range, L. R.} \\ \text{Short range, S. R.} \end{Bmatrix}$ Diameters $\begin{Bmatrix} 8 \cdot 04 \\ 8 \cdot 02 \end{Bmatrix}$ Difference, ·02

Balls of the same weight and diameter.

Weight.	Diameter.	Mortar.	Range, yards.	Difference.	
68	7·92	Long range	87	} 15	102 : 15 : : 34 : 5
		Short range	102		: : 24 : 3·5
60	7·67	Long range	30	} 4	: : 12 : 1·7
		Short range	34		
58	7·59	Long range	20	} 4	
		Short range	24		
55	7·47	Long range	13	} 1	
		Short range	12		

Hence the loss by the difference of diameters of the mortars is as the range. The enlargement of the mortars from 8·02 to 8·04 reduces the range. Now the difference in the area of the two is about ·25 of a square inch; hence may be conceived the great discrepancies observed by using, for proof purposes, old mortars and shot, of which the flaws and imperfections would soon equal this area.

The great reduction in the range, resulting from the reduction in the diameters of the shot, must next be considered.

When this becomes very great, the shot sinks deeper into the chamber of a mortar, and approaches nearer to the powder, when other relations may come into operation.

With the same mortar, same weight of ball, and well ascertained diameter of shot—

Diameter of mortar.	Diameter of shot.	Windage.	Difference.	Weight of ball.	Range, yards.	Difference.	
8·02	7·91	·11	} 24	60 {	95	} 61	The 7·91 range is taken from the last Table on Weight.
	7·67	·35			34		
	7·91	·11	} 44	55 {	105	} 93	
	7·47	·55			12		

Thus, after the first tenth of an inch in windage, the average

EFFECTS OF WINDAGE. 161

loss for each of the 2nd and 3rd tenths is one quarter of the range, for the 4th and 5th tenths about one-seventh : and the whole range would be destroyed between the 6th and 7th tenths; with very small charges.

To return to the Table.

1 tenth . ·02 : 15 :: ·1 : 75 ⎫
2 tenths . ·14 : 49 :: ·1 : 35 ⎪ Reduced loss in yards for each
3 ,, . ·11 : 17 :: ·1 : 15 ⎬ increase of one-tenth of
4 ,, . ·08 : 10 :: ·1 : 12 ⎪ windage.
5 ,, . ·12 : 12 :: ·1 : 10 ⎭

200 yards would be the extreme range, were the contact perfect, and no windage existing.

Suppose we equate the recorded ranges by the equation for difference of weight $\overline{1·02}^{n\,1.}$ Table 2.

Weight of ball.	Equated range.	Recorded range.	Difference. a	Windage.	Difference. b	$\dfrac{a}{b}$
68	100	...	...	·1		
62	110	51	59	·24	·14	·42
60	114	34	80	21	·35	·11	·19
58	118	24	94	14	·43	·08	·17
55	128	12	116	22	·55	·12	·18

The result again appears to be that the 1st tenth of windage has the greatest effect on range. Hence the great loss, on a trifling windage, to balls which previously fitted closely and tightly in the mortar. The ratios between the loss for windage in the 2-oz. and in the 1-lb. charge are so different as not to be conclusive ; $\frac{7}{8}$ is the probable ratio in range for this difference of charge.

Loss by windage, 2 oz. and 1 lb. charges.
49 : 134 :: 1 : 2·7
17 : 80 :: 1 : 4·7
10 : 79 :: 1 : 7·9
12 : 61 :: 1 : 5
Average of loss . . 5
Average of charge . 8

Range, 2 oz. and 1 lb. charges.
100 : 780 :: 1 : 7·8
51 : 646 :: 1 : 12·
34 : 566 :: 1 : 17·
24 : 487 :: 1 : 20·
12 : 426 :: 1 : 34·
Average of range . . 20

No doubt any circumstances altering the initial velocity will inversely affect the loss by windage ; the escape of the fluid will be in a ratio of the time of the passage of the shot up the bore; more fluid will escape as the transit is slower.

The difference of area may be stated a cause of the loss.

The area of a circle of the diameter of the mortar—
$$8\cdot02 \text{ is } \overline{8\cdot02}^2 = 64\cdot32 \times \cdot7854 = 50\cdot47$$
Area of a shot diameter . . . $7\cdot47 = 43\cdot8$
Difference . . . $6\cdot69$

Now the shot at this point will hardly leave the mortar, hence an area of 43 in., loaded with 53 lbs., is a measure of the fluid generated by 2 oz. of powder acting on an unpressed area of 6 in.

Diameter.	Area.	Difference.	Total loss of range calculated on the difference of area.	Table.
8·02	50·4		66 : 100 : : 2·0 : 43	49
7·92	49·2	1·2	4·2 : 62	66
7·78	47·5	1·7	5·1 : 76 .	76
7·67	46·2	1·3	6·6 : 100	88
7·59	45·3	0·9		
7·47	43·8	1·5	Total 6·6	

Hence, in some degree, the loss by windage is measured by the difference of areas.

In the 1-lb. charge :
               29 : 134 :: 66 : 304.   Table 354.

In the 2-oz. charge :
               29 : 49 :: 66 : 111.   Table 88.

The greater the weight, and the less the charge, the larger will be the loss by windage, as is shown that ·24 of windage in the 2-oz. charge reduces the range one-half; but this reduction of range requires 6 or 7-tenths with the 1-lb. charge.

Thus a clever officer, with attention to an increase of charge, may compensate for an under-gauge shell, one that otherwise might be thrown aside as unserviceable.

Thus it requires 8 oz. of powder, or four times the 2-oz. charge, to restore to a ball 7·27, or of a windage ·73, its original range. The result on trial was 107 yards from a new 8-in. mortar, in which 2 oz. would give 102 with a 7·97 ball.

EFFECTS OF ELEVATION. 163

Elevation.

COMPARATIVE PROOF OF ELEVATION.

Charge, 2 oz. ; weight of ball, 67 lbs.
Diameter of ball, 7·92 ; diameter of mortar, 8·02.

Elevation.		Range in yards.	Difference.	
Degrees.	Minutes.			
16	,,	46		
25	,,	64	+18	
35	,,	78	+14	
45	,,	83	+05	
55	,,	76	−07	
65	,,	62	−14	
75	,,	38	−24	
77	25	32		Height of curve 45 yards.

The result of this experiment confirms the parabolic theory that the range is as the sine of the double angle of elevation, for—

$$S \angle 90 : 83 :: S \angle 35 \times 2 : 78·09 \quad \text{Per table 78}$$
$$\text{,,} \quad : \quad :: S \angle 25 \times 2 : 63·5 \quad \text{,,} \quad 64$$
$$\text{,,} \quad : \quad :: S \angle 16 \times 2 : 43·9 \quad \text{,,} \quad 46$$
$$\text{Hence also} \quad S \angle 5 \times 2 : 14·4$$
$$S \angle 1 \times 2 : 2·8$$

Also that there are two elevations giving the same range, those equally distant from 45°.

Also that the range at 15° is equal to half the range at 45° = $\frac{83}{2}$ = 41·5, per table at 16° = 46. As well as to (a), the altitude due to the projectile velocity.

Ten degrees on either side of 45° only cause the range to vary, as $\frac{78}{83} - \frac{76}{83}$.

An attempt was made to measure the height of the curve by attaching a string to the ball; the result of four rounds at 77° 25′ was a range of 32 yards, and a height of 45, which reduced to the perpendicular with a base of 16, will be 42. The mortar could not be elevated higher. This trial gives 44 for the height of the curve with 90° elevation, and exhibits an initial velocity of 96 ft. in the second.

For 44 yards × 3 = 132 ft. height of curve a = space.

Now the space is the same as the square of the time :

16 ft. : 1″ :: 132 ft. : 8·2″, square root, say 3″.

EFFECTS OF ELEVATION.

The velocity acquired is as the time:
$$1'' : 32 :: 3'' : 96.$$
The initial velocity is equal to that acquired by a body falling through (a), or the space of 132 ft.; or for a period of 3".
The time of flight also equals the time of falling through $4a$,
$$132 \times 4 = 528.$$
16 ft. : $\overline{1''}^2$ :: 528 ft. : $33''$, square root, say 5·7.

According to the projectile theory, Hutton, vol. ii. p. 156, for 90° Elevation:

$V = \sqrt{4ag} = \sqrt{44 \times 3 \times 4 \times 16} = \sqrt{8448} = 96$, Initial Velocity.
$T = \dfrac{sV}{g} = \dfrac{96}{16} = 6''$. for s of 90° $= 1 =$ Flight.
$R = 2aS = 0$: for s of 180° $= S = 0 =$ Range.
$H = as^2 = 132 \times 1^2 = 132$ Height of curve.

For 35° Elevation:

$R = 2aS : 2a = 264$, log $= 2\cdot421604$
    Sine 70 $9\cdot988724$
              $\overline{2\cdot410328}$ $n\, n = 257$ ft., or 85 yards. Table 78.

$T = \dfrac{sV}{g} = \dfrac{\text{Log } 96 = 1\cdot982271}{\text{sine } 35 \quad 9\cdot758591}$
           Log 16 $\overline{1\cdot204120} = 0\cdot536742\ n\ n\ 3''\cdot 4$

$H = as^2 = \dfrac{\text{Log } a =}{\text{sine } 35 /^2} = \dfrac{2\cdot120574}{9\cdot517182} = 1\cdot637756 = 43$

$V = \sqrt{\dfrac{g\, n\, R}{s\, c\, 35°}} = 93\cdot 5.$

For a charge of 1 lb., when $R = 800$ yards. Elevation 45°:
$V = \sqrt{\dfrac{gR}{s\, c\, 45''}}$ $800 \times 3 \times 16$, log $= 4\cdot584331$
              $9\cdot698770$
            $\overline{2)4\cdot885561} = 2\cdot442680 = n\ n\ 277.$

T. $t. \therefore $ V.
    $32)277 = 8'' = t =$ Time.
A or $a =$ Space $= t^2$
    $1^2 : 16 :: 8^2 : 1024 = a =$ altitude due to initial velocity.
Also $a :: \dfrac{V^2}{4g} = 1198$ also $a \therefore \dfrac{45° R}{2} = \dfrac{2400}{2} = 1200$ ft.
All evidences of the correctness of the theory at low velocities.
Altitude due 1 lb. $= \dfrac{1024}{132} = 7\cdot 7$ ratio of altitudes.
  ,,   ,,   2 oz.
$a \therefore V^2 \therefore a$ of lb. $\dfrac{\overline{277}^2}{\overline{96}^2} = 8\cdot 3.$

These are about the ratios of the charges, or eight to one.

Recoil.

	Cwt.	qr.	lbs.
Weight of mortar	8	1	0
,, bed	11	1	6
Total	19	2	6

Charge, 2 oz.; diameter of mortar, 8·02; of ball, 7·92; weight, 67 lbs.

Nature of Platform.	Range.
Platform composed of sleepers laid flat on pucka brick work, over these a plank platform of 2½ in. thick, boards well secured	86
A platform of fascines, 1¼ feet in diameter, of dalwood sticks, laid on the bare earth. A plank, 1 ft. broad, 2 in. thick, under each cheek of the mortar bed. .	86
Platform of fascines as above, but no planks between the cheeks and the fascines	86
Bare hard soil, covered with the natural light grass	88

The result was, that so small a charge as 2 oz. had no power to move so heavy a mass as the bed and mortar.

MUSKETRY EXPERIMENTS.

Each set of these experiments was concluded with the same description of boards; and it is regretted that the whole series was not so concluded. But the disadvantages of the thin boards were only found out as the experiments progressed.

Tables.	Letters for Reference.		Charge, 6 drams.	Measure of Elasticity.	$\frac{D}{A}$, &c.
	A	Boards, ½ in. Interval, 1 in.	17		303
2 and 5	B	Boards, ½ in. No interval	11	6	432
1 ,, 3	C	Boards, 1 in. Interval, 1 in.	6·8		758
4 ,, 6	D	Boards, 1 in. No interval	5·16	1·64	1·

The gain by the elasticity of the half-inch boards is 6. Hence, if 17 : 6 :: 1 : ·35. If the elasticity is inversely as the thickness of the boards, the loss for inch boards will be ·17. Hence, 6·8 will lose 1·15 ∴ 6·8 — 1·15 = 5·65 ; table 6 gives 5·16. Much depends on the density of the wood, and on the screwing up of the frame. I assume 6-in. boards, with no interval, as the measure of the usual initial velocity of the common musket, with 6 drams of powder, equal to a point blank range of 250 yards. Hence each board is 41·6 yards. The planks are of mangoe wood.

No. I.
WINDAGE.

Boards, 1 in. Barrel, length . 3 ft. 2½ in. Ball, brass.
Interval, 1 in.   ,, weight . . 4lb. 14 oz.   { ⅖ths copper.
Distance, 30 ft. ,, diameter . ·78 in.   ⅗ths tin.
                  ,, touch hole . ·09 in.

No. of Rounds.	Diameter of ball.	Difference.	Weight of ball.	Difference.	Two Drams.		Six Drams.			
					Boards pierced.	Average.	Boards pierced.	Average.		
			Drams.							
1 } 2 } 3 }	·6		8		·2 } ·3 } ·3 }	·26	4 } 4·4 } 4 }	4·23	Table at ·675	2· 6·33
1 } 2 } 3 }	·625	·025	9	1	·5 } ·4 } ·4 }	·43	4·5 } 4·8 } 4·8 }	4·7	Average.	1·44 6·2
1 } 2 } 3 }	·650	·025	10	1	1·1 } 1· } 1· }	1·03	5 } 5 } 5 }	5·		
1 } 2 } 3 }	·675	·025	12	2	1· } 1·1 } 1·1 }	1·06	6 } 6 } 7 }	6·33		·41 ·96
1 } 2 } 3 }	·7	·025	13	1	1· } 1·5 } 1·7 }	1·4	7·8 } 6·5 } 8· }	7·43	2 drs. 6 drs.	
1 } 2 } 3 }	·725	·025	14	1	1·5 } 2· } 1·7 }	1·73	9·5 } 9 } 8 }	8·83	·675 1·5 7·13	
1 } 2 } 3 }	·750	·025	15	1	2·3 } 3· } 3· }	2·76	8 } 12 } 10 }	10	Mediums. Diameter . Boards, 2 drs. ,, 6 drs.	Medium loss Loss.
1 } 2 } 3 }	·775	·025	oz. dr. 1 1	2	3· } 4· } 5·5 }	4·13	Ball lost at this round.			

Totals . . . { Of all . . 12·80
              { Up to ·750 . 8·67

Memo. Ball ·6—10 drams powder—6·5 boards.

In all these experiments there appears to be requisite a certain relation of all the parts to render the result complete : as a certain relation of space to the quantity of powder to be fired.

Thus we find the two-dram charge not to afford proportional results with the six drams fired from the same barrel.

The momentary impact of a column of fluid on a hemisphere may be supposed only one-half the pressure on the area of the great circle. The areas are as the squares of the diameters ; hence the velocity communicated will be as the square of the diameter. But the momentum will be as the velocity and weight of the ball. The weights are as the cubes of the diameters ; hence the result on the boards may be assumed as the fifth power of the diameter. The friction against the barrel will be more in a heavy body.

We will suppose the column of fluid from the charge to move up the length of the barrel with a velocity of 6, without any ball before it ; when loaded with a well-fitting ball, let the velocity of the mass, ball and fluid, be reduced to 5 ; next suppose the barrel to be fitted with a ball of only half the area : the result is, supposing a perfect division in the barrel, there would be two columns of fluid, one moving up the barrel with a velocity of 6, and the other with a velocity of 5, or less. As there is no partition between the columns, either a vacuum could take place at once, or the continuity of the two could only be supported by the loaded column being still further reduced by the pressure of the ball against the vacuum, by which its velocity would be diminished say to 4 ; thence a double loss would take place from the windage, first, in the portion of the ball unpressed upon by the column of fluid, which would make the velocity of a reduced ball less than

---

* The resistance to a sphere in a *discontinued* fluid is half that to a cylinder of the same diameter ; but I can hardly agree with the application of this law to the action of gunpowder impinging on solid matter in a close chamber. But the idea of working out the question of the effect of windage, if fanciful, is very ingenious.—EDITOR.

the assumed 5; and, secondly, in the loss of the fluid forced into the vacuum.

Hence all circumstances retarding the velocity of the ball increase the loss by windage. For the second loss of fluid, friction, &c., let one power of the diameter be taken, and other circumstances being the same, the momentum on the boards may be as the fourth power of the diameter of the ball.

D^4	:	d^4	: :	B	:	b.	
6^4	:	7^4	: :	4·23	:	7·8	Table 7·43.
,,	:	$7·5^4$	: :	4·23	:	10·3	,, 10, and
6^4	:	1^4	: :	4·23	:	·0030	
7^4	:	1^4	: :	7·43	:	·0031	
$7·5^4$	:	1^4	: :	10	:	·0031	

for the value of ·1 in diameter, supposing all other circumstances in proportion.

The loss from windage varies inversely, as the velocity of the ball, or the charge: directly as the friction, weight, or diameter of the ball.

Thus we see that the manifest imperfections of the native guns and cannon, and balls, in this respect of windage, are met by very large charges of powder, and probably a denser fluid from inferior powder.

If we revert to the remarks on this subject by Antoni, we find, p. 124 :—" In the month of July, 1759, the Commander De Vincenti, Colonel of Artillery, made the following experiments with two 16-pounders of the same weight and length, but of different calibres: the calibre of A was divided into 813 parts, and that of B into 819 of the same parts; the guns were fired horizontally, mounted on their carriages upon platforms perfectly horizontal. The shot were of two kinds, and grazed on an even piece of ground, about 5 ft. below the axis of the gun; the shot of the first kind had the diameter = C divided into 784 of the above mentioned parts, and weighed $\frac{1}{3}$ lb. more than the proper weight; the diameter = D of the second weighing $\frac{1}{5}$th more, was divided into 774 of the same parts. Common grained powder was used, the charge was 4 lb. 2 oz., put into flannel cartridges, in order to collect it exactly in the

EFFECT OF DIFFERENCE OF WINDAGE.

same manner at each discharge. The wads were of junk; two gunners gave three strokes with the rammer to the one over the powder, and two to that over the shot." The following table shows the result:—

	No. of rounds.	Length of ranges Of the gun A. Yards.	Of the gun B. Yards.
With the shot of the diameter = C.	1	188	249
	2	198	197¾
	3	196¾	224½
	4	198¼	245
	5	224⅛	248½
	6	197	213½
With the shot of the diameter = D.	1	221⅔	199½
	2	193	213
	3	226	199¾
	4	223	199

That is, with the 4 lb. 2 oz. of powder from two 16-pounders:

Diameter of shot.	Diameter of bore, 813		Difference.	Diameter of shot.	Diameter of bore, 819		Difference.
	Windage.	Range.			Windage.	Range.	
·784	29	200	+16	·784	35	233	−30
·774	39	216		·774	45	203	

Windage.	Range.	Difference.
29 ...	200	−33
35 ...	233	best
39 ...	216	−17
45 ...	203	−13

Tried according to the formula $D^4 : d^4 :: R : r$, the result would be:

Diameter.	Range.	Loss.	Range.	Loss.
·784	200	11	233	12
·774	189		221	

showing that this formula is not very far from the truth, even on data nearly 100 years old. The subject in those days appears to have been more considered with reference to the destruction of the bores of ordnance, than with reference to the result from the powder.

Antoni considers, that windage may be too small, and assumes the windage 35 of the range 223 yards to be the correct value ; $\frac{784}{819}$, or 1 to 958 in the diameters.

No doubt the friction on the bore is the cause of decreased velocity, as is also windage. There will be a point where the two should meet.

Captain Broome found that a 16 to the pound ball, forced from a barrel nicely adjusted to a 17 to the pound ball, decreased the effect.

A certain quantity of air is also necessary to the complete explosion of the charge ; hence I am prepared to expect, that the loss from small windage is not so great as has been usually represented, and seldom such as could not be made up by a slight increase of charge. We notice in the experiment on this head, that with a charge of three times $\frac{3}{1}$ C, a difference of diameters in the balls of $\frac{6}{7\cdot75}$ has been compensated for. May not much shot and many guns be unnecessarily condemned on this head ?

New balls were subsequently made by me of the weight of one ounce, and the diameter of 7·75 ; these in two cases,—one for Table 3, and one specially for this Table,—gave

	2 drams charge.	6 drams charge.
Table 3 . . .	3·5	6·8
Special . . .	3·8	6·8

showing that above the windage of $\frac{75}{78}$ there is deterioration resulting from friction, and, perhaps, from want of air. These two losses being superior to the gain by the non-escape of fluid.

Indeed, if to be depended upon, this result would prove the

friction of ·025 in excess of the proper point, to be equal to ·075 of the loss of fluid by windage, and to diminish the result in $\frac{6\cdot33}{10}$. See table D, 6·75. Now $\frac{75}{78}$ = ·961, is nearly the same ratio with $\frac{784}{814}$ = ·958, established above by Antoni as the best point of windage, or ratio between the diameter of the bore and the diameter of the shot.

If Antoni's ratio of best effect is increased by $\frac{819}{813}$ or 1·007, the ratio of the bores of his two guns, the loss will be ·85 = $\frac{200}{233}$, while if our ratio be increased by $\frac{775}{750}$, or 1·03, the loss is $\frac{6\cdot8}{10}$ = ·68.

This diminishing result is so very far removed from the accepted theory of rifle balls and tight wads, and ramming home, that a suspicion of mistake is excited.

But I think I can partly account for this decrease of effect with increased diameter of ball in another manner.

By Table 2, on length of barrel, we establish, that with a windage of $\frac{\cdot73}{\cdot77}$ to $\frac{\cdot75}{\cdot78}$ the barrel was too long by $\frac{11}{15\cdot3}$ of result.

Friction reduces the result by drawing back the point of best effect in the bore, and thus creating superfluous length.

It is thus resolved: that at the point of best effect the windage and length are in equilibrium, and the loss from windage = 0.

> Let R = the range of the point of best effect.
> a = the loss by windage.
> b = the loss by increase of length.

Then if the windage is increased, R a will be the result.

But if the windage is decreased, it increases the length of the barrel by friction and want of air, which creates the loss (b). Hence we have R + a − b for the result.

The scale will stand

	Ratio of diameters.	Difference.	Result.	Difference.	Remarks.
R·a	9·29	−0·32	8·83	−1·17	Loss by windage.
R·best effect	9·61		10		Loss by friction from increased length.
R + a − b	9·93	+0·32	6·8	−3·2	

Hence if the barrels are not well proportioned to R, there may be a *loss* by tight balls, or balls tightly set home, or, strange to say, by *superior powder*, that is, powder of quicker ignition.

This receives strong confirmation from Antoni's experiments, where

A *decrease* of windage of ·06, gives a loss of 33.
An *increase* of windage of ·06, gives „ 17.

Hence also it follows that equal powders will preserve the same ratios from the same piece in all charges, but that in different pieces of other proportions of length and of calibre, these ratios may not continue the same. The ranges of our muskets of olden days will be found longer than at present, although the powder is now superior; that is of quicker ignition.

This want of identity of proportions will account for the difference found between proof-mortars, as those of Dum Dum and Ishapore, and evinces that powder superior in range from a short mortar may be inferior for a long gun proof.

No. 2.

LENGTH OF BARREL.

Boards, ¼ in. Ball, diameter ·73 in. Musket, diameter ·77 in.
Interval, none.   „   weight 16 drs.   „   weight 4·13 lbs.
Distance, 30 ft.   „   length 3 ft. 2·5 in.

	Charge M. P. 2 drs.			Charge M. P. 6 drs.		
Length.	Boards pierced.	Average.	Length.	Boards pierced.	Average.	
ft. in.			ft. in.			
3 2·5	3·5 / 4·5 / 4 / 3	4	3 2·5	11 / 11 / 11	11	
3 0	3 / 3 / 3	3	3 0	10 / 10 / 16	12	
2 10	4 / 4 / 4	4	2 10	11 / 16 / 12	13	
2 8	1·5 / 2 / 2	1·85	2 8	12 / 12 / 11	11·6	
2 6	3·5 / 3 / 4	3·5	2 6	10 / 13 / 14	12·5	
2 4	4·5 / 4·5 / 4·5	4·5	2 4	12 / 15·5 / 13·5	13·6	New boards.
2 2	5 / 5·5 / 6	5·5	2 2	15·5 / 13·5 / 15·5	15·33	Much recoil.
2 0	4·5 / 5 / 4·5	4·6	2 0	13·5 / 14 / 12	13·17	New ball.
1 10	4·5 / 3·5 / 5·5	4·5	1 10	13·5 / 15 / 15	14·5	Great recoil.
1 8	4 / 4 / 5	4·33	1 8	14 / 13 / 13	13·3	
1 7·25	4 / 4 / 5	4·33	1 7·25	11·5 / 11 / 11·5	11·33	{ Length of barrel reduced to one-half.
0 ·95	1·5 / 1·5 / 2	1·66	0 ·95	4·25 / 4·5 / 5	4·58	{ Length of barrel reduced to one-fourth.

The correct length of the barrel may be defined, in relation to the initial velocity, that which admits the perfect evolvement of all the fluid and heat, and concentrates all the explosive force on the ball. The moment the explosive force remains stationary or decreases, *if the friction along the barrel be greater than the resistance from the external air, then it is better the ball should leave the barrel;* and any increase of length, as regards initial velocity, is disadvantageous.

Benefit, of course, may be derived from forcing the ball into a higher curve, and thus increasing its range.

As the explosion of the charge is progressive, it would warrant the assumption that the length of the barrel depends on the size of the charge, combined with the degree of inflammability of the powder.

It may be that the fluid from a certain quantity of powder will drive before it both ball and the remaining powder; and that an increase of effect may result from the evolvement of fluid in transit,—the first being a fixed amount, and the second depending on the length of the charge.

We may notice, in the Table, that the results gradually increase both in the 2 and 6-dram charges until reaching the point of 2 ft. 2 in., which appears to give the greatest result, whence both are progressively retrograde; marking 2 ft. 2 in. as the best length under all the circumstances recorded. There exists also an appearance of equilibrium in this length, for the results being as the charge is a proof of the correctness and of the absence of disturbance.

$$5\cdot 5 \times 3 = 16\cdot 5. \text{ Table } 15\cdot 33$$

If the disadvantage of superfluous length be as the friction, it will clearly be as the time of its continuance, and hence be measured by the length of tube; and if the disadvantages of shortness lie in the *non complete* concentration of the fluid, this is a want of time measurable by the length of the barrel.

If we convert the lengths into decimals, when the charges are the same, the loss by the increased length from friction or by diminished length from want of concentration will be found as the length.

For, under friction,

$$2\cdot 16 \quad 3\cdot 16 \;::\; 4 \;:\; 58$$
$$,, \quad\quad ,, \;::\; 11 \;:\; 16$$

EFFECT OF LENGTH OF BARREL.   175

and for want of concentration,
$$1\cdot 6 : 2\cdot 16 :: 4\cdot 33 : 5\cdot 8$$
$$\text{,, ,, } :: 11\cdot 33 : 15\cdot 29$$
nearly the quantities in the Table.
When the length is the same,
$$1\cdot 66 : 4\cdot 58 :: 1 : 2\cdot 7$$
$$4\cdot 33 : 11\cdot 33 :: 1 : 2\cdot 7$$
$$5\cdot 5 : 15\cdot 33 :: 1 : 3$$
$$4 : 11 :\cdot 1 : 2\cdot 75$$
which are nearly the ratios of the charge $\dfrac{3}{1}$

It may be remarked in Table No. 5, on the increase of charge, that it was requisite to increase the charge of 6 drams to 8 drams for the purpose of raising the result from 11 boards to 15 boards; hence ⅛ of the charge is lost in compensating for the extra length between 3 ft. 2 in. and 2 ft. 2 in.

From the totals it would appear that 1 ft. of the fluid from the 2 drams was equal to 1·57 boards; but to 5·34 from the 6-dram charge.

A column of a certain base and height is converted into fluid in a certain time or space. This point being settled, any variation in the result will be as the variation in the space. The space may have a relation to the base of the column, hence the length divided by the diameter may be a good measure, so that $\dfrac{2\cdot 16}{\cdot 77}$ will indicate 28 calibres as a correct length. The space may be that required to form the highest density of the fluid from the powder. For Bengal powder 2 ft. 2 in. appears the best length with 6 drams on a base of ·77.

Hence wads, tight balls, ramming home, &c., which increase the time, will in a certain degree improve a musket's range, if shorter than the correct length, but depreciate the result from one of the proper length, or from one longer than required.

Long barrels are best calculated for slowly igniting powder; hence the long native matchlock of India, and the short rifle of England are suited to the different qualities of their powders.

If we turn to Antoni on this subject, at page 83, he remarks: " To obtain the initial velocities, four muskets of different lengths

176   EFFECT OF LENGTH OF BARREL.

carrying a 1-oz. ball, were fired with 7 drams of fine war powder, under a mean state of the atmosphere :—"

Length of barrel from the ball to the muzzle.		Initial velocities, Feet in a second.
ft.	in.	
0	11	1037
1	10	1390
3	8	1736
4	8	1815

That is

    Length of B.   Range.
      1 : 2   :: 1 : 1·3
      1 : 2   :: 1 : 1·25
  or { 1 : 2   :: 1 : 1·6 }   Obtained from the next proportion of
      { 1 : 1·3 :: 1 : 1·04 }   3 ft. 8 in. to 4 ft. 8 in. and $\frac{1815}{1736}$.

Take the average
      1 : 2   :: 1 : 1·38

Our table gives
  or { 1 : 1·47 :: 1 : 1·4 } The result of increase from 2 ft. 2 in.
      { 1 : 2   :: 1 : 1·9 } to 3 ft. 2·5 in.

Starting from the length 2·16 ft. as the point of best effect for 6 drams of Bengal powder, and from 4·66 as the best point for 7 drams of Antoni's powder, we have 1·9 in result for the ratio of an increase of 2·2 in length to the Bengal, while a corresponding increase will only give to Antoni's 1·6 in result.

Again if

    drs. Initial velocity. drs.
     7 :   1815   ::   6 : 1558
           Length.
     7 :   4·66   ::   6 : 3·98 = 3 ft. 11 in.
    Length and result.   Length for 6 drs.
     2 :   1·38   :: $\frac{3·99}{4·66 \text{ length for 7 drs.}}$ = ·85 × 1815 = 1542, for the initial velocity of
6 drams, according to Antoni's Table.

It appears 1542 ft. of initial velocity of Antoni is measured by 15·33 boards one inch thick; or each board is equal to 100 feet.

In fact, it takes a column of fluid of a certain measurement to give a certain result; if you reduce this column, you reduce the result.

What would result from increasing the length of 9·5 in. three times?

                        Boards.
     2 : 1·9 :: 3 : 2·85 = 4·58 × 2·85 = 13
     9·5 × 3 = 28·5 = 2 ft. 4·5 in. The Table gives 13·6 at this length.

The result varies as the length × by the charge; hence the result at 2 drams, with length 2 ft. 4 in., should equal the result at 6 drams, with length 0 ft. 9·5 in., which it does. (See Table.)

At Dum Dum experience proved that a charge well adjusted to a short carbine, gave nearly equal results in a long carbine, and that 2½ drams with the long carbine gave better results than a larger charge.

·This length of barrel causes the remarks we so often hear, that such a maker's powder is "very hard hitting." A sportsman with a short barrel, previously using a slowly igniting powder, finds a great improvement in a more quickly inflaming powder, and hence his remark.

The diagram below exhibits a measure of the explosive force of the powder at each point of the length of the barrel.

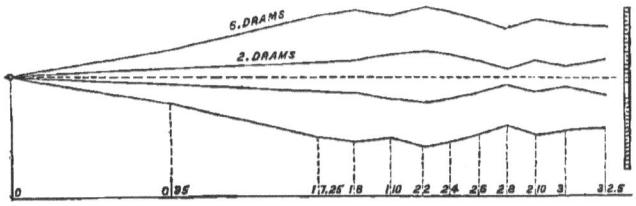

LENGTH OF BARREL.

We usually find that inferior fowling pieces burst some way up the barrel; where the increasing force of the powder meets the diminished thickness of metal.*

The figure also points out the position for any reinforces to the metal.

I should have wished a trial to have been made under progressive decrease to the thickness of the metal of the barrel, but it could not be managed.

* I cannot agree with these theories; the force would be much greater at first, and the calculations of power exerted would be different in any calculation of this kind, with varied qualities of powder and size of grain. The resistance the compressed column of air meets with from any trifling circumstance in the bore of a barrel, a little snow, paper, even a feather, might cause the barrel to burst near the muzzle.—EDITOR.

No. 3.
TOUCH HOLE OR VENT.

Boards, 1 in. Ball, diameter . ·775 Barrel, diameter ·78
Interval, 1 in. ,, weight . 16 drams. ,, weight . 4·14 lb.
Distance, 30 ft. ,, length . 3 ft. 2½ in.

Charge, M. Powder, two drams.				Charge, M. Powder, six drams.			
Touch hole. Diameter.	Boards.	Average.	Remarks.	Touch hole. Diameter.	Boards.	Average.	Remarks.
·09	3, 4·25, 3·25	3·5		·09	6·5, 7, 7	6·8	
·1	5, 3, 3	3·66		·1	8, 7, 7	7·33	
·12	3·5, 3, 3	3·1		·12	7, 7, 7	7	
·14	2·75, 3·5, 3	3·8		·14	8, 7, 7	7·33	
·16				·16			
·18	2·75, 2·75, 3	2·83		·18	7, 7, 6·5	6·8	
·2	2·75, 3, 3	2·0		·2	8·3, 8·3, 8·3	8·3	New boards.
·22	2, 2, 2·5	2·16		·22	7·5, 7·5, 8	7·66	
·24	2, 2, 2	2	Much unburnt powder ejected at the touch hole.	·24	7, 7·5, 8	7·58	New ball.
·26	1·5, 1·5, 2·2	1·66		·26	8, 8, 8	8	
·28	2, 2, 2	2		·28	7, 8, 7	7·33	
·3	1, 1·5, 1·5	1·33		·3	6, 6, 6	6	
·34	1, 1, ·75	·91		·34	5, 5, 6	5·3	Much unburnt powder ejected with force.
·39	3·3, 2, ·75	1·03		·39	3, 3, 5·5	3·8	Touch hole being ¼ the diameter of the bore.

SIZE OF VENT.

	Average.
From ·1	= 3·66
	·39 = 1·03
	·29 = 2·63 { per ·1 of touch-hole, ·9 boards.

	Medium.
From ·1	3·66
	·39 1·03
	2) 49 4·69
	·245=2·34 { boards. Table at ·24 = 2 boards

	Average.
	·2 = 8·3
	·39 = 3·8
	4·5 per ·1 touch-hole, 2·4 boards.

	Medium.
	·2 8·3
	·39 3·8
	2) 59 12·1
	·295 6 Table at ·3 = 6 boards.

We remark in both charges, 2 drams and 6 drams, that contrary to expectation, the effect increases with the size of the touch-hole up to a point, and then commences to decrease. That in the 2-dram charge ·1 gives a greater result than ·09 ; that in the 6-dram charge the effect increases up to ·2, and then retrogrades, proving that a column of air may be necessary to the full development of the fluid, and that this column has a relation to the size of the charge, 2 drams requiring ·1 and 6 drams ·2 of touch hole.

This fact receives confirmation from the experiments recorded in Antoni (p. 46), as follows :—

"We will conclude this chapter by showing experimentally how much the difference in the size of the vent affects the force of the shot. A musket was taken $\frac{8}{10}$ of an inch in diameter, and 33 in. in length of barrel. The axis of the large screw which closes the breech was perforated with a hole $\frac{5}{10}$ of an inch in diameter, to which three screws were successively applied ; the first exactly closing the opening, and consequently forced all the fired powder to pass through the muzzle ; the second had in its axis a hole or vent $\frac{1}{10}$ of an inch in diameter, through which a part of the fluid might escape ; and the third had a vent of $\frac{2}{10}$ of an inch in diameter. The musket thus prepared was loaded each time with 10 drams of fine powder, put into cartridges, and with an iron ball 1½ oz. in weight ; the wads were rammed down with equal force by the same man.

"The experiment began by firing the musket with the screw $\frac{1}{10}$ in. diameter ; afterwards with that of $\frac{2}{10}$; and at length without any vent in the screw.

"The medium of the penetration of the balls in 24 rounds is as follows :—

In discharges
- With the vent entirely closed . . . 6 inches.
- „ $\frac{1}{10}$ of an in. in diameter . 8 „
- „ $\frac{2}{10}$ „ „ . . $6\frac{1}{2}$ „
- „ $\frac{5}{10}$ „ „ . . 4 „

"It results from this experiment that, when there is no vent, less powder is fired, and that which does take fire burns more slowly. If the large vent be left open, and a sheet of paper stretched at 2 ft. from it, the paper will be pierced full of holes by the powder forced through the vent at the explosion. Soldiers firing in line are often pricked in the face by grains of powder driven with force from the muskets on their left; the common opinion that these grains are a part of the priming is erroneous."

When the vent was nothing, 0, the result was 6; when the vent was ·1, the result was 8; nor are Antoni's results on the increase from ·1 to ·2 very different from those of the Table.

8 : 6·3 :: 3·6 : 2·8 Table gives at ·2 — 2·9 boards for 2 drams.
8 : 6·3 :: 7·3 : 5·7   „   „   8·3 boards for 6 drams.

but all the circumstances were not similar.

The whole extract is confirmed in the present experiment.

Again we may remark, that the ejection of unburnt grains is noted at ·24 with 2 drams, but not until ·34 with 6 drams.

The loss appears to be directly as the diameter of the touch-hole. A similar opening for fluid in the form of windage of one-half the diameter of the ball would reduce the effect to ·6, in place of to 3·8.

The result is, that up to ·3 of an inch the size of the touch-hole is of no material value in the point of effect.

No doubt much inconvenience would be felt when firing from closed ranks and files with very large touch-holes.

We may note also the little real value of a point on which much stress is placed as a matter of theory; and that the enlarged touch-hole of a native musket used by men not in rank and file is of less real importance than it is usually considered to be by

European writers. A bad powder, to be well ignited, may require the air from a large touch-hole.

Perhaps many muskets and guns are unnecessarily condemned on the account of enlargement of the vent.

If we take ·2 for the most advantageous vent for 6 drams, and ·1 for 2 drams, then if these be in equilibrium, the result should be as the charge.

$$\frac{8\cdot 3}{3\cdot 6} = 2\cdot 3 \text{ for the result.}$$

$$\frac{3}{1} = 3 \text{ for the charge, and } \frac{2}{1} \text{ for the diameter of the vent.}$$

A very small portion of the fluid can escape directly from the touch-hole, as the bulk of the fluid is soon carried up the bore. Increased calibre would probably augment the loss on this head, for the column of fluid pressing on the touch-hole would be as the diameter of the bore.

I can understand that the size of the touch-hole may alter materially the point of concentration of the fluid; first, by the removal of the resistance in the rear; secondly, by the lateral escape of the fluid, and also by a greater or lesser admission of oxygen.*

This point of concentration will be where the maximum of heated fluid overtakes the rest of the powder, propelling before it the ball.

Alterations in the touch-hole may counteract other variations: as, for instance, a small opening may delay the complete ignition, and thus remedy the loss experienced by too great a length of barrel. Change in any one of the principles of construction may require corresponding alterations in all other parts.

* The inconvenience of the escape from the vent laterally is now avoided by the vent being placed vertically, as in the percussion fire-arms. I am also rather inclined to attribute the better ignition of the powder, with a large vent, to the great movement amongst the grains which a more rapid escape of the fluid by the vent may allow, and thus more perfect inflammation, as I cannot imagine any air can enter against the opposing current of the expanding fluid of the gas from the inflamed powder.—EDITOR.

No. 4.
DISTANCE.

Boards, 1 in.   Ball, weight, 1 oz.   Barrels, length, 3 ft. 2½ in. and
,, interval, none.   ,, diameter, ·733.   1 ft. 7·25 in.; diameter, ·77.

Distance.	Long Barrel.				Short Barrel.				Another ball, diameter ·55.
	6 drams.		2 drams.		6 drams.		2 drams.		
		Average.		Average.		Average.		Average.	
0 ..	{ 8·75 8·5 8· }	8·41	{ 4· 2·75 3·75 }	3·5	{ 7·25 6·5 8·25 }	7·5	{ 3·5 2·5 2·5 }	2·8	5·5
30 ft. ..	{ 7·5 8· 8·5 }	8·	{ 4· 3·5 3·5 }	3·66	{ 5·5 5·75 6·5 }	5·9	{ 2·5 4·5 2·5 }	3·16	...
60 ft. ..	{ 7·5 9· 8· }	8·16	{ 2·25 2·25 2·25 }	2·25	{ 5·25 5·75 6·25 }	5·75	{ 2·75 2·75 2·75 }	2·75	3·75
120 ft.	{ 6·5 6·5 6·25 }	6·41	{ 1·5 2·5 2·5 }	2·16	{ 3·4 4·5 4·5 }	4·13	{ 1·25 2· 2· }	2·5	2·5
240 ft.	{ 3·5 4·25 2·75 }	3·75	1·5	1·5	{ 2·5 3·25 2·75 }	2·83		...	·75

Distance, 0—
From stand . 8·41
Shoulder of sergeant . 6·5

Distance, 240 ft.—
From stand . 3·75
Shoulder of sergeant . 3·25

Distance.

Whatever may previously be the case, at the moment of leaving the barrel, the momentum may be considered as generated by a single impulse; hence, $m = b\,V$. In the effect on the boards, we have a measure of m; as b is constant, m will be a measure of V.

If we take the effect on the boards as the value on the velocity remaining in the ball after passing over any distance, when the distance is 0, the result is the measure of the total velocity of which the ball is susceptible, *i. e.*, the initial velocity.

In the differences between the results of any two distances, we have a measure of the velocity lost by the resistance of the air, gravity or other causes operating during the flight—

m of $o = V$.

m 240 feet $= v$ ∴ $V - v$ is the measure of the resistance of the air of 240 feet in the trajectory of the ball.

Distance.	6 drams Long Barrel.			2 drams Long Barrel.		
	Boards.	Difference.	Total.	Boards.	Difference.	Total.
Feet.						
0	8·41	...	...	3·50		
120	6·41	2·	...	2·16	1·34	
240	3·71	2·66	4·66	1·5	·66	

Where R, the resistance, is measured by 2 for 120 feet, by 2·66, for the second 120 feet, and by 4·66 for the whole distance, with 6-dram charge.

If R is as V (according to some authors V^2.)

$$V : v :: R : r \frac{v R}{V}$$

8·41 : 6·41 :: 2 : 1·5. The table gives 2·66 for 120 × 2.

If a table for an increase of 240 feet were completed on the formula $\frac{v R}{V} = v$, it would run thus:

Distance.	6 drams Long Barrel.			2 drams Long Barrel.		
	Boards.	Difference.	Total.	Boards.	Difference.	Total.
Feet.						
0	8·41	...	...	3·5		
240	3·75	4·66	...	1·5	·2	
480	1·68	2·07	6·73	·65	·85	2·85
960	·38	1·3	8·03	·2	·45	3·3

Distance.	6 drams Short Barrel.			2 drams Short Barrel.		
	Boards.	Difference.	Total.	Boards.	Difference.	Total.
Feet.						
0	7·5	...	...	2·81		
240	2·83	4·67	...	1·75	1·05	
480	1·13	1·7	6·37			
960	·28	·85	7·22			

184   RESISTANCE.

If we compare the resistance under different lengths, but the same charge—
$$8\cdot41 : 7\cdot5 :: 4\cdot66 : 4\cdot1.\text{ Table, } 4\cdot67$$
$$3\cdot5 : 2\cdot8 :: 2 : 1\cdot4.\text{ Table, not given}$$
it will be as the ratio for the lengths of barrel, which by Table 2 under the respective length is $\frac{4}{4\cdot33}$ or nearly 1.

If under the same lengths but different charges—
$$8\cdot41 : 3\cdot5 :: 4\cdot66 : 1\cdot9.\text{ Table 2}$$
$$\text{,, } : \text{,, } :: 1\cdot68 : \cdot68 \quad \text{,, } \quad \cdot65$$
$$\text{,, } : \text{,, } :: 8\cdot03 : 3\cdot3 \quad \text{,, } \quad 3\cdot3$$
The resistance will be nearly as the charge.

If we reduce the values of r of each of the experiments to the values they would afford had they started from the initial velocity of the long barrel and 6 drams—

$$v : V :: r : R = \frac{Vr}{v}, \text{ we have for 240 feet}$$

6 dram long barrel		4·66
2 ,, ,,		4·80
6 ,, short barrel		5·2
	3)	14·66 = 4·88

for the value of the resistance to a ball of ·775 diameter impelled from a musket with 6 drams of powder, giving an initial velocity of 8·41 planks, during a progress of 240 feet.

For 120 feet we have—

Long barrel . . $\begin{cases} 6 \text{ drams} & . & . & . & 2 \\ 2 \text{ drams} & . & . & . & 3\cdot2 \end{cases}$

Short barrel . . $\begin{cases} 6 \text{ drams} & . & . & . & 3 \\ 2 \text{ drams} & . & . & . & 3\cdot7 \end{cases}$

$$4) \; 11\cdot9 = 2\cdot9 \text{ as R for 120 feet.}$$

$\frac{4\cdot88}{2\cdot9} = 1\cdot8$, ratio of resistance for $\frac{240}{120}$ feet, or double, $= 2\cdot$

$4\cdot88 - 2\cdot9 = 1\cdot98$,, the second 120 feet.

$\frac{2\cdot9}{1\cdot98}$, ratio of resistance between 1st and 2nd space of 120 feet

$= 1\cdot4 \therefore \sqrt{\frac{240}{120}} = 1\cdot4$

Hence the resistance is as the velocity impressed; and as the square root nearly of the distance.

If we turn to the results with a ball of reduced diameter, and in the same mode calculate $R = \dfrac{V\,\imath}{v}$ for the ball of ·55 diameter. For 120 feet we have $R = 4\cdot59$, and for 240 feet $R = 7\cdot26$, compared with R of the ball ·7·75 diameters, we have $\dfrac{4\cdot59}{2\cdot9} = 1\cdot5$, and $\dfrac{7\cdot26}{4\cdot88} = 1\cdot4$ for the respective distances.

Now $\dfrac{D}{d}$, or $\dfrac{\cdot775}{\cdot55} = 1\cdot3$, or R is inversely as the diameter of the ball. The resistance will be as the surface of the ball, that is, d^2, and inversely as its weight, that is, as d^3. Hence, R is as $\dfrac{d^2}{d^3} = \dfrac{1}{d}$.

$2\cdot9 \times \cdot775 = 3\cdot7\ \dfrac{4\cdot88 \times \cdot775}{\cdot6} = \cdot6\cdot3$ the resistance on a ball of ·6 diameter for the above distances of 120 and 240 feet.

This supposes the initial velocity equal in both cases, but reduced to the state of actual velocities, we have $3\cdot7 \times \dfrac{5\cdot5}{8\cdot41} = 2\cdot4$. Table 3. ∴ $V - v$ of diameter ·55 $= 5\cdot5 - 2\cdot5 = 3$ for 120 feet, $6\cdot3 \times \dfrac{5\cdot5}{8\cdot41} = 4\cdot15$. Table gives $4\cdot75$; $5\cdot5 - \cdot75 = 4\cdot75$ for 240 feet. Hence the resistance varies directly as the initial velocity, and inversely as the diameter of the ball and the square root of the distance.

$$R \therefore \dfrac{V}{1} \times \dfrac{1}{d}$$

$V = \dfrac{5\cdot5}{8\cdot41} = \cdot65\ D = \dfrac{\cdot775}{\cdot6} = 1\cdot3 \times \cdot65 = \cdot845 \times 4\cdot66\ R$ of 240 ft. $= 3\cdot932 =$ to resistance of 240 to ball ·6 diameter.

$2\cdot9 \times \cdot845. = 2\cdot4$. Table gives $3 = R$, for ball ·6 at 120 ft.

$2\cdot4 \times \sqrt{2} = 1\cdot41 = 3\cdot36$. Table gives $4\cdot75$, for ball ·6 at 240 ft.

The result shown in the table in next page, increases in a ratio almost equal to the ratio of the increase of charge; in small quantities the increase is a shade greater than in the larger. Eight drams gives the highest effect, with the given length of the musket: at which point the result is nearly that of the average up to itself— $\dfrac{72\cdot5}{36} = 2$ result $= \dfrac{15\cdot3}{8} = 1\cdot91$ charge.

From eight drams the effect slightly decreases. As a general rule, we may predicate that all circumstances being in equilibrium, the result is nearly as the charge within a regulated maximum.

No. 5.

INCREASE OF CHARGE.

Boards, ½ in.   Ball, brass.   Musket barrel, length, 3 ft. 2½ in.
,, close together.   ,, diameter, ·73.   ,, weight, 4 lbs. 13 oz.
,, distance, 30 ft.   ,, weight, 1 oz.   ,, diam. of bore, ·77 in.

Charge.	Difference.	Boards.	Average.		Remarks.
Drams.		Pierced.			
1	0	2· 1· 2·	1·66		
2	1	3·5 4· 4·5	4·		
3	1	6·5 7· 6·5	6·6		
4	1	8· 9· 12·	9·6		
5	1	9·5 9·5 9·5	9·5		
6	1	11· 11· 11·	11·		
7	1	13· 13· 14·	13·3		
8	1	16· 14· 16·	15·3		
9	1	14·5 14·5 14·5	14·5		
10	1	14· 13· 15·	14·		
55	Totals.	...	101·	$\frac{101}{55}=1·83$	
36 {	Totals to 8 drams.		72·5	$\frac{72·5}{36}=2$	

The following experiments, bearing on the subject of charge, prove how useless is any excess of powder above a certain point.

INCREASE OF CHARGE.

The boards in this differ from the previous experiment on charge in $\frac{11}{6\cdot 8}$, reducing the 14 boards to 8·6 for 10 drams. This result does not greatly vary from the 8 with 12 drams under different ball, barrel, and powder. The strange point is, that 40 drams did not burst the barrel. When destroying the useless arms at Kundahar, I found that three balled cartridges, when placed one over another, burst the barrels with facility.

Boards, 1 in.
,, interval between each, 1 in.
,, distance, 30 ft.

Ball, brass.
,, diameter, ·75.
,, weight, 1 oz. 2 drs.

Musket barrel, length, 3 ft. 2½ in.
,, weight, 4 lb. 13 oz.
,, diameter of bore, ·78.

Charge.	Difference.	Boards.	Average.	Remarks.
Drams.				
12	0	8· 8· 8·	8·	
14	2	9· 9· 10·	9·33	
16	2	10· 11· 10·	10·33	
18	2	12· 11· 10·5	11·1	Reports very loud; recoil on the holding frame very heavy. Towards the muzzle the metal became so hot as to be hardly touchable by the hand.
20	2	11· 11· 11·	11·	
24	4	11· 12· 11·	11·33	
28	4	... ...		
32	4	11· 11· 11·	11·	
36	4	... ...		
40	4	10· 11· 11·	10·16	

188 SIZE OF GRAIN.

No. 6.—SIZE OF GRAIN.

Boards, 1 in.; no interval between them. Ball, diameter ·75; weight, 1 oz. Musket Barrel, length 3 ft. 27 in.; bore, ·78; touch-hole, ·09; total charge of powder, 6 drams.

Rounds.	Kunkur.	Ordnance.	Musketry.	Rifle.	Dust.	Total drams.	Boards pierced by the shot.	Average.	Remarks. B
1	...	...	...	...	...	...	3·25		
2	6	...	...	...	...	6·	3·	3·08	
3	...	...	...	...	...	...	3·		
1	...	...	...	...	...	...	4·25		
2	...	6	...	...	...	6	4·50	4·41	
3	...	...	...	...	...	...	4·50		
1	...	...	...	...	...	...	4·50		
2	...	4	2	...	...	6	4·50	4·50	
3	...	...	...	...	...	...	4·50		
1	...	...	...	...	...	...	5·50		
2	...	3	3	...	...	6	5·50	5·41	4·77
3	...	...	...	...	...	...	5·25		
1	...	...	...	...	...	...	5·25		
2	...	2	4	...	...	6	5·25	5·25	4·9
3	...	...	...	...	...	...	5·25		
1	...	...	...	...	...	...	4·		
2	...	...	6	...	...	6	5·5	5·16	
3	...	...	...	...	...	...	6·		
1	...	...	...	...	...	...	6·25		
2	...	...	4	2	...	6	6·75	6·8	
3	...	...	...	...	...	...	7·50		
1	...	...	...	...	...	...	8·75		
2	...	...	3	3	...	6	6·50	7·16	6·21
3	...	...	...	...	...	...	6·25		
1	...	...	...	...	...	...	7·50		
2	...	...	2	4	...	6	7·25	7·5	6·56
3	...	...	...	...	...	...	7·75		
1	...	...	...	...	...	...	7·		
2	...	...	...	6	...	6	7·5	7·27	
3	...	...	...	...	...	...	7·25		
1	...	...	...	...	...	...	6·25		
2	...	4	...	2	...	6	6·25	6·33	5·34
3	...	...	...	...	...	...	6·5		
1	...	...	...	...	...	...	7·25		
2	...	3	...	3	...	6	5·75	6·83	5·82
3	...	...	...	...	...	...	7·50		
1	...	...	...	...	...	...	6·5		
2	...	2	...	4	...	6	5·75	5·91	
3	...	...	...	...	...	...	5·5		
1	...	...	...	...	...	...	9·		
2	...	2	...	4	...	6	7·	7·66	
3	...	...	...	...	...	...	7·5		

Note.—A line of coarse cloth was laid on the ground to the boards, and a thin curtain suspended perpendicularly to intercept grains unburnt. The result was, that with Kunkur nearly half a dram was ejected unburnt, and with the Ordnance many grains were observed. With the dust the report was very heavy.

Description of Charge.		Charge, 6 drams.	Charge, 2 drams.
Powder as taken up from the corning sieve; the Kunkur extracted and the dust sifted, but the powder was not glazed or much dried.	Long Barrel, 3 ft. 2·5 in.	$\left\{\begin{array}{l}6\cdot5\\5\cdot75\\6\cdot5\end{array}\right\}6\cdot25$	$\left\{\begin{array}{l}2\cdot75\\2\cdot5\\3\cdot\end{array}\right\}2\cdot75$
	Short Barrel, 9·5 in.	$\left\{\begin{array}{l}2\cdot5\\3\cdot\\2\cdot75\end{array}\right\}2\cdot75$	$\left\{\begin{array}{l}0\cdot75\\0\cdot75\\1\cdot\end{array}\right\}0\cdot83$

In Table 2 we have these lengths of barrel with pure musketry-powder. The results of which, reduced by $\frac{D}{B}$, will give $\frac{5\cdot16}{6\cdot25}, \frac{1\cdot7}{2\cdot75}, \frac{1\cdot97}{2\cdot75}, \frac{\cdot71}{\cdot83}$, being all in favour of this mixture, and against pure unmixed musketry grain.

Size of Grain.

Thus with unmixed powder the result appears to be, in some ratio, inversely as the size of the grain rising progressively from Kunkur to dust.

Of the mixtures that yield the best result in which the smallest grains predominate.

That the total result is not the simple aggregation of the shares of the compound (*vide* Column B), but that something is gained by mixture.

The order appears to be—
Rifle and Musketry.
Rifle and Ordnance.
Musketry and Ordnance.

When the composition, as in a fuze, is compact, the fire destroys the surface, creates the fluid, and expands it by the heat. Thus, in one inch, a certain quantity of fluid would be generated and raised to a certain temperature. Supposing no heat to escape in the burning of the second inch, more fluid would be created, but whether the heat of the total fluid of the two inches would be raised to a higher point is questionable.

SIZE OF GRAIN.

But heat must escape into the surrounding medium, hence it is probable that the heat evolved in the second inch would not increase the temperature of the fluid of the two inches.

As the fire and fluid are unable to penetrate beyond the surface of the compact composition, the elasticity of the earlier portions of the fluid may be weakened or destroyed ere the whole is evolved.

In the charge of powder, the compactness is as the size of the grains. Between the grains are interstices by which both the fire and the fluid can penetrate.

The fire will therefore advance and inflame a second layer of grains ere the first are quite consumed. While some are expiring others will be commencing to inflame in the proportion of the density of the cake and the facility of the fire passing through the interstices of the grains. This ratio will be determined by the diameter of the sphere of fire.

The heated fluid, more subtle than the fire, will expand, carrying with it burnt and unburnt grains; but as the space enlarges, the fire will be less powerful, the distance between the grains will become longer, the supply of oxygen will become less, until reaching a point where the fire will be unable to touch and inflame the grains in advance. These with the fluid will be carried on and expelled unburnt from the barrel.

It takes a longer time to inflame the surface of a large than of a small grain. Large grains evolve the fluid slower, circulate the fire with less rapidity; hence more grains are expelled unburnt, or are only burnt in the flame and fire issuing in a mass after the ball has left the barrel; these add not to the velocity of the ball.

The object appears to be, a size of grain that shall continue to burn, evolve fluid, and raise the heat, as long as the flame takes to penetrate the entire mass, and that the elastic fluid should be kept rather behind than in advance of the flame, so as not to force any grains beyond the reach of the fire; this will constitute the sphere of fire.

A certain depth of charge to a certain length.

Large grains burn slower and create more heat, while small ones, lying in the interstices, better conduct the flame as a train.

These experiments show the desired effect to be best obtained by musketry as the base; and rifle as the train.

A large evolvement of heated fluid, with a rapid passage to the flame, are points to be justly apportioned.

The Table exhibits the following ratios:—

$$\frac{m}{r} = \cdot 70 \; \frac{o}{m} = \cdot 85 :: \frac{o}{r} \cdot 70 \times \cdot 85 = \cdot 595, \text{Table } \cdot 606 = \frac{4 \cdot 41}{7 \cdot 27}.$$

A mixture of a smaller kind of grain appears decidedly to improve the result from a larger grain. I think the Ishapore powder is too regular, and that it will be found that almost all other powders, English, Continental, Madras, Bombay, and Indian contain a mixture of small with larger grain.

The higher the cake is pressed, the smaller should be the grain.

The use of the percussion caps has caused a reduction in the amount of charge; the percussion composition is more powerful, the inflammation of the charge is quicker, and the fire of the percussion powder is thrown into the charge.

I believe with percussion caps, a larger grained powder may be used with advantage. And I think that one properly proportioned mixture of powder would answer for all purposes, and save expense.

Column B contains the result by composition of the effects of the unmixed grains. A dram of musketry powder of Ishapore manufactory contains about 3000, and of common ordnance powder 1200, separate grains.

THE EFFECT OF PRESSURE, OR PLACING ADDITIONAL WEIGHT BEFORE THE BALL.

Boards, 1 in. Ball, diameter, ·74. Barrel, length of long, 3 ft. 2·5 in.
 ,, interval, 0. ,, weight, 16 drs. ,, length of short, 9·5 in.

	Charge of 6 drams.			
	4 drams of Sand between Powder and Ball.		6 drams of Sand between Powder and Ball, set as usual.	
	Boards.	Average.	Boards.	Average.
Long Barrel .	5·5 6·5 6·5	6·16	8· 6·75 7·	7·25
Short Barrel	2·75 2·75 3·3	2·93	4· 3·5 4·	3·83

192   EFFECTS OF PRESSURE.

The previous experience of the barrel of 9·5 in. is in Table 2 B reduced to D, the result is ·4·58 × ·4·32 = 1·97. Hence, with the short barrel, by 4 drams of sand placed before the ball, the result is increased from ·1·97 to ·2·83 = ·1·49; and by 6 drams of sand ·1·97 to ·3·83 = ·1·86. The long barrel gives an increase of 1·25 for 6 drams of sand over the usual result of this barrel of 6 boards. The result clearly proves the advantage of pressure in very short barrels, with its questionable advantage or propriety in those of increased length.

LONG LAHORE MATCHLOCK.

Boards, 1 in.   Ball, diameter, ·5.   Barrel, length, 4 ft. 2 in.
„ interval, 0.   „ weight, 6 drs.   „ bore, ·55.
                                     „ weight, 6 lbs. 5½ oz.

Charge of Powder, Bengal Musketry.	Boards.	
	Difference.	Average.
2½ drams	4·5 6· 6·	5·5
3½ „	6·75 6·75 6·75	6·75
5 „	8·75 8· 8·	8·25
8 „	7·5 9· 9·	8·5
Trident's Powder.		
3½ drams	5·25 8· 6·	6·41

The charge 2·5 is 8 drams $\times \dfrac{\cdot 5 \rvert^3}{\cdot 75 \rvert^3}$, or as the cube of the diameters of the shot.

„ 3·5 is the last increased in the proportion of $\dfrac{4\cdot 2 \text{ ft.}}{3\cdot 2 \text{ ft.}}$ for length of barrel.

„ 5 and 8 drams were taken at random.

The range with the Trident's powder is curious, being equal to that of the best powder in these small quantities.

In the musket the Trident's result, compared with the Ishapore powder, was $\frac{6}{4\cdot 62}$, in the mortar $\frac{92}{15}$; as if the force of the powder were in some inverse ratio of the diameter of the charge. This Trident's powder had been in the Moyapoor magazine since A.D. 1834.

In the long charge which 5 drams must constitute with a barrel of such small diameter as ·55, we note no additional force from 3 additional drams.

VARIOUS PROOFS.

Description of Powders.	M. Barrel, 6 drams Charge. Board 1 in., Interval 1.	8-in. Mortar, 2-oz. Charge, 67 lb. 12 oz. Ball.	Gun Eprouvette, 2-oz. Charge.	
	Average.	Average. Yds.	Average. Deg.	Min.
Bombay powder, received from Dum Dum .	7·33	80	21	58
"Trident," dated when placed in magazine 1834	4·62	15	14	36
"Good Hope," 1826	4·5	66	17	40
"Perseverance," 1829	6·3	59	19	17
Ship "Mysore," 1815	4·25	10	13	44
Danish, H. D. Majesty's ship "Galathæa"	7·91	...	...	
Dartford, from Bazaar . . .	9·25	115	25	37
Decayed Urhur wood (charcoal) . .	8·3	87	...	
Well damped with water, redried . .	6·08	75	18	46
Very damp, and clotted in lumps, redried .	...	76	18	46
M. P. of 1846 from Dum Dum, dried .	7·5	91	23	8
O. P. after exposure to sun from 10 to 4 .	...	100	20	55
O. below,* M. above; 3 drams O., 3 drams M.	6·25	...	...	
M. below, O. above	6·25	...	...	
M. below, R. above; 3 drams M., 3 drams R.	6·	...	...	
Ishapore musketry, fresh . . .	...	94	...	
Bombay, 3 years old, sifted to size of above	...	87	...	
English sporting	...	130	27	40
Ishapore rifle	...	91	24	11
Madras common manufacture, 1844 . . { M. ... { O. ...		86 89	22 20	34 16
Spanish, from a Spanish man-of-war . .		70	17	43
English powder received from H.M. ship "Sphinx" . . . . . . { M. ... { O. ...		108 99	24 20	31 10
English sporting	...	130	24	40
Ishapore rifle, 30 hours glazed . .	...	93	24	

* That is, 3 drams Ordnance powder first put into the barrel of the musket, and then 3 drams musketry.

COMPARISON BETWEEN THE EFFECT ON BOARDS AND RANGE.

Musketry of 1847.		Ball.	Charge.	Boards, 1 in. Interval, 1 in.	Average.	Range by Commandant's Report, Dum Dum.	Range per dram.	Range per board.
Common Musket	Weight, 4 lb. 3½ oz. Length, 3 ft. 2¾ in. Diameter, ·78	Diameter, ·75 Weight, 1 oz. 2 dr.	6 drams	6·75 7· 6·75	6·83	244	41	35·7
Musket Fusil	Weight, 3 lb. 10½ oz. Length, 3 ft. ½ in. Diameter, ·7	Diameter, ·64 Weight, 11 dr.	6 drams	5·5 5·5 5·5	5·5	203	33·8	37
Carbine	Weight, 2 lb. 10 oz. Length, 2 ft. 2 in. Diameter, ·7	Diameter, ·64 Weight, 11 dr.	4 drams	5· 4·75 5·	4·91			
Pistol	Weight, 1 lb. 2 oz. Length, 8½ in. Diameter, ·66	Diameter, ·64 Weight, 11 dr.	4 drams	2·75 2·5 3·	2·93	199	49	67
Pistol	Weight, 1 lb. 2 oz. Length, 8½ in. Diameter, ·66	Diameter, ·64 Weight, 11 dr.	3 drams	2·5 2·5 2·5	2·5	147	49	59

N.B.—The superiority in effect of the old heavy musket is evinced.

TABLE OF RECORDED RANGES. 195

TABLE OF RECORDED RANGES OF GUNPOWDER, TAKEN FROM DIFFERENT AUTHORITIES.

Date of Year.	Authority.	Nature of Powder.	Its proof.	Shell weight.	8-inch Mortar.		24-pounder Gun.				Remarks.
					Weight of Charge.	Range.	Weight of Charge.	Range.	Length of Gun.	Eleva- tion.	
1675	"Light to the Art of Gunnery."	..	Not stated	..	If used only to project stones.		Demi-cannon charge 2½ diameters of ball in length, 8 or 10 lbs. ac- cording to the metal. 536 yards called a long point blank range.				
1789	Pocket Gunner, Edi- tion 1813.	..	..	..	lb. oz. dr. 1 0 0	Yards. 1116					
1808	Madras Gunner.	..	..	..	1 0 0	700					
1809	Practice Reports at Jauzenow, near Cawn- pore, 5 January.	Bengal fine	..	..	0 13 0	648	lbs. 8	Yards. 1000	Feet. 9¼	Deg. 2	⎧ From the Medium Tables published by General Horsford, Commandant. But such Medium Tables made at head- quarters are not to be depended upon for general work, because the experi- ments are made with instruments of the best description, and with too much care. In the remarks to these tables it is stated the powder was dried, mixed, and sifted, which would add much to its force. I also suspect that cloth-holders to fix the shells were used. There is much discrepancy between the 56 yards with 3 oz. and the 1000 yards with 15 oz. 4 drs.
1810	Pocket Gunner, Edi- tion 1813.	..	10-in. mortar, 96 lb. shell, 2lb. charge, 1000 yards range.	..	..	..	6	832	6¼	2	
1810-11	MSS. Medium Tables of Dum Dum Practice.	Bengal fine	..	46lb. 0oz.	1 1 4	1000					
1812-13	..	..	8-in. mortar, 50 lb. shell, 3 oz. charge, 56 yds. range.	46 0	0 15 4	1000					
1813-14	MSS. Medium Tables of Practice at Agra.	Allahabad Pit musketry.	8-in. mortar, 50 lb. shell, 3 oz. charge, 68 yds. range.	..	1 0 9	1050					Remarks as above for 12 and 13.
1813-14	Medium Practice Tables, Dum Dum.	Bengal M cylinder	8-in. mortar, 50 lb. shell, 3 oz. charge, 79 yds. range.	..	0 14 0	1000					Remarks as above for 12 and 13.

TABLE OF RECORDED RANGES OF GUNPOWDER, TAKEN FROM DIFFERENT AUTHORITIES—(continued).

Date of Year.	Authority.	Nature of Powder.	Its proof.	Powder's age.	Shell weight.	8-inch Mortar.		24-pounder Gun.		
						Weight of Charge.	Range.	Weight of Charge.	Range.	Length of Gun.	Elevation.	Remarks

Date of Year.	Authority.	Nature of Powder.	Its proof.	Powder's age. Yrs.	Shell weight. lb. oz.	Weight of Charge. lb. oz. dr.	Range. Yards.	Weight of Charge. lbs.	Range. Yards.	Length of Gun. Feet.	Elevation. Deg.	Remarks
1820	Card given by Sergt. Armour, of Addiscombe, considered to be of Woolwich authority. Woolwich Printed Cards	.	.	.	.	1 0 0	1156	.	.	.	.	
19th May 1826	Comparative proof of Indian Powders at Woolwich.	Waltham Abbey Glazed, Alder Cylinder LG., Dec., 1825.	.	.	41 10	1 0 0	650	8	{702 / 1042}	.	P. R. 1¼	
	Ditto, ditto	Returned from H.M. Ship Tribune, after being 3 years at sea.	.	4	41 10	1 0 0	652	8	{516 / 993}	.	P. R. 1¼	This powder was not re-stored, which is considered necessary after a three years' trip to sea.
1825-27	Average of Dum Dum Practice Reports, by Agency MSS. Book.	.	.	.	.	1 0 0	750	.	.	.	.	
1828	{ Select Committee Proof, 1828.	Ishapore, 1824-25 Allahabad, 1824-25 Madras Bombay French of 1820, Ordnance	. . . . Portee 236	4 4 . 8	41 11 41 11 41 11 65¼	1 0 0 ,, ,, ,,	587 758 571 278 612	. . . . .	. . . . .	. . . . .	. . . . .	These powders were of various sorts and ages, tried for some specific object of the time. See Appendix for the account of this experiment.—EDT.
1835	Average Tables from Merrit practice, by Maj. W. Anderson.	Ishapore of 1825-26; Allahabad, 1825-27.	.	10 9	46 0	1 0 4	786	8	{445 / 1152}	.	P. R. 2	

RECORDED RANGES.

Year	Description	Notes		Charge	Range		P.B.	Remarks
1839–40	Average Practice Tables, by Colonel C. Graham, C.B., Ferozepore.	.	46	0 15 14	800 866	8	360 1180	P.B. 2
1840–41	Ditto, ditto	.	46	1 0 0	866	8		
1858–48	Average of the Commandant's Proof, for 11 years in succession.	Ishapore M, one year old when tried.	46	1 0 0	812	8	794	1 0	This is the average of trials at Dum Dum, taken each year on the powder made during the previous year.
1847–48	Rough Magazine Report, Dum Dum practice, 3rd February, 1847.	Ishapore mus-ketry. 63 yards.	44	0 15 0 / 1 2 0	696 / 975	8	1149 / 894	9 6 { 2 15 / 1 15	
1847–48	Tables of Practice at Ferozpoor, by Capt. J. Anderson, Bengal Artillery.	Ishapore of 1843–44. Usual proof range 71 yards.	.	1 0 0	863	8	.	.	
1859	The Artillerist's Manual, by Capt. Griffiths, R.A., Woolwich.	.	.	1 0 0	750	8	360 / 755 / 1125	50 cwt. 9 ft. long. P.B. 1 2	On the whole, there is no recorded fact giving to the common run of powder in its average state, from an 8-inch mortar, with 1lb. charge, and a 45 lb. shell, a range of more than 750 yards, which could be depended upon as certain.

APPENDIX.

Experiments on varied proportions of Ingredients in Gunpowder.

DURING the years 1851-1853 I considered it advisable to ascertain if any variations in the proportions of the ingredients, or other changes in manipulation, would be attended with improved results in the range of powder.

To determine the first point, I was careful that a well-marked increased quantity of each ingredient should be made. For an excess of saltpetre, I adopted a set of quantities which I found as those of the Hounslow manufactories, viz.—

Saltpetre	. 78
Charcoal . .	. 14
Sulphur . .	. 8
Total .	. 100

Here is given a quantity of three pounds more saltpetre than in the common Ishapore powder.

For an excess of sulphur was used the proportions obtaining at Madras—

Sulphur .	. 11
Saltpetre . .	. 75
Charcoal .	. 14
	100

giving an extra pound of sulphur to the composition of 100 lbs. of powder.

For an excess of charcoal, I used—

Charcoal	. 16·5
Saltpetre . .	. 75·
Sulphur	. 8·5
	100

having 1½ lb. of charcoal additional. This was named "Experimental Powder."

Charcoal was also prepared from very old unserviceable teakwood staves, and was denominated "Teak Powder."

Powder was also made with unfused nitre; but in all other ingredients and respects like the established manufacture.

Next was made powder from the usual materials, but without the previous grinding, sifting, or mixing by the mixing barrels; much in the mode in which the ingredients are mixed in England and at Madras. The unpounded materials were thrown upon the mill-bed and evenly placed by hand before the mill was started. It required 600 revolutions before the composition was considered fit to be passed to the press.

In 1853 I tried further experiments, as I had formed an opinion that the cake of our powder was too dense, and of too uniform a consistency, and that a more porous cake would certainly improve the range of the Indian powder of the large grained Ordnance size.

First. I substituted wire sieves in place of the silk used with the saltpetre and sulphur. This powder was all called "Wire Powder."

Second. I used silk sieves with the sulphur; as its great density and its smaller quantity rendered advisable that it only should be reduced to the finest particles possible. This powder is denominated "Sulphur Silk Powder."

In January, 1853, was set up a new mill received from Europe, manufactured at Dartford by Messrs. Hall and Co., on the principles obtaining in England. The essential difference of this mill is, that every part of it is composed of iron, cast or wrought; the runners do not follow each other, but overlap about one-half in their runs, so that the area of the bed is necessarily much larger.

The runners are of the diameter 6 ft. 5 in., the breadth of the faces 1 ft. 3 in., and these are slightly convex from the centre. The ploughs are single, and no turners follow the runners.

The result of the trials of all these powders is given in the following Table. The custom obtained at Ishapore, to try all experimental powders at the same time with the common manu-

PROOF OF EXPERIMENTS.

Average of the Proof Report of 1850-51.

Description of Powder.	When made.	Density.	Mortar, 2-oz. Charge.	Eprouvette, 2-oz. Charge.	Mortar, 1-lb. Charge.	Appearance when new.	Hygrometric value, 20 being established for Ishapore.
			Yards.	Deg. Min.	Yards.		
Hounslow proportions	May, 1853	M 266	81	21 22	586	Heavy and dull, density high	23
Madras ditto	Dec., 1850	O 285	85	18 13	406	}	
		M 267	91	22 21	721	Cake very hard; less specks visible than in common manufacture	18
		O 282	94	19 41	588	}	
Experimental—additional charcoal	May, 1850	M 260	94	22 20	698	Much as usual	19
		O 274	92	19 43	477	}	
From old teak charcoal	May, 1850	M 259	77	20 42	532	Cake as usual, but light coloured	20
		O 272	79	18 30	386	}	
Unfused nitre	Dec., 1850	M 258	103	23 7	855	Cake not quite so hard as common powder	20
		O 274	101	20 26	653	}	
Unpulverised composition, 600 rev.	Dec., 1850	M 261	103	23 51	931	Cake very hard, but many specks visible of saltpetre; dark colour	18
		O 275	106	20 39	702	}	

Average from Proof Reports, 1853.

All wire sieve powder	4 Feb. 1853	M 258	97	23 11	820	Cake not dense, structure coarse, specks of sulphur very visible, also some of saltpetre	19
		O 274	96	19 56	...	}	
Sulphur silk powder	17 Feb. 1853	M 255	104	24 13	938	Structure less coarse, specks of saltpetre visible	18
		O 268	105	20 43	774	}	
Iron Mill	Jan. 1853	M 257	103	23 6	831	Not quite so dense as common manufacture	20
		O 274	103	20 11	...	}	

facture on the 20th of each month, and to record the results. The averages of the year are thus obtained.

No common manufactured powder was submitted to the hygrometric proof, so that I only give my judgment in this respect as to how the powders would stand comparison.

But as the atmospheric proof is chiefly determined by purity of materials, and as the ingredients were from identical heaps, no excessive differences were to be expected, nor were such found.

From the above results, may be predicated that the Hounslow proves that no addition is required to the saltpetre.

The Madras indicates that an addition of sulphur would not be objectionable, but not at the expense of the charcoal. The Experimental favours no reduction of charcoal.

The Old Teak powder shows that every kind of charcoal is not equally good for powder. The unfused nitre is an improvement apparently. In the manipulation of these powders there would result no saving of expense.

The unpulverised composition is worthy of extended consideration, as some general principles may be gathered from it, and great saving of expense might be obtained. The intermotion amongst the ingredients thrown unpulverised into the mill, is much greater; they do not at once set down into cake under the runners, much previous handling is spared, and the incorporation takes place at once, as the surfaces are fresh, and adherence is thus, as it were, by first intention. There exists vividness about the cake; the grain, as porous, contains more air, and explodes quicker.

The All-Wire sieve powder contains ingredients far less handled, and the powder is less dense, but the structure appeared too coarse, as the wire was in too large meshes. The intermotion and intermixture of the unpulverised is absent.

The Sulphur Silk powder meets all my objections, the density is less, and the structure more porous; while the sulphur being more pulverised than the saltpetre has the result of an additional quantity, and binding the whole better together gives increased firmness to the grain.

Iron Mill.—The result of this lies in the less intermixture and motion, by reason of the single plough and absence of the turners; although the grinding action may be enhanced by the double centres of motions from the runners revolving in different tracks.

Were I called upon to fix a standard for the proportions, it should be—

Saltpetre	74·5
Sulphur	10·5
Charcoal	15·
	100

ground as at present, but silk sieves only to be used for the sulphur. One half an hour's turning to be diminished from the mixing barrels, and forty revolutions deducted from the mills. A greater mixture of sizes of grains to be admitted in the Ordnance powder.

CARE OF POWDER IN MAGAZINES.

1. On their arrival, the barrels should be carefully and closely inspected, to ascertain if they exhibit any appearance of damp, or of the powder being altered as to colour, grain, or texture.

2. If the Magazine is supplied with a permanent set of the patent barrels, these must be cleaned out, and care taken that when the felt of the heads is decayed, such be replaced by new numdah.* This will render quite unnecessary any filling up of the crevices with putty; a bad plan, always contaminating the upper surface of the powder. The powder must then be carefully transferred to these patent barrels.

3. If the common barrels are to be retained in the Magazine, the heads should never be taken out, as grains of powder entering between the seams entirely preclude their again being completely closed up. Any investigation into the condition of the powder can be made by drawing the bung.

4. The barrels on the racks are to be constantly rolled about; the more they are turned over and moved, the less will the powder be liable to cake or hold the damp.

* Indian felt.

5. The hoops should be constantly but *carefully* set home.

6. Should there be available near the Magazine a court-yard protected from the danger of fire, it would be of the greatest advantage to the powder, if once or twice during the year, the barrels were in an unopened state exposed on powder-cloths to the very hottest sun of the season for the whole day. In this state the hoops should be well set home. This operation will dissipate any contracted damp both from the powder and from the barrels.

Damaged Powder.

I have seen, in former days, much gunpowder condemned as unserviceable, and thrown into rivers. I now know that such powder only required to be redried and resifted to be fully serviceable for all common exercise purposes.

All that is necessary being that a small walled enclosure, free from danger of fire and accident by concussion, should be selected at a good distance from the Magazine.

In this court powder-cloths should be spread, and the powder thinly laid out to the thickness of an inch, and be constantly turned over in the sun for eight hours of a very hot day.

Towards the evening, the powder, having been passed through a sieve, No. 2 of 1156 meshes to the square inch, and all fine dust and dirt extracted, may be returned to the barrel.

This operation is analogous to the restoring of the English system.

Only a few barrels should be manipulated at once.

Recovery of Saltpetre.

From powder, damaged beyond recovery, or from the dust extracted from powders redried, every magazine ought to be able to supply itself with saltpetre for every required laboratory purpose.

Or if no damaged powder is available, the same result may be obtained by using common bazaar saltpetre.

A half-hogshead barrel must be prepared to stand over a

common copper cooling pan (see plate) ; holes must be drilled in the bottom, and a stratum of fine sand, one foot deep, filled in ; over this is to be placed a false bottom, also pierced with holes.

Four times the weight of powder, of pure well-water, must now be added to the damaged powder, and well worked together in a separate half-hogshead.

This mixture must be transferred to the filter by degrees, whence it will soon run in a clear stream.

This water must then be transferred to a magazine boiler, and over a fire, in a safe corner, be thickened down by evaporation to one half its quantity, when it will be found that crystals of pure saltpetre will form on any bit of common earthenware on which it is dropped.

This being the case, the liquor may be poured into a second cooling pan, and allowed to remain twenty-four hours, when a fine crop of clean crystals will be obtained.

The drawn-off water may be again reduced over the fire, and again placed to cool, and the operation continued until no water remains. Should the crystals be discoloured, they may be reboiled with a very small quantity of clear spring water.

By this operation 40 or 50 lbs. of pure saltpetre may be recovered at the expense of a little firewood, from every 100 lbs. of damaged powder ; and each magazine can thus supply itself with this necessary article. Care must of course be taken, as in all operations with powder, that only a small quantity be manipulated at one time, and in a place free from danger, and distant from other magazines. Much advantage would result if a few men for employment as sirdars of powder magazines, went through a course of duty at the powder works, and were instructed in the various manipulations.

Empty Barrels.

Barrels for return to the powder works should be carefully taken to pieces. Teak wood is becoming daily more valuable and scarce.

The staves and heads should be as little thrown about as possible, for every chip from the edges has to be cut out, and a very slight reduction in size renders both heads and staves useless.

I am inclined to recommend all the component parts being tied up, in rather heavy bundles, as they are then less liable to be thrown about and broken.

For ten empty barrels weighing about $2\frac{3}{4}$ cwt., I would suggest the following style of packages :—

Hoops, 40	Bundles 1, weight of each $\frac{3}{4}$ cwt.	Total $\frac{3}{4}$ cwt.
Heads, 20	,, 1, ,, $\frac{1}{2}$,,	,, $\frac{1}{2}$,,
Staves, 164	,, 3, ,, $\frac{1}{2}$,,	,, $1\frac{1}{2}$,,
	Bundles 5	$2\frac{3}{4}$ cwt.

One hundred barrels requiring about a ton. The hoops are never to have the rivets taken out. Each bundle is to be secured by two pieces of iron wire plate riveted.

The heads and staves are to be well tied with common lashing, and, if found necessary, in coarse gunnoy; as indicated in the sketch. (See plate.)

REPORT ON THE NEW IRON MILL.

This Mill was sent out from England and set up in January, 1853; it was constructed at Dartford by Messrs. Hall and Co., on the pattern of those used at their works; every part of it is composed of iron cast or wrought. The question of its advantages may be best disposed of under three heads :— the Mill; the result on cost of powder; the result on the goodness of the powder.

The Mill: its cost, exclusive of the house and foundations, stands at about 3,900 rupees; the gun metal mills when new cost 37,000 rupees each.

At first the workmen were timid in approaching the cast-iron mill, but this fear soon subsided.

No turners follow to turn up the composition, and the ploughs are single; hence the composition earlier settles into cake, and

SECTION OF A CHARCOAL OR SULPHUR MILL
PROPOSED TO BE ERECTED AT THE MADRAS POWDER MILLS.

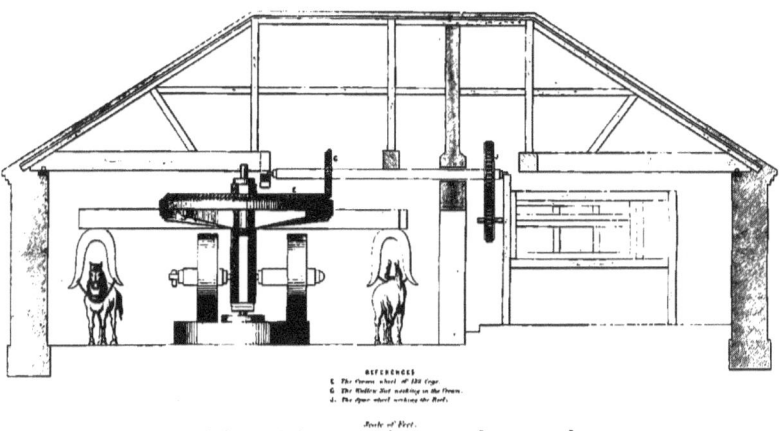

REFERENCES
E. The Crown wheel of 188 cogs.
G. The Endless Nut working in the Crown.
J. The Spur wheel working the Bolt.

Scale of Feet.

being very much less tossed about and worked, the density of the cake is less, and the incorporation not quite so complete as with the old mills; perhaps the 240 revolution cake of the new mill, is equal to the 180 revolutions of the old mills.

The iron mill has only been worked about four months; no abrasion of the surface or bed or runners is apparent. The diameter of the runners is so great as to render the work much more light on the cattle than with the old mills.

The construction is simple, the workmanship superior; I am of opinion, that the bed should be cast with a solid kerb like that of the bronze beds.

Result on the Cost of Powder.

There will be a reduction in the cost of the block, of labour, and motive power, and of the manufacturing charges generally, so as to diminish the cost of the barrel of powder.

Result on the Goodness of the Powder.

I have always expressed my opinion that the density of the Ishapore powder is too high, that such gives slightly decreased ranges, though perhaps it improves the powder by better resisting deterioration under change and climate. Hence that some of our labour in milling is thrown away, for there can be no reason why Bengal powder shall require 240 revolutions, if 100 is found ample at Madras.

The following result bears out this theory; but the experience from the cast iron mill is only derived from a limited time of working, and hence is not entitled to full confidence.

Comparative Report.

Description of Powder.		Density.	Mortar, 2-oz. charge.	Eprouvette, 2-oz. charge.	Mortar, 1lb. charge, 68lb. ball.
				Deg. Min.	
Common manufacture,	M	261	95	22 11	719
average of 1849-50 .	O	277	93	19 33	473
Cast iron mill, average	M	257	103½	23 6	831
from one barrel . .	O	274	103	20 11	not taken

On the whole nothing has appeared, at present, to detract from the good opinion entertained in England for this class of mill.

The reduction of cost to one-tenth of that of the gun metal mills, is fully sufficient to warrant the introduction under any contemplated changes.

REMOVAL OF THE POWDER WORKS.

[COLONEL ANDERSON having been called upon by the Government to give his opinion on the subject of the removal of the powder works to the upper provinces, and abandoning those of Ishapore, furnished the following admirable Report, which is well worthy of the attention of the Indian authorities."—ED.]

To clear the way to a complete view of this question, I consider it must first be determined, whether it be necessary to manufacture all the powder required for the Presidency of Bengal at one place. To this question I reply in the negative ; because the art is no secret, and the diffusion of more correct principles would be advantageous. I myself experienced the greatest trouble in getting up some supplies of powder, when the Kundahar force was in prospect of being deficient.

The country is now far too extended to be easily supplied from one distant manufactory, the danger of transporting so explosive an article is excessive, and the expense of carriage very great.

The art itself is not one of very difficult attainment, nor does it require so very expensive a block as was formerly deemed desirable.

Political reasons would also point to the great weakness of the advanced positions being dependant on one very distant source of supply, to which the communication might easily be interrupted by any disturbances in the intervening countries.

I believe the only advantage to be permanently relied upon is that from one manufactory the strength of the powder will be more uniform ; but the powder of both Bombay and Madras so nearly resembles the powder of Bengal, that no inconvenience has resulted.

Two blocks may, in a trifling degree, increase the cost of the production, but this depends so much on local circumstances as only to be settled in each individual case.

I think it may be considered as established, that it is not necessary to manufacture all the powder in one place.

But the probable form into which any future European war will glide, of large fleets of heavily armed men of war requiring immense supplies of powder, points, I consider, to the impolicy that the chief port of India, and capital of the empire, should be dependent on a distant supply of so necessary a munition of defence. Our new provinces to the eastward, in Burmah, must also be duly considered.

Consequently, I consider that it would be highly advantageous to retain Ishapore, and also to establish other distinct works.

It next becomes a point of consideration whether such shall be at Allahabad or any other station.

The advantages of removal to Allahabad are general, for the nearer the works of production are situated to the place of consumption, so far, in some ratio, will be reduced the cost in expense of carriage. This I believe to be the only real advantage that would attend the removal to Allahabad.

I have no data on which to proceed to the special advantages, but I do not hesitate to say that I believe the cost of production will be greater at Allahabad, the powder inferior, and the danger of manipulation augmented, and that such were the reasons which induced the former Government to give up Allahabad.

The only recommendation to Allahabad is the existence of some antiquated works, ill adapted to modern improvements, and repairable at an expense which would nearly cover a new set of works in a better position.

Removal to the Punjaub

Presents all the general advantages expected from removal

to Allahabad in a greater proportion as the distance is greater. The Sekhs manufactured very fair powder, of which, to my analysis, the saltpetre was good. I am informed that all the materials are plentiful, and that the cost of the powder was not great, but on this point I can only speak on the evidence of others.

But special advantages must accrue, for I have no doubt that if we can obtain a suitable position on some of the lower hills, a better description of wood for charcoal will be obtained than is found in Bengal or the Doab, and that under a more temperate climate we shall obtain the only points of difference existing between Bengal and English powder.

From the second line of the army, say between Lahoor and Loodiannah, magazines beyond Delhi and Agra might be cheaply supplied with powder. The English materials might be imported up the Indus. Sulphur exists in Scinde. Saltpetre, I conclude, but am not well advised, is also plentiful, and firewood should not be scarce; but these points require to be well ascertained.

A slight inspection of the sketch shows that a set of powder works placed near Lahoor will exhibit one powder manufactory

at each corner of a quadrangle nearly containing the entire country of our Indian Government. These might be so worked as to keep up the proportionate quantity of all the nearest magazines, while the Ishapore works, increased if requisite, would also be in a position to supply the demands of the navy or the magazines of Ceylon.

Everything points to the great desirableness of establishing works in the Punjaub, should inquiry support the asserted plenty of materials.

I suspect the system of the English Government is to keep the works necessary for the quick preparation of a large quantity of powder, in preference to holding in store large amounts of a dangerous and deteriorating article; such should be the Ishapore works.

I consider the locality of the Ishapore works to be admirable, and such as could not easily be elsewhere obtained.

To the west they are bounded by the broad river Hoogly, greatly in favour of transit by water; to the north runs a deep nullah, not fordable by men on foot; to the east there exists a narrow strip of land, which I have suggested should be annexed, lying between the works and a rice jheel; while to the south is ample space included in the agency grounds between the works and the village of Nuwahgunge.

The damp climate is superior for manufacturing gunpowder to the very arid one of the Doab.

With the addition of an eighth mill, and from time to time the improvements I have suggested, the Government would have at its command an excellent set of works, capable of turning out 15,000 barrels of powder in eight months.

No two of the three powder works in India are working on the same system. We differ on almost every point. Our proportions are not the same. The other two Agencies do not use either mixing barrels, the patent charcoal cylinder furnaces, or silk sieves, all very expensive arrangements. I give to my powder 240 revolutions to the charge, while only 100 are employed at Madras, and, I suspect, at Bombay.

All the Madras agents have visited these works, as also have some, I believe, from Bombay; they have all carried away ample information and samples, but no rejoinder has ever been returned as to the advantages derived, or what improvements have or have not been introduced :—no intercommunication exists. Moreover, the probability is great, that full advantage is not taken of our relative positions as to supply, nor do I doubt that the arsenals of each presidency contain much powder-work machinery that might be made available for new works in the Punjaub.

Now, by September, I hope the accounts of last year will be closed, and every arrangement made for the advantageous opening of next year's manufacture; should the Government deem such advisable, I shall be most willing to proceed to Allahabad and the Punjaub, returning down the Indus, and thus viewing and inspecting the works both at Bombay and Madras; from which inspection and intercommunication I have no hesitation in saying that I think pecuniary saving would result.

(Signed)   W. ANDERSON.

Powder Works, Ishapore.
June, 1853.

ANALYSIS OF ISHAPORE POWDER MATERIALS.

BY DR., (NOW) SIR W. B. O'SHAUGHNESSY.

AT the request of Colonel Anderson, powder agent, Ishapore, I have carefully examined samples of the various materials used by him in the manufacture of gunpowder, and with the subjoined results.

Saltpetre.

The once refined, called at the Agency "first boiled," contains—

First boiled, common salt (per cent.)   . .   ·06
Second boiled,   ,,   ,,   . . .   ·00162

The fused saltpetre is absolutely pure.

The residuum of the saltpetre refinery contains, per cent.—

Common salt (per cent.)   . . . .   68·4
Water   . . .   . . .   8·3
Saltpetre   . . . . . .   4·
Sulphate of soda and lime   . . . .   8·1
Sand   . . . .   . .   11·2

100·0

ANALYSIS OF ISHAPORE POWDER MATERIALS. 213

Sulphur.
Both the refined and pulverised were absolutely pure.

Charcoal.
From the Urhur, on careful combustion in the assay muffle, there were obtained—

Of saline and earthy matters, in 100 parts . 3·50
From the Jointee wood charcoal, as above . 3·00

After exposure to the air, in December, 1849, the pulverised Urhur charcoal parted with 1·30 per cent. of moisture. The Jointee charcoal, under the same circumstances, lost 3·6 per. cent.

Samples of both the charcoal powders, treated with distilled water, gave solutions alkaline to test papers, and giving copious precipitates, with the usual tests, of salts and sulphate of soda, and a slight indication of lime.

The common salt was ascertained to be precisely—

1·40 grains from 900 grains of Urhur, and
1·20 grains from 900 of Jointee charcoal.

100 grains of the coarse variety, treated with distilled water, and filtered, gave a considerable *black* precipitate; treated with ammonia,—

It yielded chloride of silver . . 0·30 grains.
and sulphuret of silver . . 4· ,,

thus indicating the presence of 0·06 grains of sulphur in a soluble state, probably combined with potassium or sodium, in the gunpowder.

This fact is interesting, and, as far as I am aware, has not been noticed before. It probably proceeds from the reaction of the sulphur on the alkaline matters contained in the charcoal.

As the soluble sulphurets are very deliquescent, the presence of the sulphuret now detected must, in some slight degree, deteriorate the powder, causing it to attract moisture from the air.

(Signed) W. B. O'SHAUGHNESSY.
Calcutta Mint,
February 25, 1850.

Note.—I have already mentioned the importance of attending to the purity of the charcoal used in the manufacture of gunpowder, as well as its quality; and the above analysis shows the great necessity of attending to it, as, with the other two ingredients perfectly pure, a deteriorating property in gunpowder may proceed from the charcoal.—EDITOR.

REMARKS ON THE TEMPERATURE OF THE DRYING TERRACES.
BY COLONEL ANDERSON.

THE powder leaves the terraces generally heated to about 110° Fahr.; during the night it falls a little towards the uniform temperature of the magazine, which seldom varies much from 80°. The area of the old terraces at Ishapore was 8,148¾ superficial ft.; of the proposed new ones, 9,040 superficial ft.

Date.	Hour.	Thermometer placed in the powder.	Density.	Remarks.
1847		°		
22nd May	1 P.M.	96		Exposed on the copper terrace in the usual manner.
	3 ,,	120	+ 1	
	5 ,,	119		
23rd May	5 A.M.	94		Cooling down in the magazine.
	7 ,,	92	− 1	
	9 ,,	94		
	2 P.M.	96	+ 1	On the terrace.

RANGE OF THE THERMOMETER AT EVERY THREE HOURS DURING THE DAY, ON THE 8TH APRIL, 1848.

In the powder magazine at		6 A.M.	95° Fahr.
		9 ,,	108° ,,
On the drying terraces at		Noon.	130° ,,
		3 P.M.	112° ,,
		6 ,,	109° ,,

It was found that the copper terraces added about 10° to the temperature obtainable from the mere ground; the differing thickness of sheet copper varies this slightly.

Thus, the gunpowder exposed on these terraces is three times raised, by degrees, from a temperature of 80° to that of 130°; amply sufficient to evaporate any remaining moisture.

The raw materials of the gunpowder exposed for the three days to the sun, only exhibited change in the colour of the charcoal. During the second day this became rather whitish in colour, and during the third day quite pale, being a very remarkable change. On being removed to the shade, after some time, it returned to its original colour, *black*.

Annexed is the report on the appearance of the powder during its three days' exposure to the sun :—

DENSITY AND APPEARANCE OF THE GUNPOWDER DURING THE THREE DAYS, AND THE PROGRESS OF ITS BEING SUNNED AND WINNOWED.

Quality of powder.		Density.	Remarks.
1st day	{ Musketry	260	} Dampish appearance, and grain a little soft.
	{ Ordnance	270	
2nd day	{ Musketry	258	} Grain firmer, hardly any dust perceptible.
	{ Ordnance	270	
3rd day	{ Musketry	256	} Grain firm and good, no appearance of dust.
	{ Ordnance	271	

REGISTER OF THERMOMETER TAKEN AT THE DRYING TERRACE OF ISHAPORE AT 11 A.M. DAILY FOR EIGHT MONTHS, 1843-44, 1844-45, 1845-46.

	Powder.	Sun.	Shade.	Powder.	Sun.	Shade.	Powder.	Sun.	Shade.
October	127	91	83	...	...	...	118	90	80
November	123	88	79	126	94	84	120	91	80
December	...	...	...	120	89	87	115	84	73
January	117	89	76	123	92	80	117	80	76
February	123	90	80	123	93	83	119	89	79
March	132	95	89	133	96	86	127	94	83
April	139	99	90	131	94	89	131	96	86
May	136	98	92	133	95	90	131	95	89
	897	650	589	889	653	599	978	719	646
Average	128	$92\frac{3}{4}$	84	127	$93\frac{1}{4}$	$71\frac{1}{4}$	$122\frac{3}{4}$	$89\frac{3}{4}$	$80\frac{3}{4}$

AVERAGE REGISTER OF THERMOMETER AND DENSITY OF POWDER KEPT AT THE MAGAZINE FROM THE 23RD OF OCTOBER, 1848, TO 23RD MAY, 1849, AT ISHAPORE.

Month.	Thermometer in the powder.	Therm. in the sun.	Therm. in the shade.	Density.	
				Musketry.	Ordnance.
1848, October .	125	94	86	266	291
,, November.	121	89	78	268	288
,, December .	118	88	77	268	284
1849, January .	113	85	74	268	283
,, February .	121	92	85	269	284
,, March . .	125	91	83	267	282
,, April .	139	97	87	263	276
,, May . .	132	100	90	262	274
,, Total . .	994	736	660	2131	2262
,, Average .	124	92	$82\frac{1}{2}$	266	$282\frac{3}{4}$

EXPERIMENT OF THE EVAPORATION OF WATER EXPOSED TO THE SOLAR HEAT, IN A COPPER COOLING PAN ON THE GROUND AT ISHAPORE IN 1848.

Date.	Hour.	Thermometer in sun's rays.	Water by weight.	Loss by evaporation.	Depth of water.	Remarks.
			lb. oz.	lb. oz.		
April 8 .	1 P.M.	113 Fahr.	5 8			The atmosphere during the three days cloudy, with a moderate wind. The copper pan is 25 in. diameter at the top edge, and 20·5 at bottom, depth 9 in.
,, ,, .	3 ,,	114 ,,	3 0	2 8		
,, ,, .	4·30 ,,	95 ,,	2 2	0 14		
,, 10.	9 A.M.	106 ,,	10 0			
,, ,, .	12 noon.	116 ,,	8 6	1 10		
,, ,, .	3 P.M.	110 ,,	6 4	2 2	Inches.	
,, 13.	6 A.M.	81 ,,	10 0		·65	
,, ,, .	9 ,,	101 ,,	9 $3\frac{1}{2}$	0 $12\frac{1}{2}$	·60	
,, ,, .	12 noon.	109 ,,	7 14	1 $5\frac{1}{2}$	·50	
,, ,, .	3 P.M.	114 ,,	6 2	1 12	·40	
,, ,, .	6 ,,	90 ,,	4 8	1 10	·27	

Calculating by specific gravity, 10 lbs. of water, exposed on a circular base of 20·5 in. would give a depth of ·83 of an inch, and 4 lbs. 8 oz. of water would require a depth of ·37. The difference is ·46 by rough measurement. I made the difference ·38. This will give an evaporation of ·26 of an oz., or 4·16 drams of water per square inch in twelve hours, under the circumstances detailed.

Note.—As an evidence of the dangerous power of the sun's rays in India, Colonel Anderson states that some sporting powder, exposed at Dum-Dum in a chilumchee (a broad brass basin used for washing, in the apparatus of an Indian toilet) to the sun's rays, exploded in the presence of several gentlemen; some part of the polished metal no doubt acting as a reflector, and concentrating the rays on the powder.

I have myself experienced the danger of allowing globular glass bottles, filled with water, to stand in a place exposed to the sun's rays, both in India and at the Cape of Good Hope, the rays being concentrated into a focus, as with a burning-glass, and producing combustion both in cloth and wood.—EDITOR.

INQUIRY

INTO THE CIRCUMSTANCES ARISING FROM THE CHEMICAL EFFECTS OF THE PRODUCTS OF GUNPOWDER, WHEN FIRED IN CLOSE CHAMBERS, SUCH AS THE BORES OF CANNON, MUSKETS, &C.

THIS is a most important subject for an artillerist to study, and it appears to me to be a very singular omission, that in all chemical books, or others specially connected with the subject of gunpowder which I have had access to, this inquiry seems to have been generally entirely passed over, or by no means pursued and explained as it ought to have been.

About thirty-eight years ago, when I was in the situation of agent for gunpowder, and for the manufacture of war rockets of my construction, at Allahabad, in the Bengal Establishment, I made a great number of experiments with compositions resembling gunpowder, which were fired in various modes in close chambers, and I then became convinced that a true explanation of such combustion had, at that time, never been placed before the public, neither has it to the present day, so as to explain satisfactorily the phenomena presented.

For instance, it is commonly known to all practical artillerists, that a great increase in the quantity of gunpowder to that of a common charge does not produce that greater range of the projectile or shot placed before it that might have been expected; and this has generally been accounted for by the supposition that a great portion of this enlarged charge is blown out of the muzzle of the gun without being inflamed, but the circumstances to which I attribute the cause of its not being inflamed have never before been stated.

Again, it has been proved by experiment that cannon loaded to the muzzle, and afterwards closed up with an immovable plug, and fired in the usual manner at the vent, have neither been burst by the effect of the combustion, nor has the charge of powder exploded in the usual way, but has issued out of the small vent in a violent current of inflamed expanding gases, and occupying some seconds of time before the whole charge was consumed.

Such trials of an excessive quantity of powder so fired, have also, erroneously, in my opinion, been considered as proofs of the great strength in resistance to fracture, of cannon, fire-arms, or cylinders used in the experiments; and my reasoning is founded upon the explanation which I shall now proceed to offer, and, I trust, satisfactorily explain.

At another part of this work, the nature and analysis of the three components of gunpowder are stated; it is therefore unnecessary to enter on that subject here, as I wish to confine myself to the effect which the gaseous products of inflamed gunpowder produce at the moment of combustion.

Taking then the principal part of the volume of the gaseous product to consist of carbonic acid, carbonic oxide, and nitrogen gases, of which the former is much the greatest in quantity, we have a gaseous compound which is not only a non-supporter of combustion, but actually *extinguishes it*.

Thus, suppose we take an open-mouthed jar or receiver, filled with carbonic acid gas, which being more than half as heavy again as atmospheric air, will remain unmixed; if we introduce a burning body into it, even ignited phosphorus or sulphur, it will be immediately extinguished.

If we lay the finest ignitable tinder, or mealed or grained

gunpowder, on the bottom of the jar, and ignited particles of steel are struck off from a flint above the opening, their ignition and their luminosity instantly disappear directly they enter the gas, and neither the tinder nor the gunpowder will be fired.

If, in a volume of carbonic gas, under high pressure of several atmospheres, gunpowder is laid in a loose train, and the end of the train is fired by a hot iron or other means, the combustion will not proceed, and the rest of the gunpowder will remain unconsumed.

We have only therefore to consider, that the moment one grain is fired in a charge of gunpowder, it produces its volume of gas, and every contiguous grain, as it inflames, adds to this volume, so that the whole vacant space between the grains will become filled with it in a highly concentrated state, acting with a pressure of from 1500 to 2000 atmospheres. There can be no wonder then that the grains which are furthest from those first inflamed will not take fire under such a compression of a *flame-extinguishing gas*; hence if they are not driven out of the muzzle perfectly unignited, as many grains constantly are with every charge of gunpowder that is fired, yet, having been exposed to a heat of high intensity, *a portion of these*, meeting the atmosphere, the oxygen of which permits their combustion, will inflame, partly producing that flash of flame beyond the muzzle and over the vent which is seen at every discharge, but lending no assistance to the propelling power.

That many grains of gunpowder escape combustion altogether has been constantly proved. It was found to be so in Dr. Hutton's experiments at Woolwich. I have often proved it myself, and Major Alfred Mordecai, in his published experiments made at Washington Arsenal, in 1847-48, with a 6-pounder and a 12-pounder gun, records that in several instances the solid grains of gunpowder, unconsumed, reached the face of the ballistic pendulum placed at the distance of thirty feet from the muzzle of the piece of ordnance used.

In many instances where screens of paper or cloth have been placed over the vents at some feet distance, solid grains of gunpowder have passed through or been attached, quite uninflamed, though passing through the narrow space of a vent, under intense heat.

It may be considered a singular circumstance, but I have found some of these unconsumed grains, under examination, to have lost their portion of sulphur, which appears to have been volatilised by the heat, only the proper proportions of charcoal and saltpetre remaining in them.

It is a mistake, then, to suppose that an excessive charge of gunpowder is a proof of the power of resistance of the metal of a gun or cylinder, when the ends are closed up, and the escape of the expanding gases is only allowed through the vent :—the presence of the compressed volume of incombustible gases preventing the quick ignition of the grains. Yet this has been considered to be the case in regard to trials with the Armstrong, Whitworth, Blakeley, and other guns, as also by Mr. James Longridge, an eminent civil engineer, in his experiments on the strength of cylinders. The pressure under such trials, I believe, to have been far less severe than that which a cannon sustains when fired with a full charge, especially when rifled, and having a heavy weight or shot placed before it to be propelled.

It may be argued, that if the volumes of gases are extinguishers of combustion, as I represent them to be, the combustion of part of a large charge of powder would totally prevent the remainder being consumed; but we must recollect, that every grain of gunpowder contains within itself the elements of combustion, when exposed under common circumstances to a certain degree of heat, about 800°, necessary to cause the chemical affinities of the materials in its composition to enter into action: and as the heat of fired gunpowder is of far greater intensity, we can in no other possible way explain the circumstance of any grains being unconsumed, and especially as escaping through the small space and intense heat of a narrow vent, except the fact of their being encompassed with a highly compressed volume of non-combustible, flame-extinguishing gas, which prevents the charcoal and sulphur from being ignited, as they would certainly be if surrounded by atmospheric air; and to this cause we must attribute the retarded ignition of charges of gunpowder in pieces of artillery or cylinders closed at the ends, as above stated.

Now, the consideration of such circumstances is of great importance, not only in regulating charges of gunpowder, but also in the forms of the chambers in which it is confined to be exploded.

It has been generally supposed by writers on artillery subjects, that the flame of fired gunpowder penetrates immediately to the extremity of the charge, through the interstices between the grains, and thus ignites the whole charge; but if it was so, then in the instances of the experiments with the cannon having the muzzles plugged up as above stated, or the cylinders having the ends immovably closed, the ignition of the charges would not have been delayed, as it proves to be in such experiments, by, as I have before stated, the condensation of flame-extinguishing gas; and it is an argument that the quantity of atmospheric air contained between the grains, which may be increased by using cartridges, not filling the chamber, is advantageous, as yielding an additional supply of oxygen, the best supporter of combustion, which will, in a degree, neutralise the action of the carbonic acid gas, and consequently promote the quicker ignition of a greater quantity of the grains, producing a greater propelling power from the same charge of gunpowder than when less atmospheric air is present: and this has been found to be the case in actual artillery practice on the continent, and, I believe, at Woolwich, although the advantage gained has been attributed to a wrong cause.

I will merely add here, that in the year 1855, in the number of the Mechanics' Magazine for August, in a paper I wrote on the subject of projectiles, is the following paragraph :—

" Are we, therefore, at once to admit that there is a limit to the range to which we can throw a projectile by the means of gunpowder ? I say, certainly not. Whether it is one mile or twenty miles, the range can be effected. For it would be very easy to ignite the largest quantity of gunpowder that could be accumulated in one hundred points at once, by means of electrical action properly applied, and thus, instead of the slow progression of igniting by one vent or touch-hole, we should precipitate the production of the elastic gas one-hundredfold! The only difficulty would be to construct a piece of ordnance strong enough for the purpose; but this perhaps may be done, and the range of projectiles may be thus increased to distances never before contemplated."

By such means also, employing electricity to ignite a large charge in several places at once, we can overcome the natural obstacle to quick inflammation, which the carbonic acid and other gases present in long charges, and obtain that superior initial velocity in the projectile which seems to be the desire of the present day. And I am given to understand, that Sir William Armstrong used this means, having two electric wires to ignite the charge at different points, with the 12-pounder of his principle of construction, in the experiment at Shoeburyness, in April last, when he obtained an initial velocity with an 8-lb. shell and 2 lbs. of powder, of 1740 ft.

But I have also a project, by the complete alteration of the form of cannon, by which this desirable object may be obtained, which I shall bring forward, if suitable opportunity offers, at a future day.

Having thus stated my explanation of the circumstances which, I believe, have an important effect in the explosion of gunpowder, I will just refer to a printed paper which is laid upon a table in the Military Department of the International Exhibition, as the explanation of the retarding causes of the combustion of powder in narrow tubes may be derived from my theory.

Mr. Vallance heads his paper, which I give below, as describing his " patent improvements in placing and igniting the charge in fire-arms and ordnance," and he states as follows :—" When gunpowder, gun cotton, a mixture of hydrogen and oxygen gases, or other explosive compound, is placed in a narrow tube, and ignited at an open end, the explosion is changed from a sudden flash to a gradual and rocket-like combustion, and the narrower the tube, the slower is the charge in burning. By taking advantage of this, and placing the charge of a gun in a conical chamber, having the base of the cone at the furthest end from the muzzle of the gun, and igniting it in front, and so proportioning the diameter of the chamber and the angle of the cone to the length of the barrel as for the whole of the charge to be ignited just before the shot leaves the muzzle of the gun, the greatest velocity may be given to the shot, although very gradually started from a state of rest, and consequently the recoil of the gun, and the bursting strain on the barrel, may be reduced to a minimum.

"In this manner I have fired repeatedly three drams of powder, and two ounces of shot, from the thinnest drawn trumpet tube, with all the effect of the best fowling piece, and I have also fired from the shoulder many times a six-ounce bullet, and six drams of powder, without any unpleasant effect from the recoil."

I have given the whole paper, because I consider that experiments of this description are always worthy of notice and consideration, and as such I trust they will be considered by my readers.

If Mr. Vallance had stated any results of comparative trials of ranges, and penetration of bullet fired from his conical-chambered barrel, as compared with others of the common cylindrical bore, it would have been more satisfactory, as rapidity of ignition is certainly a prime element in causing the strain upon the metal of fire-arms, independent of other causes, as rifling, &c.

Such trials, among others also, are convincing facts that the proof of the strength, or propelling force of gunpowder by the Gun Éprouvette, is not to be depended upon, especially when different powders are examined in comparison, and some very singular effects were found to be produced when I made the following experiments with fired charges of gunpowder, which I will now relate.

I took a strong musket barrel, and removed the breech-plug. To make sure that the barrel was perfectly cylindrical, I passed a steel cylinder, armed with four well tempered steel cutters, through the barrel. This cylinder was mounted on an axis of sufficient length to be supported by sockets at each end, to each end of which, crank handles were attached, and by gradually turning the same, and moving the barrel horizontally, the interior was made truly cylindrical and polished. I then bored a small touch hole, exactly in the centre of the barrel, a cartridge containing three drams of powder was then introduced, and by regular measured rods placed exactly equi-distant from each end; steel plugs flat at the end next the cartridge, and acorn-shaped in front, were shoved down to the cartridge on each side. At the distance of 5 ft. from each end of the barrel, two stems of plantain trees, which were equally fresh, soft, and juicy, were cut off with perfectly flat faces, and placed as targets to receive the projectiles. The charge was fired by a match, and the two balls penetrated equally $17\frac{1}{2}$ in. into the stems of the plantains.

I then screwed in the breech plug, placed the cartridge next it, then the shot, and fired at the usual touch-hole, the ball having the range of the whole length of the barrel; the penetration was $29\frac{1}{2}$ in. This was repeated three times, with nearly similar results. A half cwt. of iron was placed against the breech, to prevent any recoil. I then placed the cartridge, the same weight of powder, in the middle, having stopped up the usual vent with a screw, and leaving the air only behind the cartridge. The charge was fired by the middle vent. The penetration of the shot was 28 in., or only slightly differing from the penetration when the shot was placed close to the breech, the air in the after part of the barrel acting like an elastic cushion, and, I think, greatly assisting the combustion of the powder, as the report was sharper, and I was surprised to find, on removing the heavy weight at the breech, and replacing it by lighter ones, that the force of the recoil was greatly weakened by this cushion of air, and that a weight of 7 lbs. completely sustained it.

To prove that the fire of an exploding cartridge, placed in the middle of this barrel, and fired, will not communicate its fire to another, placed at the end vent of the breech, I fired the central 'cartridge several times, without causing the explosion of that next the breech; and I conceive this circumstance to arise from the formation and compression of the carbonic gas preventing the fire being communicated.

I find by the American papers, that a young mechanic, of New York, Mr. Cochran, has invented and experimented with a cannon having a mechanical elastic cushion or volute spring behind the charge, and that his ranges are equal to those without it, if not superior, while the shock of the recoil is greatly lessened.

EDITOR.

GUN COTTON, OR PYROXYLE.

FROM COLONEL ANDERSON'S MSS.

ACCORDING to the investigation by Dr. W. B. O'Shaughnessy, of the Calcutta mint, this explosive material resolves itself into an acid nearly allied to the active principle of the fulminating powders, a species of cyanic acid.

Cyanogen is a compound of carbon and nitrogen, which, acidified by oxygen, compose cyanic acid, detonating and expanding under the operation.

Cotton is composed of carbon and water. One hundred parts of the best cotton are saturated with a mixture of equal measures of sulphuric and nitric acid; all superfluous acid being expressed by force, or neutralised. The cotton thus prepared and well dried, weighs 120 parts.*

The rationale of the explosion is thus proposed:—The sulphuric acid absorbs the water of the cotton, and leaves that substance as carbon to combine with the oxygen and nitrogen, which it does with detonation and force. Further investigation is not yet settled. The affinities come into action at a temperature of 375° Fahrenheit. A violent blow will also explode this substance.

$$\text{Cotton} \begin{cases} \text{Carbon} \\ \text{Water} \begin{cases} \text{Hydrogen.} \\ \text{Oxygen.} \end{cases} \end{cases}$$
$$\text{Nitric acid} \begin{cases} \text{Nitrogen.} \\ \text{Oxygen.} \end{cases}$$
$$\text{Sulphuric acid} \begin{cases} \text{Sulphur.} \\ \text{Oxygen.} \end{cases}$$

* There are various receipts for preparing this material.—EDITOR.

less dangerous than gun cotton, and is quite strong enough as a propellant for safe use with any cannon that have yet been made.

Reports, however, are constantly published in the public journals, either of some improvement in the preparation of gun cotton, rendering it more safe and suitable to fire-arms and artillery, or that some new preparations, no doubt deriving their propellant power from the same chemical principles, are to astonish the world as substitutes for gunpowder. Thus, only a few days back, in the "Times" and "Standard" of the 8th July, and other papers, there appeared the following :—

"GUNPOWDER SUPERSEDED.—Apart from the ancient discovery of Berthold Schwartz, and the more novel invention of gun cotton by Professor Schönbein, the feat has just now been repeated in another way by two officers in the Prussian and Austrian services. Of these Hauptman Schmidt, a captain of artillery at Berlin, is the original discoverer, whose idea was subsequently imitated and improved by Colonel von Uchatius. The latest explosive material consists of the flour of starch, which, boiled in a peculiar way with nitric acid, possesses a far greater projectile force than the gunpowder in ordinary use. It has also the great advantage of not fouling the piece to any appreciable extent, and, from the nature of the materials used, is produced at a far cheaper rate. Another point in its composition, which recommends it especially for fortresses and magazines, is the facility with which the ingredients are mixed together, thus rendering it possible to keep them separate until wanted for actual use. In this state the powder is non-explosive. The experiments now in course of progress in Vienna and Berlin, are said to leave little doubt as to its general adoption in the Austrian and Prussian armies."

From the preparation with nitric acid, and the vegetable matter acted upon, there can be little doubt that it assimilates to gun cotton; but it may still be doubted, until satisfactory experiments prove the contrary, if it will supersede the admirable and well-established agent for projectile force which gunpowder is universally acknowledged to be ; and the question may well be asked, would the wonderful exactness of the ranges of the rifles at

Wimbledon and elsewhere have been obtained, had charges of gun cotton been used?

Although it has been found that gun cotton does not generate so much heat as gunpowder when fired, and the residue it leaves is trifling, yet its chemical effect on iron or steel, if the moisture it forms is not carefully wiped out, would seriously damage the surface of the bore, and therefore be very injurious to rifled barrels, and it is probable that this new composition, having the same elements, would be equally deleterious.

EDITOR.

ATTEMPTS TO USE OTHER COMPOSITIONS AS SUBSTITUTES FOR GUNPOWDER.

NOTWITHSTANDING the acknowledged advantages of gunpowder, yet at various times experimentalists have, from different causes, endeavoured to form a substitute, some with a view to economy, others hoping to gain superior force.

The astonishing violence of the detonation of the fulminating powders made from metals, as gold, silver, and mercury, is found useless as a projectile force, and destructive to the tenacity of the metal of guns or cannon, and they are therefore well set aside; but we will notice below a few compositions that have been tried.

1st. Powder made with nitrate of soda.

This salt was used in the place of nitrate of potash, and a compound made with some proportions of sulphur and charcoal, as are usually employed in common gunpowder. It was found to inflame more difficultly, its detonation was weaker and slower, and its projectile force much less than that of gunpowder made with nitrate of potash. This salt also subdeliquesces on exposure to the air, so that no powder made with it would keep.

2. Powder made with nitrate of ammonia.

This composition was made at Essonne, in France, by Mons. Robin; but it was found that with a charge of 6 oz. the shell from a mortar was not projected.

The composition also inflamed very slowly, liquefying without detonating; it is also very deliquescent, its water of crystallisation cannot be separated without a difficult process, and it soon imbibes moisture on exposure to the air.

3. Powder made with oxymuriate of potash, or hyperoxymuriate of potash, now named chlorate of potash.

This astonishingly powerful compound was first made known by Bertholet, in 1785, who proposed to substitute it for common gunpowder. When Bertholet first formed this salt, he named it oxygenised muriate of potash—afterwards Mr. Kirwan shortened the term to oxymuriate of potash—because, as chlorine is produced by distilling black oxide of manganese and muriatic acid, Bertholet thought that it was a compound of muriatic acid and oxygen. But in 1809, Sir H. Davy proved that it contained no oxygen, and called it chlorine, from its yellow colour; and this term was afterwards adopted by chemists.

This discovery set aside at once the old opinion that any atmosphere which supported combustion was respirable and innoxious, and that without the presence of oxygen combustion could not take place, for if any animal inhales chlorine, in a pure state, it produces instant death, and some substances will inflame in it spontaneously.

What Fourcroy says of this salt will convey an excellent idea of its nature. (See Vol. iii. of his Chemistry.) He says, "that it appears to include the elements of thunder in its particles," and that "Nature seems to have concentrated all her powers of detonation, fulmination, and inflammation in this terrible compound." If three grains only of this composition are struck with a hammer upon an anvil, the report is as loud as that of a gun. There is great danger in mixing this composition, and too much circumspection cannot be used in making experiments with it. It explodes instantly on any violent stroke—often by friction only, and sometimes spontaneously, or when at a state of rest, and no known cause for its combustion can be ascertained. Several individuals have lost their lives, or been dreadfully wounded, in their attempts to manufacture gunpowder with this salt, and the lives of the two first workmen employed by Bertholet were sacrificed to the experiment; for immediately they began to triturate the ingredients, they exploded with dreadful violence, which destroyed the building, and proved fatal to these unfortunate men. This was in 1788, and the accident was supposed to have occurred principally from the ingredients not having been reduced to extreme tenuity, as subsequent trials have succeeded in manufacturing this dangerous compound without accident, and the above melancholy fate of the two workmen employed by Bertholet did not deter others from attempting the manufacture under careful precautions.

Mons. Riffault, one of the members of the Imperial Administration of Powder and Saltpetre in France, prepared, with great caution, about 8 oz., by slowly triturating the materials when moistened; he then formed it into grains by pressing it through a sieve, but he did not dare to dry it completely, and in this moist state, with a charge of 8 oz., he tried its force in an old mortar éprouvette, which, with a charge of 6 oz. of the best cannon powder, would project a solid globe 240 yards. The new composition threw the globe (with a velocity that the eye could hardly follow it in the air) to the distance of 500 yards, where it penetrated deep into the earth.

Mons. Cossigny made many experiments with this kind of gunpowder, using a process which seems to be almost free from any danger. He first made a strong solution of the salt in a certain quantity of water, then adding the proportions of sulphur and charcoal, and stirring the mixture gently, he evaporated the moisture to dryness.

His proportions were 75 chlorate of potash, $12\frac{1}{2}$ sulphur, and $12\frac{1}{2}$ of charcoal, in 100 parts.

He also tried to increase the force of gunpowder by substituting a portion of this salt for a part of the nitrate of potash.

First Experiment:—$37\frac{1}{2}$ parts of chlorate of potash, $37\frac{1}{2}$ of nitrate of potash, $12\frac{1}{2}$ parts of sulphur, $12\frac{1}{2}$ of charcoal.

The detonation of this was very strong, above that of common gunpowder.

Second Experiment:—3 parts of saltpetre; 1 of chlorate of

potash; 1 of sulphur; 1 of charcoal. The detonation of this was also very strong.

Third Experiment:—3 parts of saltpetre; 2 of chlorate of potash; 1 of sulphur; 1 of charcoal. This was stronger than the last, but when made without any saltpetre, the composition is strongest, being more than double that of gunpowder.

It was soon found, however, that fire-arms of the common standard would not sustain, without danger of bursting, the violence of the explosion, even with a small charge; and when the arms were made stronger, they were soon injured by the vehemence of the combustion, and its active oxidation of the metal.

Experiments were afterwards made with it for the purpose of firing a charge of common gunpowder in cannon and fire-arms by means of a priming of this compound, which should be exposed in a peculiar kind of lock to a violent blow.* It answered this end completely, but the vent and lock were soon oxidated by the small quantity thus used (only an eighth of a grain), and the danger attending the transport of this composition soon caused it to be abandoned, even for the purpose of priming, because a new preparation of silver was found to be superior for this purpose.

Several attempts were made under Bonaparte to make use of these gunpowders in his campaigns, and it is reported that, in one campaign, they were actually used.

It is certain, however, that the disadvantages and dangers attending the use of compositions containing chlorate of potash, greatly overbalance any advantages that can be gained from their superiority in projectile force.

A white powder for fulminating may be made from—

    Saltpetre . 3⎫
    Salt of tartar 2⎬ parts by weight.
    Sulphur . . 1⎭

A small quantity of this explodes with great violence, if ex-

---

* I suspect these experiments in France must have preceded the invention of the Rev. Mr. Forsyth for this purpose in England.

posed to a moderate heat for a quarter of an hour. Chlorate of potash and arsenic mixed, also inflame with astonishing quickness and incredible force. Many others might be named, but chemical works can easily be consulted for their prescriptions.—EDITOR.

REMARKS ON CHARCOAL.

THERE is, perhaps, no ingredient in the composition of gunpowder which is more important, supposing the others pure, than the charcoal. It has been remarked by French chemists, that the English use too much charcoal in the composition; and Chaptal, who searched carefully into the subject, says, the proportions which yield the best gunpowder are,

77 Saltpetre
14 Charcoal } "Chemistry Applied to the Arts," vol. iv. p. 142.
9 Sulphur

There is every reason to believe that these proportions of charcoal and sulphur might be advantageously introduced, and many private manufacturers in England have certainly done so.

Not only in France, but at Woolwich, Mr. Cruickshanks, who devoted much attention to the subject many years back, found on examining the residues of fired gunpowder, that the *unconsumed charcoal* amounted to, generally, one third of the quantity used in the composition. As the residue or foulness of the bores of cannon and fire-arms is of serious importance, now that we have rifles in common use with the army manufactured with the utmost truth and delicacy of bore, surely it would be as well if careful experiments were made on this subject, leading, perhaps, to a judicious improvement in our national gunpowder; and as charcoal is so high an absorbent of moisture, any reduction of its proportion would be highly important for sea service.

Chemical analysis must fail in exactly determining the best proportions of the ingredients for gunpowder made with varieties of charcoal.

Here may be remarked the effect in the loss of gas from the willow from overheating. I do not, however, consider this trial satisfactory, unless the composition was as intimately mixed and milled as it is in gunpowder; but it shows the great superiority of black dogwood in proportion to that of other woods.

I was in hopes of having obtained from France a statement regarding a peculiar preparation of charcoal for gunpowder by Mons. Violette, which is fully detailed in the Annales de Chimie et de Physique, Paris, 1848, in which the inventor has given a very ingenious mode of preparing charcoal, which he terms "charbon rouge," from its red appearance. It is made by passing superheated steam through the wood in the retort, until it is charred by a degree of heat not exceeding 400° of the centigrade thermometer, so as to preserve a portion of the hydrogen gas which, at a higher heat, would be driven off, and M. Violette, with powder made with this charcoal, obtained very high ranges in projecting shells and shot.

It has been stated, of late years, that the use of this charcoal for gunpowder in France has been given up, as it was injurious to the fire-arms, and I wished to learn whether this was the case, and what was the cause; whether the gunpowder was too strong for the guns, or whether it was from any deleterious action on the metal chemically; but I have not been able to obtain a satisfactory answer, or I should have described the whole process, as it seems an important one.—EDITOR.

REMARKS ON SIFTING AND SIZE OF GRAIN.
BY COLONEL ANDERSON.

The manufactories of gunpowder appear to work with different sieves.

Madras
- O. { 10, 14, 18 } Hence Madras O contains a great deal of larger and a portion of smaller grain than that of Bengal.
- M. { 18, 24, 30, 36 } The Madras M, uniformly smaller than that of Bengal.

Bombay
- O. { 10, 18 } As Madras.
- M. { 18, 36 } As Madras.   { 14 to 36 } are proposed, which will be very large musketry.

Bengal
- O. { 13, 17 } Small.
- M. { 17, 34 } Large.

England
- O. { 10, 24 } I suspect, more mixed, contains both larger and smaller than Bengal.
- M. { 24, 36 } Smaller than Bengal.

The following is the composition of the Ishapore powder, in sizes of grains:—

Sieves.	Ordnance two months old.	Density.	Ordnance sifted to utmost.	Musketry two months old.	Density.
5	—		—	—	
4	·86		·32	—	
3	·13		·61	·47	
2	·00		·06	·50	
1	·01		·01	·03	
Total	1·00	280	1·00	1·00	263

The Table below gives the result obtained by sifting English and Bombay powders:—

	English Ordnance 6 years old.	Density.	English Ordnance sifted to utmost.	Density.	Bombay Musketry, 5 years old.	Density.
5	·20		—		—	
4	·32		·59	English Musketry 6 years old.	—	
3	·33		·28		·35	
2	·1		·09		·45	
1	·05		·04		·16	
Dust	—		—		·14	
Total	1·00	272	1·00	267	1·00	254

I made the following experiments on the run from the Corning House:—

No. I.

COMPARATIVE PROOF OF GUNPOWDER taken at Ishapore on the 22nd of November, 1844, with powder of the different sizes of grain, that was passed through the upper and retained by the next lower sieve.

Description of powder.	Charge 1 lb. 65½ lbs. ball iron. dia. 7·85.	Charge 2 oz. 68 lbs. ball iron, dia. 7·92.	Remarks.
Ishapore powder of 1844-45. Large grain. Retained on No. 5 sieves.	Yards. 453	Yards. 77	KUNKUR. Firm sharp grain.
Ishapore powder of 1844-45. Retained on No. 4 sieve.	618	87	ORDNANCE. Similar and regular grain.
Ishapore powder of 1844-45. Retained on No. 3 sieve.	793	93	MUSKETRY. Long and flat, less round grain.
Ishapore powder of 1844-45. Retained on No. 2 sieve.	827	89	RIFLE. Rounder and smaller grain.
Ishapore powder of 1844-45. Retained on No. 1 sieve.	437	53	FINE. Dusty; brownish colour, small grain.
Dust, with a few minute grains . . .	288	35	DUST. Dust, with a few minute grains, brown colour.

The above powder was not glazed, nor winnowed on the drying terrace; hence the different kinds contain some small portion of dust.

No. II.

COMPARATIVE PROOF OF GUNPOWDER taken at Ishapore Powder Manufactory, on the 3rd December, 1844, with powder passed through the following sieves, all the larger grain extracted being the complement of the run of the Corning House.

Description of powder.	Charge 1 lb. with 65½ lb. ball iron, dia. 7·84.	Charge 2 oz. with 68 lb. ball, proof ball, dia. 7·93.	Remarks.
Powder as passed through the Corning House sieves	Yards. 685	Yards. 68	This contains O. M. R. F. Dust. Unglazed, colour dark brownish.
Ditto, ditto, No. 4 sieve .	678	76	This contains M.R.F. & Dust. Unglazed dark slate colour.
Ditto, ditto, No. 3 sieve .	486	52	This contains R. F. and Dust. Unglazed, dark black colour.
Ditto, ditto, No. 2 sieve .	340	38	This contains F. and Dust. Unglazed, black colour.
Ditto, ditto, No. 1 sieve .	356	43	This contains Dust. Unglazed, black colour.

Towards elucidating the question of grain, I also made the following combinations of various sizes and sorts :—

	8-in. mortar. Charge, 2 oz. 68 lb. ball.
	Yards.
Press cake, 10 pieces	12
,, 20 pieces	16
,, 30 pieces	20
,, 40 pieces	24
,, 50 pieces	27

Next from the common run of powder, giving an average to the officer on proof duty of ordnance, 96 yds., musketry 97. I made up 2 oz. charges in the following proportions :—

Ordnance . 96 ⎫ Average proof of officer on duty.
Musketry . 97 ⎭

Proportion. O. M. R.	Yards.	
$\frac{7}{8}$ $\frac{1}{8}$	105	
$\frac{6}{8}$ $\frac{2}{8}$	110	
$\frac{5}{8}$ $\frac{3}{8}$	102	
$\frac{4}{8}$ $\frac{4}{8}$	99	
$\frac{3}{8}$ $\frac{5}{8}$	92	Mortar No. 8, an average
$\frac{2}{8}$ $\frac{6}{8}$	90	mortar, was used.
$\frac{1}{8}$ $\frac{7}{8}$	96	
$\frac{2\cdot54}{8}$ $\frac{2\cdot54}{8}$ $\frac{2\cdot52}{8}$	96	
$\frac{4}{8}$ $\frac{2}{8}$ $\frac{2}{8}$	97	
$\frac{3}{8}$ $\frac{3}{8}$ $\frac{2}{8}$	89	
$\frac{2}{8}$ $\frac{4}{8}$ $\frac{2}{8}$	89	
$\frac{3}{8}$,, $\frac{4}{8}$	89	
$\frac{2}{8}$,, $\frac{5}{8}$	93	
$\frac{1}{8}$,, $\frac{6}{8}$	90	
1	92	

To indicate the improvement by a slight mixture of musketry with the ordnance powder; the difference would be infinitely more remarkable in long charges.

Sort of powder.	8-in. mortar. M. 2-oz. charge. 68 lb. ball.	Pendulum Eprouvette.	Density.	Remarks.
M. O.	Yards.	° ′		From a very inferior, bad
2 oz. ,,	66	23 1	256	mortar, rejected for
$\frac{5\cdot35}{8}$ $\frac{2\cdot65}{8}$	59	22 9	270	proof, No. 173.
$\frac{4}{8}$ $\frac{4}{8}$	66	21 21	274	This mortar is 20 yards
,, 2 oz.	69	20 29	276	in range, inferior to
$\frac{2\cdot65}{8}$ $\frac{5\cdot35}{8}$	70	21 6	280	No. 8.

There is an indication of the Eprouvette arc, falling progressively with the density and with the larger grain.

The mortar range with 2 oz. rising with the density and with the larger grain.

To ascertain how far the mixture and size of grain caused the difference between Ishapore and English ordnance powders, I compounded some Ishapore of the same quantities of the same sizes as the English; the result was—

	8-in. mortar. 2-oz. charge. 68 lb. ball.	Pendulum Eprouvette.	
	Yards.		
English war powder 6 years old . .	107¼	22 1'	
Ishapore similar to the above . .	91¾	20 11	

So that other cause for the difference must be found than the variation in sizes, and quantities of grain.

This must be in the density of the cake, or in the weakness of the Bengal charcoal.*

ACCIDENTS.
BY COLONEL ANDERSON.

IN the manufacturing an article of the explosive nature of gunpowder, serious and fatal accidents may be expected and will occur. These have certainly taken place in the Ishapore works, but perhaps, in proportion, less than in works of a similar nature in other countries.

In former days, when pilon mills were in use, under common bamboo huts, and worked by old women and children, these explosions were constantly occurring; but in later years they have been few, and resolvable into two kinds: those from accidental presence of fire, and those from a second cause, not quite determined.

To those of the first kind there is no limit but under care and prudence.

With reference to the arrangement of the works, it is wonderful that they do not more often take place.

* See Appendix, my remarks on Charcoal.—EDITOR.

When the gloom stove was used to dry the powder, a spark once found entrance,* and the whole place was blown up with serious loss.

At Allahabad, in 1823, a long string of men was carrying barrels of powder to the drying terrace; it was supposed that one man let a barrel fall, and the whole quantity of the powder exploded, killing some men, and all the others were much burnt. Unfortunately the fire communicated to the press house and one of the counting-houses, at that time constructed of thin boards, thus sadly increasing the effect of the disaster.

The friction of the corning house wheels at Ishapore has twice caused explosion, which, considering their velocity, is not to be wondered at.

The explosion constantly of either the mixing barrels or mills, excited my curiosity, and I attempted to examine the cause. This had been identified by several agents with friction with bits of wood, or stone, or copper ; with wilful neglect or intention on the part of the workmen, and to every cause but the correct one, of concussion.

This having been denied at the commencement as a possible cause by Colonel Galloway, has since been disallowed by all ; but I made the experiment, and found it was facile in the extreme, with a very slight blow, to ignite gunpowder placed between different substances.

To a committee sent up to Ishapore by Government, I proved that, with gunpowder placed as follows, the results were,—

Iron upon iron { 5 misses / 45 explosions }
Brass on iron { 3 misses / 47 explosions } With a hammer about 4 lbs.
Iron on brass { 9 misses / 41 explosions } in weight.
Brass on brass { 20 misses / 30 explosions }

I had previously tabulated all the mill explosions I could find recorded, and had traced them to this cause of concussion on heated dry composition.

* Or perhaps it was overheated.—EDITOR.

This cause also accounts for the firing of the mixing barrels in the direct impingements of one brass ball on another.

TABLE OF MILLS EXPLODED.

Month and Date of Explosion.	No. of Mill.	Time of Explosion.	Remarks.
1821. May 9th	No. 3	9 a.m.	By lightning.
1822. Jan. 16th	No. 2	10 a.m.	
1823. Nov. 17th	No. 3	2 p.m.	
1833. ,, 30th	No. 3	12 noon.	Charge out.
1834. April 5th	No. 2	8 p.m.	[dry.
1835. April 3rd	No. 2	10 a.m.	1836. Cylinders sent to foun-
1840. Dec. 2nd	No. 1	4 p.m.	Charge just put in.
1842. Dec. 6th	No. 4	8 a.m.	Charge out.
1843. March 1st	No. 4	7 p.m.	
1844. April 3rd	No. 2	1½ p.m.	
1847. Jan. 5th	No. 3	4½ p.m.	} Only thus far was com-
1847. Oct. 31st	No. 5	12 noon.	mented upon.
1848. Oct. 27th	No. 5	4½ p.m.	Charge just put in.
1848. Nov. 23rd	No. 5	3 p.m.	,, half worked off.
1848. Nov. 25th	No. 1	2¾ p.m.	15th revolution.
1849. Feb. 24th	No. 4	9 p.m.	Charge half worked off.

ABSTRACT.

Years and No. of Explosions.		Months and No. of Explosions.		Hours and No. of Explosions.			Mills Exploded and No. of Explosions.
1821	1	January	2	A.M.	1	0	
1822	1	February	0·1		2	0	
1823	1	March	1		3	0	
1833	1	April	3		4	0	
1834	1	May	1		5	0	
1835	1	June	0		6	0	
1840	1	July	0		7	0	1—1·1
1842	1	August	0		8	1	2—4
1843	1	Sept.	0		9	1	3—4
1844	1	October	1·1		10	2	4—2·1
1847	2	November	2·2	P.M.	11	0	5—1·2
1848	0·3	December	2		12	2	6—
1849	0·1				1	1	7—
					2	1·1	
					3	0·1	
					4	2·1	
					5	0	
					6	0	
					7	1	
					8	1	
					9	0·1	
					10	0	
					11	0	
		*	*		12	0 *	
12·4		12·4			12·4		12·4

N.B.—There were only 4 mills working up to 1836; 5 mills to 1846; 6 mills to 1847.

* The second column are the additions after the report was submitted to Military Board.

We will now proceed to examine these facts, and, if possible, deduce from them some cause of these explosions, and, perhaps, eliminate their laws.

First, as regards the years. I believe, in 1820, that these mills began to work. From 1823 to 1833, I can trace no explosion. During a portion of this period, from 1828 to 1832, the works were closed, and for the whole period, my records are not very complete. From 1835 to 1840, we miss the almost annual explosion, for this reason, at the close of the season of 1835, the whole of the cylinders, axles, washers, &c., &c., were sent down to the foundry of Fort William to be refitted. The faces of the cylinders from use, having become highly concave, were turned to their original and proper form, of slightly convex.

As long as this new surface lasted, nearly five years, we have no explosions, but in 1840 they commence to reappear in their usual ratio. In 1844 I took much care, with my imperfect means, to reduce the beds to a water level, but could not turn, from want of power, the faces of the cylinders. For three years we had no explosions, but now, in 1847, they are commencing to reappear.

All this goes towards a proof, that a perfectly level bed, and convex face of the cylinder, are to be desired, and that the reverse are a cause of explosion.

This is also in accordance with the best evidence I can obtain on this subject, viz., the conversation in the hospital of the men who had suffered from the explosions, as from time to time gathered by our intelligent native doctor, Gunga Saugor.

He states all the men to say, that explosions take place from any sudden fall of the cylinder on the bed,* or any sudden contact between the raised edges of the cylinders and the high edge of the bed ; that this is their fear ; no danger being apprehended when the cylinders are once fairly in motion, moving over a good deep mass of damp composition.

* A singular accident is stated in the "Mechanics' Magazine" of the explosion of a cylinder mill at Hounslow, in confirmation of this cause of explosion, from a cricket-ball having been struck from a distance, and falling into the trough of the runners as they were moving.—EDITOR.

That a fear of explosion is always present in their minds during the first transfer of the cylinders from the old mill charge to the dry, fluffy, new composition ; that at this point, or near it, take place all explosions, a fact proved here by a reference to the abstract of mills and hours.

In regard to the months, we notice that the fewest explosions are at the cool, low temperature of February and March ; while the greatest number occur in the hot month of April ; hence may be inferred that dryness of atmosphere and of composition are disposing causes of explosion.

In regard to the hours, a most curious and highly interesting feature is brought forward—that, of all these explosions, not one has taken place during the night ;* all of them, but one, at the hours of changing charges, and chiefly during the latter portions of the day. Had negligence or want of care been a cause, assuredly during the inefficient light and want of superintendence during the night, more explosions would have taken place than during the day, but for the dampness of the atmosphere.

Hence I again argue, that dryness of composition and the act of changing charges, are truly predisposing causes.

In regard to the mills, Nos. 2 and 3 have exploded more than three times oftener than any other, because always used for the dust, and hence, having the charge changed about three times as often in them as in any other mill, dust only receiving one-sixth of the revolutions of fresh composition.

The system of watering is to be considered, and runs thus :

First starting.	At 30 revolutions.	At 100 revolutions.	At 150 revolutions.	At 200 revolutions.	At 250 revolutions.
0	½ seer.	½ seer.	½ seer.	½ seer.	½ seer or more, according to weather.

Hence the cylinders first start on perfectly dry composition, of the most minute particles.

From these simple facts I deduce, that the heat of the atmo-

---

* The great discovery of Professor Schönbein, of Bâle, of nascent oxygen, called ozone, has awakened much inquiry in its relation to the phenomena of combustion and explosion ; and as the quantity varies greatly in different months, and is more diffused in the day than in the hours of night, it is very probable that it is intimately connected with the explosions of gunpowder mills.—EDITOR.

sphere and dryness of composition are predisposing causes, and the contact of the cylinders and bed the active cause of these explosions; that the latter again exists in the want of level in the beds and convex face to the cylinder.

A further inspection of the table shows another feature illustrative of the correctness of the idea of the contact of the edge of the cylinders being the cause of explosion; viz., that we find the same will continue to explode in succession.

I have no doubt it would do so week after week, as fast as renewed, if some change was not made in the bed or in the cylinders. The bed and cylinders rub down into hollows, which containing the mass of composition, allows the cylinder to drop from a strata of composition on the bare bed, when the mill explodes.

This is believed to be caused by some accident, the mill is rebuilt, and again explodes, when some change is made; thus I am informed, after No. 2 had twice exploded, all the cylinders for the eight mills were refaced at Cossipore. After No. 4 had twice exploded, its cylinders were changed for newly faced ones. Now No. 5 has exploded thrice, I shall take it to pieces.

In 1836 all the cylinders for the eight mills were refaced. On my arrival, in 1843, only one of these sets remained untouched; therefore, in seven years, although only working five mills, my predecessors had used up the faces of cylinders for seven mills. From 1836 to 1843, eight years, my predecessors appear to have made 64,277 barrels of gunpowder, experienced three explosions, and used up the faces of the two pair of spare cylinders.

From 1844 to 1848, five years, I have made 52,397 barrels of powder, and had six explosions, and used up no spare cylinders, and this with machinery that, since its last re-setting up, had previously worked eight years, and is now thirteen years unset up.

Tables and drawings of the present state of the mills were sent to the Military Board.

No old copper or brass should ever be worked up in powder-works (such always contain the points of steel files and grains of filings, calculated to strike fire—I have seen a magnetic instrument for extracting such steel), but only new metal should be used.

ON THE MODERN IMPROVEMENTS IN ARTILLERY AND FIRE-ARMS.

It is a singular circumstance, that in the comparatively new country of the American Union improvements in cannon and fire-arms have preceded those of the old nations of Europe.

Thus in the last American war the successes against our troops were greatly owing to the skill with which their countrymen used the rifle, while our soldiers, generally, were only furnished with the common musket.

We find also that ships covered with iron plates, to be impelled as rams by steam power, and formidable floating batteries in iron-plated steam vessels, in which the heavy guns were partly worked by steam power, as Stevens's, originated, or, at any rate, were first brought into practical use, by the Americans.

It is true, that proposals for iron-plated vessels had been made by French officers of the navy, and by the celebrated General Paixhans many years back to the French Government, which were rejected by the official committee appointed to examine the project; and probably if we could ransack the old records in our public military and naval departments, where many a good principle or suggestion is now dwelling in cobwebby existence, we might perhaps claim precedence as to time; but our Transatlantic brethren were the first to bring them into useful form; and, notwithstanding the unhappy war which is now devastating that fine country, the Americans are still proceeding with their experiments and improvements; and, perhaps, without wishing to depreciate the many ingenious inventions and beautiful workmanship of English and Scotch gunmakers, Storms's American breech-loading rifle, lately invented and brought over to the International Exhibition, may be considered as the simplest, strongest, and most handy of any breech-loading fire-arm that has yet been brought before the public,[*] and we must not be

[*] Since this was written, I find that the inventor has received a medal for this arm from the Commissioners of the International Exhibition.

forgetful of the American improvements, both in machinery and weapons, of the late Colonel Colt.

In France, under Napoleon I., there were no great or decided improvements in the construction of artillery or fire-arms made, if we except the Paixhans gun and the elongated mortars; but in the reign of Louis Philippe, under the Duke of Orleans, several advances took place in 1837-38, and in the year 1848 the French had at least 16,000 men of their numerous army provided with improved rifles. In the year 1842, Monsieur Tamisier, who had been formerly a captain of artillery in the French service, was in charge of a course of instruction in musketry at Vincennes, and he constructed a rifled mortar with cylindro-conical shells to be propelled from it. The young Duke de Montpensier, then colonel of artillery, at once saw the importance of the project, and earnestly promoted it; but it must not be allowed that this Captain Tamisier was the first to propose rifled cannon, as has been asserted by some writers, as in the records of our Patent Office, amongst others, may be found a patent taken out by Mr. James Bodmer, dated 23rd November, 1813, for a method of loading cannon at the breech, rifled or plain bore, and a plate showing the spirals in the bore for rifling, accompanies the specification.

From Captain Tamisier's various improvements in introducing elongated shot for rifles both for cannon and fire-arms, we may, however, trace the progress of improvement in France; and much is due to the encouragement given him by the Duke de Montpensier's causing many experiments to be made at his own expense (in 1847) in the construction of Captain Tamisier's elongated shot and shells, in which he satisfied himself of their superior range and efficacy; the project dropped for a time, but in 1850, under Napoleon III., it was revived, and it was proved at Vincennes, that with elongated projectiles, thrown from a 6-pounder rifled bore, extraordinary, accurate, and extended ranges were made. Thus a 6-pounder rifled bore, with three grooves, projected elongated shot to a range of 1500 mètres, with a charge of 700 grammes of powder; and so great was the success of the continued experiments there, and at other places in France, that the Army of Italy brought into the field more than 200 rifled guns of a calibre of 84 millimètres, requiring, for service, only two-thirds of the men and horses usually employed with guns of the same calibre of the old construction, and these field guns projected balls of 4 kilogrammes, 3500 mètres, with such precision as to fall at that range within the area of a rectangle 80 mètres long and 40 broad.

Prussia, in 1848, had 60,000 men armed with the needle rifle, which, though not a perfect weapon, was a great improvement on their old fire-arms; and rifled and breech-loading cannon are now engaging the earnest attention of their Government.

The Austrians, Belgians, Germans, Danes, Russians, Spaniards, Italians, &c., are all providing themselves with improved cannon and fire-arms; and it may be remarked, that in the International Exhibition there is an extraordinary variety of construction from almost all the States of continental Europe.

It is well known that Great Britain, of late years, has not been behind other nations in this military display; and as to workmanship, it cannot be disputed that our experienced workmen, under able and scientific directors, stand first in the list of comparison.

It would be difficult, laborious, and, perhaps, considered an invidious task, to search into and endeavour to explain the construction and the merits of the varieties of military weapons now placed before the public in the International Exhibition; and it would be impossible to state their relative values justly, without the necessary trials under the action of gunpowder.

I may, however, remark in this place, that as an entire change has been effected, or is now taking place, in almost every department of the science of war, those nations that are neglectful, or remain unprepared in this advance,—if unfortunately they become involved in hostilities,—must suffer the evil consequences of such neglect. Those who depend upon the traction of horses for conveyance, cannot attempt to compete with the railroad speed of the present day; neither can the less powerful cannon and fire-arms of comparatively very recent date, be now brought into the field with any chance of success ; and, moreover, *the stream of advance and improvement is yet moving on!*

Only a few years ago, from the great improvements in the rifle, it was supposed that field artillery would become of greatly less importance, as the artillerymen could be struck down by the certain aim and accuracy of the rifle ball, at distances where the projectiles commonly used with cannon would be of little avail. It was supposed that by building wooden ships of war of large size (too large to enter most of our harbours), carrying formidable batteries of numerous heavy guns, a few broadsides would effect the destruction of an enemy's ship or fort ; but the improvements in the range and accuracy of cannon, as well as the projectiles used with them, are now fully keeping pace with those of smaller fire-arms ; and plated iron ships, steam rams, and a few, but heavier, pieces of ordnance, will supersede the continuance of the "wooden walls" which have been so long and so worthily our national pride.

In naval and land battles, therefore, as well as in our system of fortification, great changes must necessarily take place ; and it requires no argument to prove, that to be effective against iron-plated ships, we must have more powerful ordnance, and probably abandon the old plan of placing guns on ramparts to fire through embrasures, by which defective plan ships can run up close to the batteries, exposed to the fire of only a fraction of the number of guns planted upon them. The ramparts should be plain, and the cannon defended by moving cupolas, or shields, with proper traverses between each gun, to prevent the effects of enfilade, and to protect the unemployed gunners and those that serve the ammunition, and only high enough for those purposes. Thus the guns will be "*en barbette,*" and by having no limitation as to their lateral range, can bring the whole force of the artillery into play on any front attacked by land or sea.

A few powerful guns will then be able to effect all that can now be expected from a great number of cannon firing through embrasures.

There are now at least four serious questions the subjects of controversy and experiment relating to artillery and fire-arms.

First.—Whether cannon should be of solid metal, cast or otherwise; or whether they should be built up; or a combination of separate parts?

Secondly.—Whether to be rifled or smooth bore?

Thirdly.—Whether they shall be muzzle or breech-loading?

Fourthly.—The best form of projectile.

It is evident that experience, and trials with charges of fired gunpowder, and suitable projectiles, can alone settle these questions satisfactorily, and as our Government authorities are now directing such experiments to be made at Woolwich and Shoeburyness, with a liberal expenditure, and under able and scientific artillery officers, there is no doubt the result will be satisfactory to the nation; and we trust that the several experiences gained by such trials may be open to public inspection, or at any rate to those who have the interests of the nation at heart, and are engaged, mentally or experimentally, in such improvements.

It was the remark of Mr. Rennie, the celebrated engineer, in a public discourse relating to architecture, "that more useful lessons were given by *failures in construction* than by records of successful inventions." And this truth is peculiarly applicable to military science, both in theory or in practice.

As regards the first question, there can hardly be a doubt, that from the great skill, science, and practical abilities of Sir William Armstrong, Mr. Whitworth, Captain Blakeley, and the several great practical metal working companies that have taken up the subject of forming built-up cannon, all that can be accomplished has been, or will be, obtained; but at present it must be considered as an unsettled question, while there is every reasonable hope, from the great improvements in the manufacture of iron and steel under the Mersey Steel and Iron Works, the Bessemer, and other processes, that solid guns will be produced quite equal to any service that can be required from them; and though it is true that built-up guns, carefully manufactured, have stood very severe proofs, and admirable scientific theories have been advanced by Captain Blakeley and others in their favour, yet from the very nature of metal, there must be a want of perfect combination and solidity in the different parts, which the vibration of large charges of powder, constantly applied, will tend to increase, so that the question of durability, probably, may still rest with the solid gun after much service.*

The second question, whether they shall be rifled or smooth bore?

The experiments made by Robins in the Charter House Garden of London more than one hundred and twenty years ago, first brought to public notice the true cause of the deflection of round balls, from the looseness of their fitting, and consequent windage. The friction and striking against the interior of the cylinder through which round shot are propelled, causing a motion of rotation on their axes, at right angles to the line of flight; and, by chance, from the position of the last point of contact just before quitting the muzzle of the piece, this axis of rotation may be perpendicular, horizontal, or inclined ; and thus from the unequal action of the air on the frontal surface of the ball, one side, or half the hemisphere turning towards, and the other half turning from the line of resistance, such shot are deflected, upwards, downwards, or laterally from the proper or intentional line of flight ; and although the experiments of Professor Magnus of Berlin and others dispute this theory, yet it is sufficiently true to stand.

* Although the practice of making built-up cannon is of very early date, yet to Mr. Longridge, C.E., and to Captain Blakeley must be given the merit of working out the theory, and putting on record the reasons for, and the possibility of, forming strong cannon on the built-up principle of construction; and as Captain Blakeley's guns have stood the severest trials by fired gunpowder, and are justly in repute and demand, both at home and abroad, in several of the European continental nations, as well as in America, I am happy to find that the Jury of the International Exhibition has awarded him a medal for investigating the true relation between the sizes of the inner and the outer tubes, on which the strength of the principle of construction depends ; and I am informed by Captain Blakeley that a built-up gun of 7 inches diameter can be made for less than half the price of the solid forged one, and one of 13 inches diameter at less than a quarter the price of one forged solid.

It is true that this rotation might be prevented, as well as the loose fitting of a round shot, by attaching an expanding bottom, or sabot, preventing all windage, and the contact of the surface of the shot with that of the bore, as has been done by Mr. Bashley Britten and others; but still this would not embrace all the advantages of rifling, for by adopting this we are able to use elongated shot, which having the same, or greater weight than round shot, and being of less diameter, consequently meet with less resistance than round shot in passing through the air.

There are also other advantages in the extended ranges of rifle balls, as well as their accuracy, which must be considered in favour of using rifled barrels.

As the rifle ball in its flight rotates upon an axis coinciding with its own elongated axis, and, if properly fitted, with the axis of the bore of the piece from which it is discharged, this gyratory motion, when the piece is fired at a low elevation, from the axis of the projectile being inclined to the direct line of resistance, will cause it to be partially supported, as long as the rotation is sufficient, against the constant force of gravitation; and thus its range, although moving with less velocity than a round shot, will be proportionally prolonged and extended.

It has also been found by experiment that the velocity and consequent momentum of a projectile from a rifle increase for a short distance after it has left the muzzle of the piece from which it is discharged, which can only be accounted for by the resistance it meets with in its passing along the bore preventing the maximum of the propellant power of the fired powder being displayed for certain moments of time, till it has completed a part of its course. We have, besides the resistance offered by the spirals of the rifling, to consider the great compression, and consequent condensation of the column of air in a barrel as it is driven before the shot until it escapes from the muzzle, so that, all at once, it starts into a comparatively rarefied medium, and escapes from a spring, as it were, which held it back. At least, I thus attempt to explain this curious phenomenon, though I am not quite satisfied with the explanation, and the subject will, I hope, be one of scientific investigation and experiment.*

The question of the advantages of rifled barrels over smooth bores may be considered as settled, as far as fire-arms and the smaller description of cannon; but for heavier guns, from the loss of velocity in the shot, and the violent additional strain which a large gun with a heavy elongated shot receives when rifled, there is every reason to suppose that the smooth bore will be preferred for a portion at least of the heavy ordnance we now require.

Thirdly, whether they shall be muzzle or breech-loading ?

If we may judge from the patterns of our own country, and those of foreign nations, in the International Exhibition, the excess in number of the breech-loading principle evinces a general desire to form both small arms and cannon on this plan.

The advantages of breech-loading are eminent; and if the difficulties of construction, so as to ensure safety and durability without a complication of parts, can be overcome with our larger cannon, as they are already accomplished with fire-arms and moderate-sized guns, the general adoption of breech-loading to all fire-arms will be certain to follow.

The advantages of breech-loading are so great that its opposers generally can only advance as the principal argument against it, that the soldiers would be inclined to waste their ammunition from firing too rapidly; but discipline would soon overcome this, and therefore the objection is not worth consideration. We may state as the advantages; first, with regard to cannon, greater safety and protection to the artillerymen† and guns, because there need be

* Another explanation of this phenomenon may be, that when a rifle projectile first leaves the barrel the greatest quantity of rotary motion which the spirals of the bore cause is imparted to it: this will be the cause of violent friction on its exterior by the air it is passing through, and its quickness of rotation is certain from this cause to be diminished, and, with its diminution, also a certain quantity of resistance to the velocity of the projectile; and thus, until the shot has gained the maximum of the momentum impressed upon it by the fired gunpowder of the charge, its velocity and consequent momentum may be increased, to a certain extent of range, after leaving the muzzle of the piece from which it is projected.

† Such an unhappy and fatal accident as that which occurred at Blyth, the

less exposure, and protection by shields, &c., can be easily made ; greater ease and facility in loading and firing; fewer men are required to keep up an effective fire and serve the gun than with muzzle-loaders ; fewer loose implements are required ; and the advantages of rifling in stopping the windage by an expanding sabot or wadding more effectually and simply obtained. The heating of the chamber of the piece, from successive quick discharges, is comparatively trifling : and with cupola ships breech-loading cannon can hardly be dispensed with. With small arms, the facility of loading on horseback, the loss of the ramrod, or reversal of the cartridge, which in the hurry and confusion of the battle-field often occurs—for a time disabling the piece—cannot take place with a breech-loader.

Some objectors consider that heavy cannon cannot be made with sufficient solidity to resist the powerful strain at the breech and chamber of the exploding powder. I think this may be overcome by taking the support of the breech-plug from the trunions, by carrying a heavy and solid strap, embracing them behind the breech. I imagined that this plan had not been tried, and submitted one of this description to the War Office, which was sent to the Select Committee at Woolwich, whose reply was that the plan had been tried and failed. After I had submitted that, I found Captain Blakeley had one on a similar principle, and there is a very beautiful small model of a gun so formed amongst the Bessemer steel trophy in the International Exhibition.

With all deference to the Select Committee, I am of opinion that it is the best plan of sustaining the recoil of the breech-plug, and that if the *cause* of its failure, when tried, was explained, perhaps a modification of it would ensure success.

Fourthly, the best form of projectile ?

This opens several important questions :

The nature of the rifling and closing of the windage.

The purpose for which the projectile is intended.

other day, by which two esteemed young men lost their lives, who belonged to the 3rd Northumberland Volunteer Artillery, could not have taken place with a breech-loading gun.

VARIOUS PLANS OF RIFLES.

The resistance of the air.

The position of the centre of gravity, &c.

It is evident that experiment can best decide these questions, and from the wonderful accuracy which has attended the practice at targets with rifled small arms at Hythe, Wimbledon, and other places and with projectiles so differently shaped and formed as the Enfield, the Jacob, the Lancaster, and the Whitworth shot, it does not appear that there is cause for much difference of choice, but from what I hear from the riflemen, for long distances, there is a leaning in favour of the Whitworth shape.

It is indeed a matter of wonder that such perfect accuracy at ranges of 800 and 1000 yards should be obtained, that some of the skilful marksmen could, at these distances, hit the centre of the target, or the bull's-eye, several times in succession; and leaving out of the question the merit of the shooter, such accuracy reflects the highest credit on our national and private manufacturers of rifles, and on the excellence and uniformity of the propelling property of our gunpowder.

With the Jacob rifle, with four grooves cut rather deep, having a shot formed with four projections to fit them, and with the centre of gravity nearer the rear end of the shot than the point, the most accurate ranges are obtained from 1200 to 1400 yards, the pointed end of the shot still maintaining its true position in striking the target! This rifle has four-fifths of a turn in 24 inches, the length of the barrel.

The Enfield rifle, with the Pritchett ball, or, I believe, with a ball slightly improved by General Hay, also makes excellent practice. It has three grooves, cut slightly deeper at the breech than at the muzzle, and the spiral makes one revolution in 78 inches, the barrel being 3 feet 3 inches long, and the shot of less weight than General Jacob's, has its centre of gravity near the middle of its length.

The Whitworth rifle is used with a hexagonal shot, well fitted to his hexagonal shaped bore, and makes one turn in 20 inches, and I believe Mr. Whitworth has lately introduced a quicker spiral, even to one turn in 16 inches, which the solid form of his shot, and its flat pressure upon the faces of the hexagon, enables him to do, but such quickness of turn would probably be destructive to a soft metal shot with shallow or deep grooves. The centre of gravity in Mr. Whitworth's shot is towards the head of the shot, a little in advance of the centre.

Mr. Lancaster's plan is to use a slightly elliptic bore, with a corresponding elongated shot to fit. He gives one turn in 32 inches; and the most accurate practice and great length of range have been obtained with his rifles.

Here, then, we have four different kinds of rifles, having different quicknesses of spiral, and shot of quite different forms, yet all making excellent practice; and therefore with small arms it does not appear that any one has great superiority over the other; but when we approach the subject of rifling heavy guns or cannon, the nature of the rifling, and the shape of the shot so as to give the least resistance in moving through the air, and the least strain upon the gun at starting, are circumstances of serious consideration.

Mr. Whitworth, in the specification for his patent "for improvements relating to elongated projectiles," states that according to the purpose to which they are to be employed, the fore part may be more or less pointed, or curved, or flat-fronted, having the rear part of his shot, behind the centre of gravity, *tapering to the rear*. And he states that compared with his projectiles formerly used, which had pointed fronts, and non-tapering rears, that the former, that is tapering to the rear, give from one-fourth to one-third greater ranges. He uses a flat end to the taper, as that shape, he asserts, gives greater steadiness to flight.

Now this tapering to the rear is a subject of serious consideration when we want *velocity of flight*, and I advocated this principle in a paper written in the "Mechanics' Magazine," in August, 1855, and in a lecture at the United Service Institution, as a form which the prime instructor, nature, teaches us, in the shapes of birds and fish; and the idea was afterwards taken up by Mr. Bridges Adams and others. From the great advantage of this shape, that by a proper non-metallic wadding, all the advantages of rifling, and perfect protection to the bore of the gun from injury by a solid hard metal shot, can be obtained, I consider will only be a work of time to demonstrate; and experience alone is wanting to establish the superiority of *rear-tapering shot*.

The form and grooves of a rifled barrel, as well as slowness or quickness of turn, though not of much importance in small barrels having to propel but a moderate weight of projectile, are of serious consideration when, in large cannon, that weight is greatly increased.

With all rifles, however, it may be laid down as a rule, that with increased quickness of turn the length of the barrel may be reduced; and that as the length of the projectile is increased, the greater should be the quickness of the turn, to ensure its most perfect direction. It is evident, however, that with this increase of quickness of turn, whatever may be the shape of the grooves, and whether numerous or few in number, the strain on the metal of a large gun must be dangerously increased.

If the grooves, or mode of rifling in a large gun, also, are so formed as to cause the action of the projectile to assume the lateral force of a wedge, as it appears to me the projectile of the Lancaster gun will do, then it must produce a dangerous strain, liable to burst the metal open, in addition to the expanding force of the gunpowder; and all rifled cannon, having their grooves formed with inclined planes, not perpendicular to the radii of the circle of the bore, must have the same dangerous tendency.

If rifling is continued to large guns, experiment alone can determine that form which can be used with the greater safety, and the best effect; it is not yet a settled question, and it is evident that different lengths of shot should be used—one kind if long, another if short ranges are required.

The great variation in the rifled ordnance, and the forms of the projectiles used, seem to determine that the question of superiority is not yet decided.

The disparity in the proportions of the thickness of metal about the breech end,* where the first and greatest strain

* Alluding to the cannon shown in the International Exhibition.

of the exploding charge is sustained, is remarkable. In the Whitworth and some other guns, in consequence of the small quantity of metal about the breech, I should be inclined to think there is a mistake in the construction; for, leaving out of the question the greater strength required in that part of the gun, it is no longer doubted, I believe, that by throwing an excess of weight of metal into the breech, the recoil is less violent, and the precision of fire more certain; and General Jacob expressly states, that if twice the usual quantity of metal is interposed between the chamber and the false breech, the recoil of the most ponderous rifle need not exceed that of an ordinary fowling-piece.

The same principle applies to cannon, whatever their size may be.

The question may well be asked, What have these improvements achieved beyond those of former artillery and fire-arms? and it may be answered, that a few years back, from windage and other causes, the length of range and accuracy of fire, both in fire-arms and artillery, were quite inferior to those now obtained, and there was, consequently, a greater waste of ammunition. The arms now used are lighter and more compact, and the quantity of gunpowder required for charges, from reduced windage and the close fitting of all balls in rifle arms, is greatly reduced, so that with the old musket at 200 yards the shooting at a mark could hardly be depended upon, while with the improved rifles, at distances from 600 to 1000 yards, a target of 6 feet by 4 can be, with tolerable certainty, hit; and the same comparative superiority in precision of fire and length of range of cannon over those of former days has been fully established.

It is useless at the present time to enter upon a discussion as to the rival merits of the various inventors of guns. Although immense sums of national money have been spent, the question of a fit gun for our army and navy is yet unsettled. It appears that Sir William Armstrong's *shunt* gun, 140-pounder, with a charge of 25 lbs. of powder and a 91 lb. flat-ended shot, has given way—on the 14th of July, in an experimental trial at Shoeburyness. According to an answer to a question in Parliament by Mr. Osborne, Sir G. C. Lewis, the Minister of War, states that it was a 120-pounder, and having been tried experimentally with a charge of 25 lbs. of powder, which was *double the ordinary service charge, it cracked near the centre.* If people will call the guns by a wrong denomination, I cannot pretend to explain ; but supposing a 120-pounder, and a plain, smooth-bored gun, the service charge for a round ball, according to the established custom, should be one-fourth of the shot's weight, or 30 lbs. of powder, —the nation, therefore, does not appear to be benefited by Sir William Armstrong's labours at present.

In the Table below, it will appear that the ranges are in favour of the Whitworth gun ; but I believe if Captain Blakeley's rifled cannon, Mr. Lancaster's, and others, had been tried at the same time, under equal circumstances, there would be very little difference in ranges or accuracy. The report will, however, serve to show the great improvement in accuracy of fire and length of range, as well as in the reduction of the charge of gunpowder with modern field artillery as compared with those in former use.

RESULTS OF EXPERIMENTS MADE ON THE 2ND APRIL, 1861, AT SHOEBURYNESS, under the Select Ordnance Committee, to ascertain the Range and Deflection of Whitworth's breech-loading 12-pounder Gun, in comparison with Sir William Armstrong's breech-loading 12-pounder.

Names.	No. of Rounds.	Charge of Powder.	Elevation.	Mean Range in Yards.	Mean difference in Ranges of the Five Rounds.	Mean Deflection of the Five Rounds.
		lb. oz.		Yards.	Yards.	Yards.
Whitworth	5	1 8	2°	1198	19	1¾
Armstrong	5	1 8	2°	1180	12	4
Whitworth	5	1 12	2°	1289	28	1⅔
Armstrong	5	1 12	2°	1256	26	5
Whitworth	5	1 8	5°	2365	119	1¾
Armstrong	5	1 8	5°	2140	11	9
Whitworth	5	1 12	5°	2471	97	1⅔
Armstrong	5	1 12	5°	2358	15	11
Whitworth	5	1 8	10°	4222	68	3
Armstrong	5	1 8	10°	3568	24	12
Whitworth	5	1 12	10°	4399	25	6¾
Armstrong	5	1 12	10°	3908	41	17

From this Table may be seen the extraordinary ranges of

these new guns and the reduced charge of powder. The range of a medium 12-pounder gun of old construction, with a charge of 3 lbs. at 2° elevation, would be about 1000 yards.

It will appear that the Whitworth gun exceeded the Armstrong in range; the mean difference in ranges is in favour of the Armstrong, the mean deflection of the shot greatly in favour of the Whitworth gun.

Captain Blakeley's cannon have been highly approved of by committees of Spanish officers in Spain, and the results of the trials with high charges are stated to be most satisfactory; the aim was very certain, and the ranges with a $6\frac{1}{2}$-inch cannon, charged with 8 lb. 13 oz. of powder, with 17° elevation, 6600 yards. This was a rifled gun. Another $6\frac{1}{2}$-inch smooth-bore, with charges from 6 lbs. to 8 lbs. 13 oz., had been fired upwards of 900 rounds without sustaining the slightest alteration, and the hooped cast-iron guns on Captain Blakeley's plan had proved perfectly satisfactory in Spain.

A rifled cannon, $6\frac{1}{2}$-inch bore, weighing 62 cwt., fired with an elongated shot weighing 61 lbs., had undergone the trial of 1366 rounds, with a charge of 6 lbs. 9 oz. of powder, the greater part of the rounds fired in rapid succession. At Woolwich, also, an experimental trial was made, in 1855, by the Ordnance Select Committee of one of Captain Blakeley's guns, 9-pounder, against a cast-iron service 9-pounder and a brass ditto. The cast-iron gun burst, the brass gun became unserviceable after standing 64 rounds more than the cast-iron one, and Captain Blakeley's gun was continued 144 rounds after the brass gun had failed, and remained perfectly uninjured. The firing continued for 158 rounds with a charge of 6 lbs. of powder, and as many shot as the gun would hold over the charge to the muzzle—a severity of proof, perhaps, that no other gun ever sustained before this trial.

The improvements in the manufacture of iron and steel by the Mersey Iron and Steel Company of Liverpool are such that we may expect strong solid guns from them;[*] and Sir G. C. Lewis

---

[*] Medals have been awarded for these improvements, in England, America, France, and Holland.

has stated in Parliament that Sir William Armstrong is making a 600-pounder gun, and Mr. Lynall Thomas a 400-pounder, besides others by different makers, amongst whom is, I believe, Mr. Whitworth. We may thus hope to see this decisive point of heavy guns fit to cope with iron-clad ships in some fair way of being settled to the satisfaction of the country.—EDITOR.

EXPERIMENTS ON THE FORCE AND PENETRATION OF SHOT FIRED FROM CANNON MADE AT WOOLWICH IN THE YEAR 1651.—*Phil. Transactions.*

" AT 200 yards distance from the platform for great ordnance were raised three butts, one behind the other ; the space between the first and the second butt was 14 yards, and the space between the second and the third 8 yards.

"The thickness of each was 19 inches, whereof 13 inches was of beams of massy oak fastened to the ground, and set so close that they touched each other. On each side, front and rear, were planks of oak 3 inches thick, jointed close, and fastened on both sides with iron bolts and strong pins of wood ; and on the back, at the ends, and on the middle, there were three crossing braces of elm, a foot in breadth and 5 inches in thickness.

" The first gun was an iron demi-cannon of 3500 lbs. weight, the shot 32 lbs., iron, the charge 10 lbs. ; the shot passed through the two first butts and stuck in the third, so that the ball was almost quite within the wood, but the timber was not shivered, nor scarce split. When the charge was 9 lbs. the same results as at the first discharge, and with 8 lbs. of powder the same.

" This demi-*cannon* was with a cylinder bore.

" The second experiment was with an iron demi-*cannon*, having a taper bore ; 3600 lbs. in weight, and 4 inches longer than the first gun. The iron bullet 32 lbs., charge of powder 7 lbs., which in three trials seemed to have the same force as the first. One of the shots piercing through the first butt and lighting near the edge of the middle butt of elm, tore it ; but, by its yielding, the bullet glanced aside off the third butt and entered into the earth.

"The third experiment was with a whole *culverin* in brass, 5300 lbs. weight, 11 feet 1 inch long, with a taper bore, being intended for a chase piece for the frigate called the 'Speaker;' the iron bullet was 18 lbs., the charge of powder, first trial, 10 lbs.; second trial, 9 lbs.; third trial, 8 lbs.; which last proportion did the best execution, and passed through the two first butts, entering gently into the third, which the two first shots struck but did not enter.

"The fourth experiment was with a whole *culverin* in brass, made at Amsterdam for the French, with this mark, 3580, being 10 feet long and not very thick at the breech; the first shot, 18 lbs. iron; charge 9 lbs. of powder; passed through the three butts, and entered one foot into the ground; it passed through the joints of the timber, two planks having been beaten off before.

"The second shot, with 8 lbs. of powder, passed through two butts, and grazed between them. The third shot, with 8 lbs. of powder, was much battered; passed through two butts, and in both butts through the middle of a massy strong beam that had not been battered.

"The fifth experiment was with an iron demi-*culverin*, having 9 lbs. shot of iron, 4 lbs. of powder; this passed through one butt, which was torn before, and entered the second butt.

"This half culverin was shot eight times, as fast as they could charge it with powder and the iron bullet, and yet was scarce luke-warm at the breech, a little more so in the middle, most at the muzzle, and this last scarce so hot as my hand, and yet the gunners in charging her wet not at all the scoop or sponge.

"The sixth experiment was with a brass demi-*culverin*; the breech of her was $13\frac{5}{8}$ inches (tried with calliper compass), the muzzle $9\frac{4}{5}$. The first shot, 9 lbs. iron, with a charge 4 lbs. of powder, passed two butts. The second shot, with 3 lbs. of powder, passed almost two butts; this proved to be the best shot, because the timbers struck were the strongest."

REMARKS.—These guns must have been of good metal, for the proportion of powder was very high compared with the weight of the shots, and from the penetration of the shot, the gunpowder, though probably not so quick of ignition as that now made, must have been of good serviceable strength. The reader will observe the great weight of the brass gun used in the third experiment : it is to be regretted that the measurements and weights of all the guns are not given, as well as the windage and nature of the wads used. The penetration of the shot and the strength of the gunpowder more than 200 years ago, as records, must prove curious and interesting to the artillerist.—EDITOR.

ALLAHABAD EXPERIMENTAL POWDER DRIED BY STEAM HEAT.

As there had been a very fatal explosion just before I was appointed to take charge of the works at Allahabad, which is supposed to have originated from an accident on the drying terrace, and knowing that in the dry season, at the time the manufacture of gunpowder is carried on, the atmosphere is filled with fine particles of dust or sand, more or less saline, I proposed to the Military Board that I should be allowed to make the experiment of drying by the heat of steam in a covered building, and I was authorised to prepare 100 barrels for this purpose.

There was an old overseer's house in the grounds of the mills, which, not being required, I used for this purpose, setting up a boiler outside the walls enclosing the powder works for the sake of safety, and bringing two small copper pipes along the wall on an incline to connect them with the building in question. Inside this building I placed two thin copper pipes, well soldered, and suspended from the roof to allow for expansion and contraction ; these were connected with the small pipes, and they were laid on such an incline that the steam passed up one and the condensed water ran back to the boiler through the other.* I set up frames in the house of the bottle-rack form, on which I placed shallow trays having canvas bottoms, which were to receive the powder in thin strata. When complete, I found I could easily regulate the heat to about 140°, which I never allowed it to exceed, as I thought the heat on the terraces exposed to the sun, often at 145° to 150°, had an injurious effect on the powder. It took about two days to dry the loaded trays of powder, the powder being gently stirred every day. The roof was very open tile-work, and therefore did not require more ventilation. When the drying was complete, the gunpowder was passed through a glazing reel to take away all dust, and carefully barrelled up.

In preparing this powder I was exceedingly careful in taking the best of urhur, or dhalwood, for charcoal; and although I consider the advantage of drying without exposing the powder on the terraces was very great, yet the powder proved so superior in strength, as the following Table will show, that I must attribute this greatly to the charcoal. I was of course very careful in bringing all the ingredients to their proper state of purity; the saltpetre, in refining, was always passed through canvas filtering bags, and was fused; the proportions of the ingredients were as usual, 75, 15, 10, and in all respects the milling was like that pursued at Ishapore, the only difference being my care in refining the saltpetre, and careful selection of the other ingredients.

---

* The large copper pipes for the steam were suspended from the roof by ropes, —so that they were near the floor. They were 5 inches in diameter, and the boiler was sunk in the ground to allow the slight inclination of the pipes to carry the condensed steam back to the boiler. There was also a small connecting pipe, outside the building, which conveyed a portion of the distilled water from the pipe running back to the boiler into a copper vessel; and this distilled water was used for watering the mill charges, a precaution quite necessary where the local water obtainable is not quite free from saline impurities. The boiler, for safety, was 100 feet from the drying-house; and the small connecting pipes in the recess in the wall rested upon friction-wheels, to allow for longitudinal expansion. On such a plan a perfect drying-house may be made. An artificial draught of air, to carry off the moisture, would be highly advantageous.

TABLES OF PROOF OF POWDERS. 265

Trial of Allahabad Powder, dried by Steam Heat.

EXTRACTS FROM A REPORT OF PROOF TRIALS MADE AT DUM-DUM IN 1828, by Order of the Military Board, to ascertain the respective Qualities of Gunpowders manufactured by the Agent at Allahabad, Captain Samuel Parlby; the Agent, Lieut.-Col. Galloway, at Ishapore; and by the other Agents at Madras and Bombay, respectively. The Allahabad powder, part of 100 barrels made for the experiment, was dried by steam heat.

Date of Proof.	Ordnance used.	Charge of Powder.	Quality of Powder.	Weight of Shot or Shell.	Where and when Manufactured.	Average Range of Five Rounds in Yards.	Remarks.
14th Jan. 1828.	10-inch Mortar.	2 oz.	Ordnance.	Shell, 85 lbs. 13 oz.	Allahabad, 1824-25 Ishapore, 1824-25 Madras, 1825 Bombay, 1825	$39\frac{3}{5}$ $32\frac{7}{5}$ $28\frac{1}{5}$ $5\frac{2}{5}$	In favour of the Allahabad powder, as compared with the next best, the Ishapore, $6\frac{3}{5}$ yards.
15th Jan.	10-inch Mortar.	1 lb.	Ordnance.	Shell, 85 lbs. 13 oz.	Allahabad, 1824-25 Ishapore, 1824-25 Madras, 1824-25 Bombay, 1825	$354\frac{2}{3}$ 255 253 $68\frac{3}{5}$	In favour of the Allahabad powder, as compared with the next best, the Ishapore, $99\frac{1}{3}$ yards.
15th Jan.	10-inch Mortar.	1 lb. 12 oz.	Ordnance.	Shell, 85 lbs. 13 oz.	Allahabad, 1824-25 Ishapore, 1824-25 Madras, 1824-25 Bombay, 1824-25	$671\frac{2}{3}$ $461\frac{1}{3}$ $558\frac{3}{4}$ $154\frac{4}{5}$	In favour of the Allahabad powder, as compared with the next best, the Ishapore, $210\frac{1}{3}$ yards.
16th Jan.	8-inch Mortar.	2 oz.	Ordnance.	Shell, 41 lbs. 10 oz.	Allahabad, 1824-25 Ishapore, 1824-25 Madras, 1825 Bombay, 1825	65 $46\frac{2}{3}$ $39\frac{1}{5}$ $10\frac{1}{3}$	In favour of Allahabad powder, as compared with Ishapore, $18\frac{1}{3}$ yards. With Madras . $25\frac{4}{5}$,, With Bombay . $54\frac{2}{3}$,,

TABLES OF PROOF OF POWDERS.

Date of Proof.	Ordnance used.	Charge of Powder.	Quality of Powder.	Weight of Shot or Shell.	Where and when Manufactured.	Average Range of Fire Rounds in Yards.	Remarks.
17th Jan.	8-inch Mortar.	1 lb.	Ordnance.	Shell, 41 lbs. 11 oz.	Allahabad, 1824-25 Ishapore, 1824-25 Madras, 1825 Bombay, 1825	$557\frac{1}{2}$ $318\frac{1}{4}$ $419\frac{3}{4}$ $97\frac{1}{3}$	In favour of Allahabad powder, as compared with Ishapore, 239 yards. Madras, $137\frac{3}{4}$,, Bombay, $460\frac{2}{3}$,,
17th Jan.	8-inch Mortar.	1 lb. 11 oz.	Ordnance.	Shell, 41 lbs. 11 oz.	Allahabad, 1824-25 Ishapore, 1824-25 Madras, 1825 Bombay, 1825	$1168\frac{2}{3}$ $709\frac{2}{3}$ 1148 371	In favour of Allahabad powder, as compared with Ishapore, $459\frac{1}{4}$ yards. Madras, $23\frac{3}{4}$,, Bombay, $797\frac{2}{3}$,,
17th Jan.	8-inch Mortar.	? oz.	Ordnance.	Solid Iron Ball, $65\frac{1}{2}$ lbs. diam. 7·85 in.	Allahabad, 1824-25 Ishapore, 1824-25 Madras, 1824-25 Bombay, 1824-25	$55\frac{3}{4}$ $41\frac{1}{3}$ $42\frac{3}{5}$ $11\frac{2}{3}$	In favour of Allahabad powder, as compared with Ishapore, $14\frac{2}{3}$ yards. Madras, 12 ,, Bombay, $43\frac{1}{3}$,,
21st Jan.	8-inch Mortar.	1 lb.	Ordnance.	Solid Iron Ball, $65\frac{1}{2}$ lbs.	Allahabad, 1824-25 Ishapore, 1824-25 Madras, 1824-25 Bombay, 1824-25	$501\frac{2}{3}$ $358\frac{2}{3}$ $449\frac{1}{3}$ $113\frac{2}{3}$	In favour of Allahabad powder, as compared with Ishapore, $142\frac{1}{4}$ yards. Madras, $52\frac{1}{3}$,, Bombay, 388 ,,
22nd Jan.	8-inch Mortar.	1 lb. 12 oz.	Ordnance.	Solid Iron Ball, $65\frac{1}{2}$ lbs.	Allahabad, 1824-25 Ishapore, 1824-25 Madras, 1825 Bombay, 1825	$1142\frac{1}{2}$ $721\frac{2}{3}$ 1135 $407\frac{1}{2}$	In favour of Allahabad powder, as compared with Ishapore, $420\frac{2}{3}$ yards. Madras, $7\frac{1}{2}$,, Bombay, 734 ,,
17th Jan.	8-inch Mortar.	1 lb.	Ordnance.	$68\frac{1}{2}$ lb. Ball.	Allahabad, 1824-25 Ishapore, 1824-25	336 255	In favour of Allahabad powder, 81 yards.

TABLES OF PROOF OF POWDERS.

Date of Proof	Ordnance used.	Charge of Powder.	Quality of Powder.	Weight of Shot or Shell.	Where and when Manufactured.	Average Range of Five Rounds in Yards.	Remarks.
17th Jan.	10-inch Mortar.	1 lb.	Ordnance.	Shell, 85 lbs. 13 oz.	Allahabad, 1824-25 Ishapore, 1824-25 .	496 384¾	In favour of Allahabad powder, 111⅓ yards.
17th Jan.	8-inch Mortar.	1 lb.	Ordnance.	Shell, 41 lbs. 13 oz.	Allahabad, 1824-25 Ishapore, 1824-25 .	808 606	In favour of Allahabad powder, 202 yards.
20th March.	10-inch Mortar.	2 oz.	Ordnance.	Shell, 85 lbs. 12 oz.	Allahabad, 1824-25 Ishapore, 1824-25 .	51¾ 32	In favour of Allahabad powder, 19⅔ yards.
20th March.	8-inch Mortar.	2 oz.	Ordnance.	Shell, 41 lbs. 11 oz.	Allahabad, 1824-25 Ishapore, 1824-25 .	79⅓ 50⅔	In favour of Allahabad powder, 28⅓ yards.
20th March.	8-inch Mortar.	2 oz.	Ordnance.	Solid Shot, 68½ lbs.	Allahabad, 1824-25 Ishapore, 1824-25 .	85 56½	In favour of Allahabad powder, 28⅔ yards.
21st March.	10-inch Mortar.	4 oz.	Ordnance.	Shell, 85 lbs. 13 oz.	Allahabad, 1824-25 Ishapore, 1824-25 .	96 73⅔	In favour of Allahabad powder, 22¼ yards.

TABLES OF PROOF OF POWDERS.

Date of Proof	Ordnance used.	Charge of Powder.	Quality of Powder.	Weight of Shot or Shell.	Where and when Manufactured.	Average Range of Five Rounds in Yards.	Remarks.
21st March.	8-inch Mortar.	4 oz.	Ordnance.	Shell, 41 lbs. 11 oz.	Allahabad, 1824-25	185	In favour of Allahabad powder, 56 yards.
					Ishapore, 1824-25	129	
21st March.	8-inch Mortar.	4 oz.	Ordnance.	Solid Shot, 68½ lbs.	Allahabad, 1824-25	177	In favour of Allahabad powder, 36 yards.
					Ishapore, 1824-25	141	
21st March.	10-inch Mortar.	8 oz.	Ordnance.	Shell, 85 lbs. 12 oz.	Allahabad, 1824-25	226	In favour of Allahabad powder, 42 yards.
					Ishapore, 1824-25	184	
21st March.	8-inch Mortar.	8 oz.	Ordnance.	41 lbs. 11 oz.	Allahabad, 1824-25	353	In favour of Allahabad powder, 101⅗ yards.
					Ishapore, 1824-25	251¼	
21st March.	10-inch Mortar.	2 lbs.	Ordnance.	85 lbs. 13 oz.	Allahabad, 1824-25	1102	In favour of Allahabad powder, 253⅔ yards.
					Ishapore, 1824-25	848⅓	
21st March.	8-inch Mortar.	2 lb.	Ordnance.	Shell, 41 lbs. 11 oz.	Allahabad, 1824-25	1755⅔	In favour of Allahabad powder, 290¼ yards.
					Ishapore, 1824-25	1465¼	

Date of Proof.	Ordnance used.	Charge of Powder.	Quality of Powder.	Weight of Shot or Shell.	Where and when Manufactured.	Average Range of Five Rounds in Yards.	Remarks.
19th August.	8-inch Mortar.	2 oz.	Ordnance.	Solid Shot, $65\frac{1}{2}$ lbs.	Allahabad, 1824-25 Ishapore, 1824-25 . Madras, 1825 . . Bombay, 1825 .	$59\frac{1}{2}$ $46\frac{2}{3}$ $39\frac{1}{3}$ $20\frac{1}{5}$	In favour of Allahabad powder, as compared with Ishapore, $12\frac{1}{4}$ yards. Madras, 20 ,, Bombay, $39\frac{1}{2}$,,
19th August.	8-inch Mortar.	1 lb.	Ordnance.	Solid Shot, $65\frac{1}{2}$ lbs.	Allahabad, 1824-25 Ishapore, 1824-25 . Madras, 1825 . . Bombay, 1825 .	649 515 561 312	In favour of Allahabad powder, as compared with Ishapore, 134 yards. Madras, 88 ,, Bombay, 337 ,,
19th August.	10-inch Mortar.	2 oz.	Ordnance.	Shell, 85 lbs. 13 oz.	Allahabad, 1824-25 Ishapore, 1824-25 . Madras, 1824-25 . Bombay, 1825 .	$41\frac{1}{3}$ $30\frac{1}{3}$ $34\frac{2}{3}$ $13\frac{2}{3}$	In favour of Allahabad powder, as compared with Ishapore, 11 yards. Madras, $6\frac{2}{3}$,, Bombay, $27\frac{2}{3}$,,
19th August.	10-inch Mortar.	1 lb.	Ordnance.	Shell, 85 lbs. 13 oz.	Allahabad, 1824-25 Ishapore, 1824-25 . Madras, 1825 . Bombay, 1825 .	$438\frac{1}{3}$ $299\frac{1}{3}$ 333 $154\frac{1}{3}$	In favour of Allahabad powder, as compared with Ishapore, 139 yards. Madras, $105\frac{1}{3}$,, Bombay, 284 ,,
19th August.	8-inch Mortar.	1 lb.	Ordnance.	Shell, 41 lbs. 11 oz.	Allahabad, 1824-25 Ishapore, 1824-25 . Madras, 1824-25 . Bombay, 1824-25 .	$758\frac{1}{3}$ 587 571 278	In favour of Allahabad powder, as compared with Ishapore, $151\frac{1}{3}$ yards. Madras, $187\frac{1}{3}$,, Bombay, $480\frac{1}{3}$,,

WAR ROCKETS.

As an improver of this formidable weapon, which has of late years greatly fallen in military estimation from causes which will be stated below, I cannot omit to urge the infinite value which good rockets, as an aid in military or naval operations, are certain generally to prove themselves to be; and, on some special cases, superior to any other.

In the preceding parts of this volume it will be seen that in the most ancient times, long before the supposed introduction of artillery and fire-arms, rockets appear amongst the eastern nations to have formed an essential part of military offence and defence. As an officer serving in the Bengal Artillery in India, my attention was early drawn to the Indian rocket, with the construction of which I became well acquainted.

Satisfied with the superiority of artillery, I never thought of bringing forward a weapon which certainly in many points it can never rival; yet, after the public notoriety of the improvements and employment of rockets in Europe by the late Sir William Congreve, I earnestly pressed the use of them in our service; and in 1814, before the Congreve rocket had been sent for, or at any rate before any supply arrived in India, I made a public offer of my services to the Earl of Moira, then Commander-in-Chief in India, to make war-rockets to be used in the Nepaul war, if sent to any magazine with proper authority for that purpose. As, however, Lord Moira had sent for a supply of the Congreve rocket from Europe, my offer was at that time declined.

Soon after this I returned to England on a short furlough to recruit my health; and believing that I could produce a superior weapon to the Congreve, fresh and suited to the climate by being made in India, I devoted a considerable sum of my own private resources, encouraged by several members of the Hon. Court of Directors of the late E. I. Company, to construct an apparatus, of my own plan and invention, for the purpose of making rockets on my return to India, employing the late Mr. Galloway, then living in Holborn, for this purpose; the circumstances attending which I shall allude to in this paper.

If we inquire, What is the principal value of a rocket as an aid or substitute for artillery? we must notice:—

First. Its extreme portability; so that wherever man can go by land or water, a supply of rockets can be carried.

Secondly. It is an arm requiring the aid of no gun or machine to project it, and exposes no front for the enemy's artillery to aim at.*

Thirdly. It can be constructed in such variety as to carry to a greater distance a heading to discharge balls with far greater

---

* Although tubes of sheet iron, or angular troughs of iron or wood, which are superior, may be used where greater accuracy of direction is required than usual, yet rockets, when laid upon the even ground, in the proper direction, if on a plain, will range with tremendous effect, and to equal distances of effective shot of common field pieces; yet if greater range and accuracy are required, a common sloping bank of earth may be used, as that of a hedge and ditch, or one made for the purpose, as occasion requires, in a few minutes.

An erroneous opinion as to the cause of the flight of a rocket has long been maintained, and repeated in many of our Encyclopædias, as in the former editions of the Encyclopædia Britannica; and I wrote to the publishers of that work and to other journals, more than twenty years ago, to explain what is the true cause of propulsion in this weapon; but the error in some of those is still continued.

A rocket-case is loaded with a composition which generates, when fired, a powerful expanding gas, as gunpowder does. This gas is allowed to escape only at the vent or tail end of the rocket, and thus half of its pressure acts towards the head end, where, not being allowed to escape, it forces the cylinder forward, and as the interior of the composition is hollowed out to a certain length longitudinally, the superficial area of the inflamed composition is thus constantly increasing as it burns, and consequently the quantity of gaseous volume; the velocity of the flight of the rocket therefore increases as long as this combustion continues. But in the construction of a rocket the whole area of the vent or tail end *is not left open, only a certain portion:* this causes the inflamed gas to be acted upon as if it were in *a reverberatory furnace,*—its heat and expansion are greatly increased by this formation, and though, if the whole area of the vent end was left open, the cylinder would still be forced forwards, its flight and range would be trifling in comparison. Thus the cause of a rocket's flight is to be explained; and the resistance of the air to the escape of the fluid at the vent, which has been erroneously supposed to be the cause, has nothing to do with it.

force and precision than a Shrapnell shell; a rocket having at 1200 or 1400 yards equal velocity and greater momentum than a cannon ball of the same diameter; or it can convey, as part of itself, a greater quantity of explosive or combustible matter than any projectile of equal diameter fired from a cannon.

Fourthly. If supplied in proper numbers, an instantaneous development of projectile power can be exerted in its formidable nature and appearance (carrying both flame and momentum) far beyond that which a moderate battery of artillery is capable of with any projectiles that can be used.

If anything is wanting to the above statement as to the value of rockets, the following extract from "The Spirit of Military Institutions," by Marshal Marmont, Duke of Ragusa, the celebrated aide-de-camp of Napoleon I. (chap. iii., Artillery), may be quoted:—

"But these projectiles acquire a vast importance under a thousand circumstances where guns are perfectly useless. In the mountains it is with the greatest difficulty that a small number of light guns, which produce but inconsiderable effect, can be transported. But the rocket combines extended range with multiplied fire. It may be established everywhere; on the crests of the highest peaks, or on the lower plateau of mountains. In the plains it converts every house into a fortress, and the roof of a village church is rendered at will the platform of a formidable battery. In one word, this invention, such as it now exists, and susceptible as it is of further elaboration, adapts itself to every variety of circumstance, to every possible combination, and must exercise an immense influence on the destinies of armies."

How is it, then, that this formidable weapon has fallen into such general contempt and dishonour? I will endeavour to explain:—

The Congreve rockets have been and still are made with *many faults of construction and combination*; * so that, in many cases,

---

* The specimens of the Congreve Rocket sent from the Royal Laboratory at Woolwich, and shown in the International Exhibition, fully exhibit *these defects of construction*, and I am prepared to state that rockets made on such a plan

DEFECTS OF THE PRESENT SERVICE ROCKETS.

they have proved as dangerous to the men who have discharged them as to the enemy towards whom they were projected, not only from a general uncertainty of flight, but also from occasionally turning completely round in the air and coming back towards the place from which they were fired.

In consequence of this faulty construction, their general irregularity and uncertainty of range has actually brought this really formidable weapon into contempt.

To show the foundations for these statements, I give the following extract from a book published by authority, "The Course of Artillery and Fortification for the Use of the Royal Military College, Sandhurst," by Captain (now Colonel) Boxer, superintending the Royal Laboratory, Woolwich, 1860.

The notice of the war rocket is thus concluded in this book :—

"The present service rocket has one serious defect—namely, great irregularity of flight. If this be overcome, the rocket would be a most formidable weapon, if used in large numbers."

Such, then, is the acknowledged defect of the Congreve rocket of the present day by the head of the Royal Laboratory.

The following extract from the letter of a General Officer serving in India will also show the utter and disgraceful failure of the Congreve rocket in India during the late mutiny.

In the battle of Golowlie, the day before the action and the capture of Calpee, in Bundelkund, the General writes :—

"At the moment of the advance of a dense mass of the enemy's cavalry on the 22nd May, 1858, our rocket-firing was a perfect failure. One or two rockets hissed off from the tubes towards the enemy, and then suddenly buried themselves in the ground, and one or two others whizzed erratically in the sky and then turned back upon their *friends* who had wished them good speed. So the General, Sir Hugh Rose (now Commander-in-Chief in India), ordered these *dangerous things* to the rear."

I could detail many other instances of this uncertainty of flight

cannot have the regular and accurate flight which they would obtain under another formation.

T

of the Congreve rockets, in Bengal, Madras, and Bombay, but it is needless to allude to them now.

In the "Times," of Thursday, 15th May, page 5, giving an account of an engagement between the combined French and English troops and the Rebels (Taepings), part of the paragraph runs thus :—

"The practice with Bradshaw's mountain howitzers was good as soon as the range was obtained, but *the rockets were a failure.*"

And in a late account in the military and naval column of the review of the Royal Marine Artillery at Portsmouth, the practice with the Armstrong and other guns was described as excellent, but that of the rockets "*uncertain as usual.*"*

It is well known that the nation has expended large sums of money on the Congreve rocket, and if this is the result of the state of the present manufacture of rockets, surely the subject should be inquired into. Perhaps, in case of invasion, no weapon would be found more serviceable in aiding the noble army of patriotic volunteers with their accurate rifle fire than good rockets in sufficient numbers; and the use of a rocket is so simple that every able man, in every village throughout the kingdom, could, in a few hours, be taught how to use them with effect against an enemy.

To prove the intimidating effect of the fire of rockets upon the horses of a body of cavalry, I may here mention the following circumstance. About the year 1821 or 1822, when that excellent officer, the late Colonel Charles Graham (then captain) was commanding the Rocket Troop at Meerut, it was his practice to make use of common penny paper rockets to accustom the horses and camels to the noise and fire produced; and the colonel commanding the 11th Dragoons, then at the station, with many other officers, having been in the habit of speaking contemptuously of the war-rocket as a weapon, had stated that if a field day took place, they would, at a charge, ride over the Rocket Troop. It happened soon after, that this

* The italics are mine.—EDITOR.

fine regiment of cavalry was exercising on the plain at Meerut, when Sir Thomas Reynolds, then commanding officer of the district, rode up, and he intimated to the commanding officer that he should like to see the regiment charge. On the inquiry, in what direction it should be, Sir Thomas happened to cast his eye upon Captain Graham's Rocket Troop (at a considerable distance from the usual exercising ground, which that officer always chose to prevent interference with other corps), and Sir Thomas said, "Oh, there is the Rocket Troop, charge on that." Captain Graham saw the Dragoons advancing towards him, heard the usual trumpet sounds for preparing and charging, and having a presentiment that the threat of riding over his troop was about to be accomplished, he ordered his men to lay a number of these paper rockets on the ground, ready to fire a volley when he gave the command, should the Dragoons advance into too close proximity. The charge, however, continued with undiminished speed, and some of the horses' heads were nearly in line with the rockets, when Captain Graham gave the command to fire : the effect was such on the horses, that the whole regiment was thrown into confusion,—one officer and several men were unhorsed, and the charge was completely broken. As some arms and military accoutrements of the Dragoons fell upon the ground, Captain Graham ordered his men to run forward and secure them, and had them brought to the lines as trophies of his victory, and a memorandum was sent round in the station orderly-book, that they might be recovered by sending to the main guard of the Horse Artillery, where they would be delivered up.

Unfortunately, one of these small paper rockets struck a dragoon horse in the soft part of the chest, and disabled it. On a complaint, and reference to the Marquis of Hastings (then Commander-in-Chief), on the subject, his lordship's reply was, that while he regretted the accident, he was glad to find that the Rocket Troop, if called into action, was likely to be so serviceable.

Here, then, is an instance of a fine regiment of Royal Dragoons, in high discipline, being thrown into complete disorder by the discharge of a few paper rockets, and from this we may judge the effect of real iron-cased rockets carrying shot and shells at their heads.

I may proceed to state, that in consequence of the home interest of Sir William Congreve with His Royal Highness the Prince Regent, and its effect on the authorities in India, I was not allowed to make any rockets, until the Congreve supplies proved so uncertain and so useless, that the subject was pressed upon the Government and the Military Board. Lord Hastings having returned to England, the excellent Mr. Adam, of the Bengal Civil Service (at the time acting as the head of the Government), deemed it proper to authorise my being allowed to prove what I could do in making rockets for the service in India. I was therefore ordered to prepare 70 rockets of different sizes to be tried against those of Sir William Congreve; and although I had no proper places to put up my apparatus, or any men who had been accustomed to the work, I did not shrink from the task, but with my own private native servants, and in the out-houses of my private house, I prepared the number required.

The trial took place on the public practice ground of the Artillery at Dum-Dum on the 31st of May, 1834, in the presence of Lord Amherst, who had lately arrived as Governor-General, Sir Edward Paget, the new Commander-in-Chief, and a large concourse of military and civil spectators.

The following was the report of Colonel A. McLeod, Commandant of the Bengal Artillery:—

"To Captain Craigie, Secretary, Military Board.

"Sir,—I have now the honour to forward a report of the experimental practice which took place here with Captain Parlby's and General Congreve's rockets, on Monday, the 31st ultimo. The detail of the report will sufficiently explain the nature of the practice; and it remains for me to add, that not only from the result of the number of rockets, which were put into the curtain by both parties, but also from the apparent flight of the missiles of the two descriptions, I can have no hesitation in giving as my opinion, that Captain Parlby's rockets had a decided advantage in the correctness of fire over General Congreve's.

"But it does not appear that Captain Parlby's rockets were propelled with the same force which General Congreve's were, although they had a considerable velocity, and sufficient to answer good purposes for field service, or even in bombarding at distances not exceeding 1800 or 2000 yards.

"With bombarding rockets General Congreve had a great superiority of range : add to this also, it must be noted that Captain Parlby's 24-pounder rocket weighs about 14 lbs. more than General Congreve's, which on some occasions, on service, might be rather a disadvantage. It may be desirable to be informed that Captain Parlby had nothing to do in directing General Congreve's rockets : I had appointed Captain Graham of the Rocket Troop for that duty, and they were managed by him, assisted by Mr. Allen (who first brought them out), and the officers and men of the troop. In fact, every justice was done in the preparation and direction, and the practice with them was extremely good.

"I have the honour to be,
(Signed) "McLeod,
"Lt.-Col.-Com., Commanding Artillery."

"Dum-Dum, June 2nd, 1824."

The following extract from the "John Bull" newspaper, of Calcutta, June 1st, 1824, written by a spectator, quite unknown to me at the time, on the subject of the experiment, is important, as it establishes my claim as the first inventor and exhibitor of rifle rockets :—

"First discharge, target distance 600 yards. Volley of nine rockets, 3-pounders, Congreve and Parlby, separate. In this discharge there was a complete failure of the Congreve rockets ; six out of the nine burst within 100 yards of the car, another fell about half-way, and the two remaining rockets went to a considerable distance right and left of the target. Of the Parlby rockets only one burst, two struck the target, and the remaining six preserved the line, and passed over it within a few feet of the top. Here, then, the superiority of the Parlby rocket is manifest, as he forms his rockets so as to have a rotary motion."

Soon after this I was appointed to the Allahabad Gunpowder Manufactory as agent, and as all the Congreve rockets in the country had become unserviceable, as was especially shown when they were required for the siege of Bhurtpore, Government determined that I should establish a manufactory for war-rockets in conjunction with the agency at Allahabad. I had only native workmen, and those who know the heat of the climate at that station will easily imagine the labour that fell upon me; but that success attended my exertions may be learnt from the following extracts of letters from Captain Graham, and from Captain Blake, who succeeded him:—

"MY DEAR PARLBY,

"I have sincere pleasure in acquainting you that I have fired 24 of your 32-pounder rockets, and 12 18-pounder rockets without a single failure. General Reynell was present the first day, and expressed himself highly gratified with your success. He lamented the want of such formidable auxiliaries at Bhurtpore. These rockets ranged beautifully, and far beyond my expectations. On the whole, I cannot but repeat my hearty congratulations on the success of your manufacture, so far as it has fallen under my observation.

"Yours very sincerely,

"Meerut, Jan. 9th, 1827." (Signed) "CHARLES GRAHAM."

Extract of a letter from Captain Blake, who succeeded Captain Graham in command of the Rocket Troop :—

"MY DEAR SIR,

"I commenced, on the 16th instant, with twelve of your 18-pounders, at an elevation of 20°: they all went with great steadiness and precision; and on the 18th I fired, at the same elevation, twelve of your 12-pounders; they went all alike, and were allowed by the numerous Artillery officers on the battery to be, in precision, force, and continued length of horizontal flight, quite unequalled by any kind of rocket they had yet seen, or expected to see. "Yours very sincerely,

"GEORGE BLAKE."

Here, then, I proved that with only native workmen, and with apparatus by no means equal to that I could make in England, I produced rockets that ranged *alike*, and that were pronounced to be, by numerous Artillery officers, *in precision, force, and continued length of horizontal flight*, quite unequalled by any kind of rocket they had ever seen or expected to see.

Just at this time Lord William Bentinck arrived as Governor-General, and as the aspect of affairs in India appeared peaceable, and retrenchment of public expenditure was his determination, both the powder works at Ishapore and Allahabad were closed for a period, and the establishments, many individuals of which at Allahabad had been employed for years at the dangerous work of making gunpowder, were discharged at one month's notice!

I had served my period of 24 years in India, and I soon after returned to England, and retired on the pension of my rank as major.

Since my return to Europe, about twenty years after I had invented and adopted, as *part* of my principle of construction, the mode of making rockets rotate in their flight, Mr. Hale took out a patent, I think in 1844, for the same principle, and proposed and carried into effect, through this principle of rifle motion, the rockets without shafts known by his name; but as such rockets must be greatly inferior to a good rocket with a proper shaft, in momentum and direction, I have little expectation that they will be generally adopted; and, though I believe Mr. Hale has disposed of the right to use his patent in America, I cannot observe that his rockets are in use on either side in that unfortunate and deeply to be regretted war.

I have made several offers at various times to the Government authorities in this country, to show, for a moderate pecuniary consideration, all the improvements which I have made in the construction of rockets; but the answer has generally been, that I must make them at my own expense, and then a trial can be made at Woolwich.

A similar answer was given me at the time Lord Vivian was Master-General of the Ordnance, and when I went to Woolwich

I was told by an old Artillery officer holding a high appointment, and who had been a fellow cadet with me at the old Royal Academy in the Warren (now Royal Arsenal), that if I showed any improvements at Woolwich, without having a full understanding as to my reward previously, in all probability all the good points would be adopted, whilst any recompense to the inventor would be out of the question.

Such has been the result of attempting for nearly forty years to improve a most important weapon, the true value of which, from being so indifferently constructed, as it is at present, is hardly known and estimated.

Vast sums of money are spending, or have been spent, in producing monster guns and mortars; as to the latter, rockets, properly made, ought entirely to supersede their use for throwing shells. Much heavier rockets, and with all the precision of shells in their range, may be made, say from 500 to 1000 lbs. weight. Yet no one would venture to make a gun to carry a projectile of 1000 lbs. weight, and the economy in production, and the facility of using such rockets would be greatly in favour of the latter. It is very true that the principle of forming a large rocket is very different from that adopted in making a moderate-sized one; but from trials I have made, I feel certain of success, if the means are afforded.

I think one writer on projectiles, Dr. Scoffern, some years back, stated that a rocket of 500 lbs. would not move, but perhaps he is by this time aware, that amongst a semi-barbarous people in Asia much larger rockets than I have mentioned have been produced; and if reference is made to the 173rd page, quarto edition, of Major Symes's Embassy to Ava in 1795, the following paragraph will be found. " The display of rockets was strikingly grand. The cylinders of the rockets were the trunks of trees hollowed, many of them 7 to 8 feet long, and from 2 to 3 feet in circumference; they were bound by strong ligatures to thick bamboos, 18 or 20 feet in length; they rose to a great height, and in descending emitted various appearances of fire that were very beautiful."

Now we have only to fancy the effect of such formidable

rockets, combined with exploding combustibles; or, which may be easily done, having their head so formed as to discharge a volley of heavy 4 or 8 oz. balls, not falling with the force of gravity, but projected perpendicularly downwards with all the force and velocity which they would obtain by being discharged from a cannon or howitzer, and we can then imagine the destructive effect of such a method of applying rockets—*for vertical fire* of such a formidable nature could be obtained from no other projectile than a rocket. But this is only one of their uses.

The first object to overcome is that of *irregularity* of flight—this I have accomplished.

The next is that they shall be safe to discharge and free from the vicious propensity of a Congreve rocket, of turning back upon its friends—this can never happen with a rocket of my construction, and I can fully explain the defect in that of the Congreve rocket which occasions it.

As an old Artillery officer, I cannot but express my opinion again, that as an aid in defending our country against invasion, considering the state of our population, and the facility by which the most formidable number of rockets could be rapidly accumulated, there is no artillery aid, to assist our noble army of volunteers, that can be compared to that which good rockets would afford on a sudden emergency.

There also is no kind of ammunition, *if properly made*, that can be so safe in store, or so little injured by time as rockets.

They can be made perfectly secure against any exposure to fire that would not heat them red hot, and rockets may be laid under water for months, and yet, when required for service, will be found free from all deterioration.

On the 3rd of March last I made an offer to the War Office to produce rockets (under certain considerations, and on the amount expended in preparing them being paid) with the following characteristics:—

1st.—That they shall not deviate from the proper line of flight more than a few feet at any time, at the usual ranges of Congreve rockets.

2nd.—That they shall never return upon those that fire them, as the Congreve rockets do.

3rd.—That made under the same circumstances, in a public manufactory, they shall not cost more than the present Congreve rockets.

4th.—That rockets of any large size shall be produced which shall equal the regularity of flight of shells from mortars.

5th.—That there shall be other advantages, which I will bring forward, rendering the war-rocket more applicable and formidable, both at short and at long distances, and that this adaptation can take place at will, in the shortest space of time in the field of action.

After some delay in obtaining an answer, and some further correspondence, I was finally informed that if I made my rockets at my own expense, the Minister of War (Sir G. Cornewall Lewis) would order a trial to be made at Woolwich. I then stated that as I was informed from good authority that the rockets now made at Woolwich are very irregular in their flight, if the Minister of War would allow a few of the Royal Laboratory rockets, and a few of Mr. Hale's, to be fired, and allow me to be present to see them, I should then be able to judge if my proposed services would be useful, or whether they had been unjustly refused.

To this I have received a reply, that Sir Cornewall Lewis regrets that he cannot comply with my request; and thus the matter rests.

SAMUEL PARLBY.

ON THE CAUSE OF THE GREAT INTENSITY OF HEAT AND INCREASED VELOCITY OF THE GASEOUS PRODUCT IN LARGE CHARGES OF GUNPOWDER.

THE heat required to melt malleable iron is about 3300° Fahrenheit, yet I have often, with particular compositions in rockets, caused the surfaces of malleable iron vents to be fused, presenting the same appearance as the points of iron or steel instruments fused by the heat called into action by a current of lightning.

It is the reverberatory action (seldom if ever taken into account by writers on the subject) caused in the *flame* of fired gunpowder, which first impinges upon the surface of a heavy shot placed before it and is then *reverberated*, that produces the great intensity of heat, and consequently increased violence of the gaseous product, in large charges of gunpowder; especially when used in guns of large calibre with heavy shot, which we are now trying to introduce; a strong argument in favour of using gunpowder very large in the grain, which will not permit so quick an inflammation, and consequently that sudden intensity of force and heat, before the shot is moved, as smaller grain, and yet will have time to exhaust itself in the length of barrel before the shot quits the muzzle, if properly proportioned.

ON THE VELOCITY WITH WHICH THE ATMOSPHERE, OR COMMON AIR, RUSHES INTO A VACUUM.

THIS inquiry is a very interesting one to the artillerist, and is deeply connected with the subject of the resistance to projectiles in their flight or range; and as many writers on this subject, even to the present day, have fallen into the error of supposing that a vacuum can take place behind a shot at very high velocity, which a little calm reasoning would have convinced them is an impossibility, it may be as well to dwell a short time upon the subject.

Our philosophers, at an early day, since the introduction of the force of gunpowder gave higher velocities to projectiles than mechanical force had been accustomed to produce, endeavoured practically to bring out a satisfactory answer to the question by experiment; and I feel satisfied that my readers will excuse my going back to the year 1686, when such experiments were made, and describing the mode of conducting them, as they will admire the simple and truly philosophical spirit that guided the inquiry, which will be found detailed in "The Philosophical Transactions" of the year 1686, No. 184, p. 193, being the substance of a paper read before the Royal Society by the celebrated Dr. Papin.

It appears that some time before this, members of the Royal Academy of Paris had tried to demonstrate the problem in the following way. A bladder was filled alternately with water and air, and the experimenters found that when the weight used to squeeze out the fluids was exactly the same, as well as the orifice to let them escape from the neck of the bladder, the air was emptied, or driven out, in one-25th of the time that was required to drive out the water; from hence they concluded that the swiftness or velocity of the air in escaping was 25 times greater than that of the water.

"This experiment," as Dr. Papin quaintly remarks, "was very well thought on, and might serve till a better should be found out; but those gentlemen could not but know that this was not perfect;" and he reasons, "that the air yieldeth much, and so the bladder, being filled with it, will become pretty flat as soon as a considerable weight is laid upon it. It is plain, therefore, that the weight bearing upon so large a space, doth not press every part with the same force as it would do if the bladder did for a while remain plump as it doth when full of water; moreover, the water itself being heavy in the bladder, makes some pressure, so that it appears that the pressure in this experiment was not quite so great upon the air as upon the water. I have therefore thought of another way which I think better to come to the same knowledge, and I do humbly submit it to the Royal Society."

Dr. Papin then argues, that quicksilver being $13\frac{1}{2}$ times heavier than water, bears as much pressure when its spring is one foot above the spout-hole, as water does when its spring is $13\frac{1}{2}$ feet high, and the height to which the water will ascend will be $13\frac{1}{2}$ times less than the height to which water will be driven by those equal pressures.*

He then proceeds, "that different fluids, bearing the same

---

* The resistance of the air not being considered.—EDITOR.

pressure, those that are the lightest must acquire the greatest swiftness, and their velocities are to one another as the roots of the specific gravities of the said fluids; and as the velocities of bodies are to one another as the square roots of the heights to which they may ascend, so, on this occasion, they are also as the roots of the specific gravities."

"If, therefore," Dr. Papin says, "we would know the velocity of air being driven, by any degree of pressure whatever, we have but to find what would be the velocity of water under the same pressure, and then take the square roots of the specific gravities of the two fluids; because as much as the square root of the specific gravity of water doth exceed the square root of the specific gravity of air, so much in proportion will the velocity of air exceed the velocity of water. For example, when I would compute what would be the velocity of a bullet shot by the pneumatic engine, as described in the 'Philosophical Transactions,' No. 179, I should first compute what was the velocity of the air itself that drove that bullet. I did therefore take notice, that on this occasion the air bears the pressure much about the same as that of the water when its spring is 32 feet high. Now, such water would spout out with a sufficient velocity to ascend 32 feet perpendicular, and therefore such water has a velocity of 45 feet per second.

"It remains, therefore, but to know the proportion of the gravity of the air to that of water, and we have found that it is not always the same, because the height, the heat, and the moisture of the atmosphere are variable; nevertheless, we may say in general, that the reason" (ratio) "between the specific gravities of water and air to be much about 840 to 1. Taking, then, their square roots, which are 29 and 1, we conclude that the velocity of air must exceed that of water 29 times, and so by multiplying 45 the velocity of water by 29, we shall find that the velocity of air driven by the pressure of the atmosphere into a vacuum is about 1305 feet in a second."

It will be perceived that Dr. Papin arrived at a perfect solution of the question by his admirable mode of reasoning, and that he was perfectly aware of the effects of the variation in the calculation, which the varied differences of altitude, heat and moisture, would occasion—circumstances that are not so much attended to as they should be when exactness is required in trying the strength of gunpowder by ranges, or by initial velocities.

It is generally allowed, now that we have arrived at greater exactness by delicate instruments, that when the pressure of the atmosphere is such that the barometer will stand at 30 inches, which is that of $2\frac{1}{2}$ feet of mercury, the air will rush into a vacuum at the velocity of about 1344 feet in a second; but the state of dryness or moisture will make a difference.

We may also put down the density of air as that of the 825th part of water, and mercury to water as 13·6 to 1, which will differ from the estimates of Dr. Papin in a slight degree. The column of water sustained by the pressure of the atmosphere may be considered as 33 feet when barometer is 30°.

The determination of the velocity with which air will rush into a vacuum has been an important element in calculating the resistance it gives to the progressive motions of projectiles passing through it, and has led many to suppose, that if a shot is moving with greater velocity, there must be a vacuum left behind it; forgetting that, as air is a highly elastic medium, the compression it receives from the front and sides of the shot will quite alter the velocity with which it will move round it to restore the disturbed equilibrium occasioned by the shot in its passage. For let us consider that the atmosphere is supposed to consist of gaseous atoms, so loose in combination as to yield to the slightest pressure, and so perfectly elastic as to return instantly that pressure is removed, and we find that with the common pressure of the atmosphere—say nearly 15 lbs. on the square inch—air will rush into a vacuum with a velocity of 1344 feet in a second; surely then the air that rushes round a shot, being highly compressed in front especially, must move round the surface to restore its disturbed equilibrium with much greater velocity than the natural pressure of the column of atmosphere gives. But if there was a vacuum caused behind a shot moving with high velocity, the particles of air rushing together and striking would cause violent detonation, and as long as a shot, *according to the vacuum theory*, moved with a greater velocity than 1344 feet in a second, its flight would be accompanied by the noise of thunder, which we know is not the case.

My opinion is, that writers on the subject of the resistance of the air on moving projectiles have not properly considered the elements of the causes of resistance. I attribute this greatly to the *friction* of the air on the surface of the ball, and as this increases with the increase of velocity, we can thus account for those phenomena of various resistances which appear to have puzzled even great philosophers.

We know that when a gun is fired there is a loud report; this is caused by the atoms of the gaseous matter of the fired powder striking upon the air with—as some have estimated—a velocity of 7000 feet in a second; and if we could project a shot with that velocity, no doubt we should have the same sound as long as the shot moved with it. There cannot be a vacuum formed on the discharge of a gun, which some have supposed, for the permanent gaseous matter of gunpowder is more than half as heavy again as common air, and will thus strike with greater force; but there is a sudden and quick collapse of the volume as it parts with its heat, which may give the appearance of a vacuum. I do not now, as I once did believe, that there is any vacuum formed even by the passage of lightning, from its rapidity of motion; but that the electric current strikes the air in its course, and thus occasions the noise of thunder, and the friction caused by its rapidity of motion produces the lightning, which I believe a shot would do if it moved fast enough.

MEMORANDA BY COLONEL ANDERSON.
Power required to Start the Cylinder Mills.

THE following experiments were made (with two single blocks, with one end of the rope fastened to each arm, the other to the weights) to ascertain the relative force required to start each mill with a charge of 95 lbs. of charcoal, which is supposed to be equal to a charge of gunpowder.

No. 1 Mill, with cylinders that have not been new faced :—

1st Trial. The composition, being stirred up as usual with the turners, took 648 lbs. to start it.

2nd Trial. The composition, stirred up, 432 lbs. started it.

3rd Trial. The composition, not stirred up, took 528 lbs. to start it.

No. 4 Mill, with cylinders new faced, and bed cut to a water level :—

1st Trial. The composition, stirred up, took 852 lbs. to start it.
2nd Trial.   Ditto   Ditto   . 336   „
3rd Trial.   Ditto   Ditto   . . 392   „
4th Trial. The composition not stirred up   420   „
5th Trial.   Ditto   Ditto   . . 392   „

Experiments made as to the Heating Properties of Coal and Firewood.

To evaporate a boiler of the mother waters, it takes 35 maunds of firewood, which is sufficient to complete the process in 24 hours.

With Burdwan coal, it was found that 17 maunds were expended, and the time in completing the process the same as with firewood.

This may be owing to the way in which the furnaces are made for the consumption of large logs of wood; but, I think, if the boilers were brought lower down, and a greater quantity of draught given by raising the chimney about one-third, the weight of coal to that of firewood would answer.

The next point to be taken into consideration is the relative cost for firewood and coal.

The price of Soondry firewood supplied here this season is 16r. 6a. 6p. per 100 maunds, so allowing that one-third the quantity of coal would answer in place of firewood, the rate per maund should not exceed 8a. 7·8p., to make it equal in price with firewood ; but if coal can be purchased at anything below this rate, and our furnaces altered so as to answer for coal, I think there would be saving in using it in place of firewood; as it is, the experiment made with the fusing pots was found to be in favour of the coal, and I think the same result would be found at the charcoal furnaces, if we had better draught, which could be easily effected by raising the chimneys. The following will show the result obtained at the several places, viz.:—

For evaporating one boiler of mother waters containing 30 maunds of saltpetre—

	R.	A.	P.
Firewood, 30 maunds, at 16r. 6a. 6p. per 100 maunds	5	11	10½
Burdwan coal, 17 maunds, at 8a. per maund . .	8	8	0
Difference in favour of firewood . . .	2	12	1½

For fusing 8 pots, each pot containing 6 maunds of nitre— it required of

	R.	A.	P.
Firewood, 20 maunds, at 16r. 6a. 6p. per maund .	3	4	6
Burdwan coal, 6 maunds, at 8a. per maund . .	3	0	0
Difference in favour of coal . .	0	4	6

In charring of cylinders of wood, each when charred containing from 22 to 25 seers of charcoal, it took—

	R.	A.	P.
12¼ maunds of wood, 16r. 6a. 6p. per 100 maunds .	2	0	9¾
Burdwan coal, 4½ maunds, at 8a. per maund . .	2	4	0
Difference in favour of firewood . . .	0	3	2¼

It requires the same quantity of sea coal as that of Burdwan to give the same proportion of heat, so that it would never answer to use sea coal, unless it can be purchased for the same price as the Burdwan.

Another thing to be considered is the quantity of charcoal received from the using of wood, and which is issued to the smiths and braziers, and amounts to about 100 ferrahs annually, each ferrah * being worth one rupee, so that about 1000 rupees is saved on this head alone; therefore, allowing that one-third the weight of coal to that of wood now expended would answer, we

* A Bengal ferrah measures 29 in. by 21½, and is 8½ in. deep.

should require about 18,000 maunds of coal yearly, and from the price of that, deducting the value of the charcoal received, it should not cost more than 6a. 9p. per maund, to equalise the value of it with the wood—not taking into consideration the expense that must be incurred in altering the furnaces, &c., to adapt them for the use of coal, so that unless a great reduction of the present price of coals (8a. per maund) could be made, no saving need be expected by its use.

Trials to find the Cause of Explosions.

3rd April, 1844.

No. 2 Mill exploded, everybody certainly doing their duty; 12¼ P.M., wind blowing very hard, much dust flying about.

Next day, on taking out the spindle of the cylinder, it was found bent two inches out of the straight line, and cracked half through, apparently the fracture of some standing, as the cylinders had for some time been known to make an unusual noise. This was the first of the cylinders turned from the concave to the convex face.

The following different experiments were made in No. 2 Mill with gunpowder, kunkur of bricks, and soorkee (brick pounded into dust), to try and find out the cause of the explosion which took place in this mill on the 3rd of this month.

Powder Works, Ishapore,
7th April, 1844.

1st Trial. With about 4 oz. of ordnance powder, mixed with the kunkur and soorkee dust of the fallen roof, spread on the bed in front of the cylinders—mill working at the rate of 3½ revolutions per minute—no explosion took place.

2nd Trial. The bed cleaned out, and two pieces of wood ⅜ths of an inch thick were put in front of the cylinders to give them a fall on the bed, with about the same quantity of powder as in the first trial. Explosion took place, after a good many revo-

EXPLOSION EXPERIMENTS. 291

lutions, the pieces of wood having been forced along the bed; mill working 3½ revolutions per minute.

3rd Trial. With the same quantity of powder only as before. Bed cleaned out, and one of the safety leathers doubled was put in front of the cylinders to give them a fall upon the bed; mill working about 4 revolutions per minute. No explosion took place.

4th Trial. Two pieces of wood, ⅜ths of an inch in thickness, were put in front of the cylinders, with about 6 oz. of powder, and a great quantity of kunkur and soorkee dust; the pieces of wood were broken into splinters, and were bruised very thin—mill working at the rate of 4 revolutions per minute. No explosion took place.

Firewood—to try Loss of Weight by drying for a month.

23rd December, 1836, weighed 50 maunds of Soondry wood that had been landed from the boats without being thrown into the water, and 50 maunds that had been in the water two days, and only that day brought to the bank to be weighed; also weighed one month afterwards, with the intent of ascertaining the quantity of water that might be in the latter.

The dry wood was marked T, 38 pieces; the wet M, 45 pieces. Weighed again, 21st January, 1837.

	mnd. srs.	Loss. mnd. srs.
The dry wood weighed	48 3	1 37
The wet weighed	45 16	4 24

Experiments with Compositions.

Experiments in firing, in a portion cut from a musket barrel of 3 in. in length, the following compositions of nitre and charcoal, each unit 15 grains. They were well mixed for 4 minutes in a marble mortar, and dropped into the barrel through the same funnel, then fired by a small piece of ignited charcoal—Urhur charcoal.

u 2

EXPERIMENTS WITH NITRE AND CHARCOAL MIXED.

URHUR CHARCOAL.

Charcoal.	Nitre.	Time of burning.	Remarks.
1	10	37″	A regular deposit of nitrite of potash left against the barrel.
1	9	24	A few beads thrown up, less potash left, and not so regular.
1	8	25	As above.
1	7	20	Burnt fiercer; less residue.
1	6	16	Burnt still fiercer, and less residue.
1	5	8	A little ash.
1	4	9	A little dust.
1	3	5	No residue.
1	2	4	No residue.

WILLOW CHARCOAL.

1	5	{17, 15}	Much potash left.

SAUL CHARCOAL.

1	5	17	Less potash left.

The Willow charcoal was much more distinct and less friable than the Urhur, and of a more brilliant shining black, but was not so finely pulverised. The Saul looked more like the Urhur. The fire, more intense and settled at the larger proportions of charcoal, say to $\frac{1}{8}$, burnt with more noise and struggling as the nitre was a shade less, as $\frac{1}{6}$. The smoke and gas was more, as the fire appeared more settled and dominant. The residues deliquesced in the air, being nitrites and oxides of potash, the base more or less prevalent having absorbed carbonic acid; the next day the whole residues had turned into liquids.

ON THE PENDULUM GUN ÉPROUVETTE.

A PENDULUM GUN ÉPROUVETTE.

A B   The Gun.
C A, C B   Suspending-rods.
E E   The axis.
F G   The graduated arc attached to the rods.
V   An index fitted to the axis at H.
H D   The prolonged arm of the index, to prevent it moving back with the recoil.
I   A small screw, to adjust the index to zero before firing the gun.
K   Pendulum to set the frame horizontally in both directions.

The pressure and friction of the index upon the head of the suspending-rods is just sufficient to keep the index in its place on the quadrant after the gun has recoiled, but not sufficient to check the recoil; and it thus shows the magnitude of the greatest vibration.

THE principle on which this instrument is constructed (a small gun suspended by arms from an axis directly above the centre of gravity, see plate) is, that when it is charged with gunpowder and fired, the expanding fluid acting equally in all directions from its centre, the fluid being resisted at the breech end of the gun by impinging upon the whole area of the base of the bore, and escaping towards the muzzle in the opposite direction as it rushes along, (where it is only met by the resistance of the air, and the friction on the sides of the bore, no ball or wad being used,) causes the gun to recoil or fly back, and up a part of the arc of suspension of which the suspending arms are radii, the axis of suspension being the centre of the circle.

The Chevalier D'Arcy, in his "Essai d'une Théorie d'Artillerie," printed in 1776, takes to himself the credit of this invention. To the upper part of the framework is fitted an arc and graduated scale, by which the measure of the greatest recoil or vibration is obtained.

The weight of the gun, length of the arms, centre of gravity, diameter of bore, and oscillation, are all elements in the calculation, and if these be not the same, no two éprouvettes will give an equal arc with the same charge of powder.

As the circumstances under which the gun is discharged are few and simple, I believe the same éprouvette will constantly and correctly give nearly the same results. The charge, accurately weighed, is introduced by a long ladle reaching to the bottom of the bore, which is pushed up to the end, and the muzzle being then raised till the axis of the bore lies at about 45°, the charge falls into a compact space, and the successive charges are similarly placed.

The friction and abrasion at the sockets with instruments so little used, and carefully preserved, when well oiled, is so very trifling as not to cause any variation.

As the gun has length of barrel, the proof by this instrument calls into play relations different from those found in the mortar proof. Combined, the two form an excellent measure of the strength of powder.

The quickness of the inflammation of powder is perfectly exhibited in the gun éprouvette; while the results are more certain than from a small charge, like two ounces, in the large chamber of an 8-in. mortar.

The arc of two different éprouvettes cannot be compared,

unless the variations of the elements above mentioned as entering into the calculation are known.

To ascertain the result of increase of charge, the following trial was made with musketry powder :—

Charge.	Arc of recoil.	1st difference.	2nd difference.
½ oz.	4° 22′	4° 22′	° ′
1 ,,	10 18	5 56	1 34
1½ ,,	16 44	6 26	0 30
2 ,,	23 36	6 52	0 30
2½ ,,	32 0	8 24	1 32
3 ,,	39 0	7 0	1 24
10·5 ,,	126 0	39 0	5 30
Average	21 0	6 30	0 55

The effect of size of grain on this instrument was ascertained thus :—

PROOF TAKEN TO ASCERTAIN THE DIFFERENCE OF RECOIL OF THE PENDULUM ÉPROUVETTE WITH LARGE AND SMALL-SIZED GRAINS OF POWDER.

Ishapore, 20th March, 1834.

Description of grain.	Pendulum Éprouvette.
	Mean of several rounds fired.
Very large grains, termed kunkur . .	18° 15′
Ordnance	20 55
Musketry No. 1	22 40
Ditto 2	24 30
Rifle No. 1	25 22
Ditto 2	25 23

As the small grain is the quickest inflamed, a larger quantity of fluid is earlier brought to bear on the interior base of the gun, hence the arc in each case is greater.

The Ishapore pendulum éprouvette was not advantageously placed or made; it was not with a cast-iron frame and wheels, as it ought to have been, and such as represented in the plate.

The present gun éprouvette at Ishapore is of the following dimensions:—

Weight	90 lbs.
Length	29·25 inches.
Diameter of bore	1·94 ,,
Length of arms	16·50 ,,

NOTE.—I believe the results from trials of the different sized grains would not differ so much if a *heavy* shot or weight is to be propelled through a long barrel, especially if rifled; and perhaps the largest grains *then* would be found most advantageous. The circumstance of varying the size of the calibre of an éprouvette to suit it for such trials seems never to have been thought of, yet with the large guns we are now introducing this is essential for a right result.—EDITOR.

VARIOUS PATENTS FOR IMPROVEMENTS IN GUNPOWDER.

IN 1815, July 3, William Congreve (afterwards Sir William) took out a patent for a new mode of manufacturing gunpowder.

I. The proportions of the composition in fine powder are to be introduced into three separate hoppers, having cylindrical brushes working beneath each hopper, and as they revolve the stream of materials fall on an endless band, by which they are deposited in a semi-mixed state on a hopper, and are there mixed by a revolving brush.

II. In the press-house the mixture is pressed, between gauged plates, into flat cakes about $\frac{1}{8}$ of an inch thick.

III. The cakes are broken to form grain in an improved granulating machine, consisting of two pair of toothed rollers— the upper one breaking the cake into coarser pieces; and the under ones, being closer, and with finer teeth, reducing the pieces still smaller; proper bands, hoppers, and sieves, being arranged to separate the large and small grains and dust. The cake is passed through the rollers by feeding apparatus.

REMARKS.—In this patent the process of mixing by brushes seems useless, and probably injurious, by causing the lighter parts to fly off and be lost from the proper proportion. The second and third improvements, however, were good, and in a greater or less degree and modification are now used in most manufactories.

In 1853, August 13, a patent was taken out by John Gwynne.

His improvement is to prepare a dust made from pulverising solidified peat or coal, so as to use it instead of charcoal in the manufacture of gunpowder.

In 1853, Dec. 15, Edward Auguste Bellford took out a patent for improving blasting powder for mining purposes. His proportions were as follows :—

$19\frac{1}{2}$ lbs. of charcoal.
68 lbs. of saltpetre.
$12\frac{1}{2}$ lbs. of sulphur.
———
100

The composition was to be mixed, pressed, granulated in the usual way, and afterwards a quantity of chlorate of potash was to be deposited in water to saturation, and the solution sprinkled over the grains of the powder. Then it was to be dried in a proper drying room heated to about 100° for four days. This powder is to be used unglazed.

REMARKS.—Although there would probably be an increase of strength from this powder, yet there would be increased danger in using it—by its readily exploding by friction, or percussion, from the presence of the chlorate on the exterior of the grains. By all means avoid the use of chlorate of potash in a gunpowder manufactory.

In 1857, August 22, Henry Hodges took out a patent, his proposal being to mix the usual ingredients, in their proper proportions, in fine powder and in a suitable vessel, and then injecting steam, so that the saltpetre is dissolved, and the ingredients are thoroughly incorporated by being stirred up.

Of late years there seems to have been much competition amongst the manufacturers of gunpowder, and several patents have been taken out on the subject. It will not, therefore, be objectionable to my readers to have some of them alluded to.

A patent was taken out on the 9th July, 1855, by Mr. Edward Hall, for such improvement.

It states that the improvement consists in regulating the temperature of the mills in which the process of milling goes on, by applying artificial heat to the beds—by means of hot water or other heated fluids, through proper hollows or channels, supplied from a boiler and properly-disposed cisterns, communicating by proper pipes—so as to keep the temperature of the bed at a higher temperature than the atmosphere. The water is pumped up into cisterns, the upper cistern being kept at the temperature of 212° by steam pipes when the atmospheric temperature is at 50°; and by carrying a current of hot water through the hollows or channels in the mills to a lower cistern, the same uniform temperature which the manufacturer desires in winter or summer may be maintained at his discretion by means of stop-cocks, &c.

REMARKS.—The patentee observes that such mills should be well ventilated above, in order that the moisture arising from the water in the charge of the bed may evaporate freely. And I understand from Mr. Hall that he derives much benefit from this improvement.

By following such a plan the sulphur in the charge must be brought to nearly a fusing heat, and thus its intimate mixture with the other ingredients may be improved and facilitated in an extraordinary degree, the warmed molecules of the sulphur at this high temperature being laminated as it were over the molecules of the two other ingredients. I have before alluded to the great benefit which gunpowder derives from the small portion of sulphur.

In 1855, July 26, a patent was applied for by Mr. Charles Goodyear for improvement in gunpowder.

His object was to apply due proportions of india rubber, or

gutta percha, with the usual proportions of saltpetre and sulphur leaving out the charcoal altogether; but as his patent did not proceed to the Great Seal, I suppose the projector found that the proposed alteration would not answer in practice, if in theory.

In 1856, April 30, a patent was taken out by Mr. Henry Edward Drayson, of the Maresfield Powder Works, Sussex, for the following improvement :—

He first dissolves the saltpetre (weighed in proper proportions with the other ingredients for a mill charge) in boiling water, using about 50 per cent. of water, or the least possible quantity to dissolve it, and then, mixing the sulphur and charcoal with the solution of nitre, proceeds to grind the mixture under the mill as usual.

He uses saltpetre that has not gone through the process of fusion, and states that the requisite labour and time of milling may be shortened by drying off part of the moisture by exposing the charge to artificial heat, to bring it to a sufficient state of dryness to be put under the runners.

REMARKS.—The only disadvantages of this proposed improvement appear to be the excess of moisture, and the liability of the saltpetre to re-crystallise when the temperature is reduced ; and that in bringing the powder after being pressed and grained through the process of drying, the grains may be left more or less porous ; not that this would affect the strength of the powder when new, but after it has been kept in store or exposed to the atmosphere.

In 1856, January 24, Mr. Edward Hall took out another patent, in which he proposes a new mode of watering the mill charge. He states that the charges of powder in a mill are moistened with water at the commencement, and after milling some time, and as often as the charge becomes partially dry, they are damped again by sprinkling water over them by hand, with a small watering pot, while the mill is in motion ; but in this way of watering, the distribution of the water is not uniform, or limited precisely to the quantity required.

The patentee, therefore, brings forward an apparatus whereby the exact quantity of water can be sprinkled over the charges in a given time, and continued with little variation for an indefinite period, by means of which the charges are better incorporated, the loss from dust diminished, and the chance of explosion lessened.

The water is distributed by small pipes which lead from a cistern above down to near the surface of the mill bed, where a horizontal perforated pipe connects, which, being attached to the mill shaft, revolves with the mill; and being provided with cocks capable of nice adjustment, and the water in the cistern being heated by a steam pipe from the boiler, can be distributed at any temperature that may be desired; and thus the mill charge is better watered and incorporated than by a man with a watering pot, as is the common practice.

On the 10th June, 1857, Mr. Frederic Koehler applied for and proceeded in part with a patent, for a new kind of gunpowder to be made,

I. Of a new discovered salt, whose chemical incorporation is—

Oxygen	38·51
Chloride	29·76
Kalium	31·73
	100·

or any Kaly-oxymuriaticum.

II. Sulphur.

III. Charcoal.

These ingredients are to be powdered fine, and mixed together in the following proportions :—

70 parts of Salt;
20 parts of Sulphur;
10 parts of Charcoal;

or in other proportions. The mixture produces *instantly* gunpowder without further manufacturing.

REMARKS.—As notice to proceed with this patent by application for letters patent was not given within the time specified, it was never completed, perhaps to the saving of the remainder of the expenses.

For, first, as the newly discovered salt was not properly described, the patent could not have stood. Secondly, the having the material in fine powder would be so objectionable, that it would never come into use for fire-arms or cannon at the present day.

The inventor, however, states, the powder made on this invention has increased power and weight, and becomes better by keeping, and that there is a further advantage, that it is not inflammable or likely to explode, as the single ingredients alone are only inflammable and not explosive.

On the 19th of August, 1856, Mr. T. W. Willett, of 89, Chancery Lane, C.E., took out a patent for improvement in gunpowder.

His first plan is to supply a jet or jets of steam to the charge of powder, instead of watering it, to give the requisite moisture to the charge, by which it is more evenly and regularly moistened; the pipes to convey the steam are carried just over the surface of the charge by proper pipes, and move round with the runners or rollers. His second plan is to supply a current of air artificially above the surface of the charge, to carry off the moisture, which current is so contrived as to carry it just above the surface of the mill charge, and not to impinge directly upon it. This current of air may be caused by a fan or other suitable means, and may be artificially heated if required, and must be a gentle current, so as not to raise the dust of the powder; and when it is desirable to hasten the drying, his apparatus is so contrived that he can reverse the current, and draw it inwards, just passing over the mill charge, and thus creating a current passing into his apparatus; but as some particles of the dust of the composition might be drawn in, the openings in the pipes for the air to pass in or out must be covered with a thin woollen cloth.

REMARKS.—In the moist climate of England, perhaps, a gentle current of warm air passing over the mill charge might be beneficial, but the reversing the current seems of little practical use, and difficult to be managed, for assuredly the moisture or vapour from the mill charge would accumulate on the thin woollen cloth proposed to cover the orifices of the pipes, and most probably, assisted by the dust of the powder, would stop the passage of any gentle current of air as proposed.

On December 8th, 1857, Mr. Thomas Willett took out a patent.

His proposal is,—I. To cause the beds of the incorporating mills to rotate in a horizontal direction, while the vertical wheels or runners only revolved upon their main axle vertically, which axle can move up and down vertically, so as to set the beds and runners at a regulated distance as required.

II. To use press plates in the press mill, with raised surfaces or ribs, so that the cakes when they come out of the press are indented and easily broken up.

III. A drum-shaped rotating vessel, heated by a steam jacket, is used for mixing the ingredients, and copper or hard wooden balls are placed in the vessel.

IV. Saltpetre in a state of solution is heated and mixed with the charcoal in a copper pan, and the sulphur is added to the rest after it has cooled down to about 50° Fahr.

V. A new kind of granulating machine is proposed, the press cake being placed upon a table having parallel metal ridges, and is pressed down by suitably arranged pressing plates, furnished with ridges also.

REMARKS.—There may be some advantages in using such a granulating apparatus, especially when powder of large grain is required.

It would be endless to enter largely on the notices of the various new patents relating to gunpowder; no doubt many of them are perfectly useless. Private manufacturers, having large capital involved, are not communicative of their improvements, and it would be well, therefore, that those who are about to enter upon the manufacture should be cautious, and by inquiry ascertain whose gunpowder bears the best character in the market, with the view of making some agreement with that firm for the disclosure of their processes of manipulation.

I believe, iron mills will quite supersede stone or gun metal; will be cheaper, stronger, and more durable; and even the granulating rollers, when made of iron and steel, are quite as safe, much stronger, and more durable, than brass ones, and, I am informed, are used in one of the best and most flourishing private manufactories in England.

Much economy in time and labour may be saved by taking advantage of improvements which are the results of *experience*, not only in the different processes of refinement and manipulation, but also in the arrangement of the buildings, all of which should be well considered in establishing new gunpowder works.—EDITOR.

THE END.

길

JOHN WEALE'S PUBLICATIONS.

In 8vo, 88 pp. Price 6d.

CATALOGUE OF BOOKS, OLD AND NEW,

INCLUDING

THE PUBLICATIONS AND PRESENT STOCK OF JOHN WEALE,

ARRANGED AS FOLLOWS:—

1. Architecture, Engineering, Design and Ornament.
2. Bridges, Stone, Iron, Timber, Suspension, Tubular.
3. Carpentry and Joinery.
4. Hydrostatics, Hydraulics.
5. Italian Architecture and Ornament.
6. Military History and Art.
7. Mines and Mining.
8. Machinery, Mechanics and Millwork.
9. Naval Architecture.
10. Painted and Stained Glass.
11. Railways, the Forming and Making.
12. Renaissance, Tudor and Elizabethan Architecture.
13. Strength of Materials.
14. Steam Engine and Steam Navigation.

WITH AN INDEX FOR REFERENCE TO AUTHORS AND SUBJECTS.

In 8vo. Gratis.

CATALOGUE OF BOOKS FOR 1861,
ON ARCHITECTURE AND ENGINEERING.

In 8vo. Price 2s. 6d.

NATIONAL DEFENCES:
THE GREAT QUESTION OF THE DAY.

By SIR W. SNOW HARRIS, F.R.S., &c.,

With Charts and Plans of Spithead, Plymouth Sound, and Fowey Harbour.

" Breathes there a man with soul so dead,
Who never to himself hath said,—
This is my own, my native land."

BRIDGES OF ALL KINDS,

FOR RAILWAYS ACROSS RIVERS, ROADS, CANALS, VALLEYS, EMBANKMENTS, &c., &c., OF IRON TUBULAR GIRDERS, WIRE, SUSPENSION, STONE, TIMBER, BRICK, &c. (SEE CATALOGUE, PAGES 8—14.)

MILITARY WORKS, ENGLISH AND FRENCH.

(SEE 6d. CATALOGUE, PAGES 45—49.)

In 8vo, with a Fourth and much Extended Edition. Price, in cloth boards, 10s. 6d.

THE WORKING OF THE STEAM ENGINE
EXPLAINED BY THE USE OF THE INDICATOR.

By JOSEPH HOPKINSON, C.E.

With several elaborate Engravings.

In 8vo, with 13 Engravings, extra cloth boards, price 5s.

PRIZE DESIGNS FOR COVERED HOMESTEADS,
ADAPTED TO FARMS OF 200 AND 500 ACRES.

Together with an Introductory Essay on the Principles and Practical Management of Covered Homesteads.

By PHILIP D. TUCKETT, F.G.S., &c.

In 12mo, in Two divisional Parts complete, price 5s., an entirely New Work.

DIVISION I.

FORMULÆ, RULES, AND EXAMPLES FOR CANDIDATES

FOR THE

MILITARY, NAVAL, AND CIVIL SERVICE EXAMINATIONS;

ALSO FOR

MATHEMATICAL STUDENTS AND ENGINEERS.

By T. BAKER, C.E.,

AUTHOR OF "RAILWAY ENGINEERING," "LAND AND ENGINEERING SURVEYING," "STATICS AND DYNAMICS," "ELEMENTS OF MECHANISM," "MENSURATION," ETC.

DIVISION II.

IRON BRIDGES.

PRACTICAL FORMULÆ AND GENERAL RULES

FOR

ASCERTAINING THE STRAIN AND BREAKING WEIGHT OF WROUGHT IRON BRIDGES,

WITH SUNDRY USEFUL TABLES.

SUGGESTIVE ALSO, WITH THE CALCULATIONS, FOR CARRYING A RAILWAY BRIDGE ACROSS THE QUEENSFERRY ON THE FIRTH OF FORTH.

By CHARLES HUTTON DOWLING, C.E.,

FORMERLY OF TRINITY COLLEGE, DUBLIN.

In folio, with 29 Plates.

A NEW WORK

ON THE

MACHINERY AND TOOLS

WHICH ARE

MANUFACTURED AT PARAGON WORKS,

SOUTH QUEENSFERRY, N.B.

BY

JAMES DUNDAS, ESQ.,

DUNDAS CASTLE.

THE FOLLOWING IS THE LIST OF THE PLATES:—

1. An 8-horse power Horizontal Engine.
2. A 10-horse power Ditto.
3. A 12-horse power Ditto.
4. A 15-horse power Beam Engine.
5. A 25-horse power Horizontal Engine.
6. A Steam Hammer.
7. A Donkey Engine or Steam Pump.
8. A Soorka or Clay Mill, with a Horizontal Steam Engine attached.
9. A Portable Hydrostatic Press or Machine.
10. A Bolt and Nut Screwing Machine.
11. A Punching and Shearing Machine.
12. A small Pillar Vertical Drilling Machine.
13. A Drilling Machine.
14. A single-powered Vertical Drilling Machine.
15. A Vertical Drilling Machine.
16. A powerful Vertical Drilling Machine.
17. A Radial Drilling Machine.
18. An Improved Foot Lathe.
19. A Slide and Screw-cutting Lathe.
20. A Slotting or Vertical Planing Machine.
21. A Self-acting Slotting Machine.
22. A small Cross-cut Nibbling or Shaping Machine.
23. A Cross-cut Planing or Shaping Machine.
24. A Self-acting Cross-cut or Shaping Machine.
25. An Improved Self-acting Planing Machine.
26. An Improved Printing Press.
27. An Improved Albion Press.
28. A Screw Press.
29. A Diagonal Paper-cutting Machine.

Price in cloth boards, £1. 1s.

JOHN WEALE, as Publisher approximating a period of half a century, continues to publish, either on commission or by purchase, works on the Constructive Arts.

DR. REID'S WORK ON VENTILATION AND WARMING;

MORE PARTICULARLY FOR

THE VENTILATION AND PURIFICATION OF ALL PUBLIC BUILDINGS, ASSEMBLIES, CHURCHES, CHAPELS, SHIPS OF WAR, PASSENGER SHIPS, MINES, ETC. ;

ILLUSTRATED BY AN AMPLE PRACTICAL DESCRIPTION,

AND

FURTHER EXPLAINED WITH SECTIONS AND PLANS IN 334 DIAGRAMS.

PUBLISHED AT £1. 1s., NOW REDUCED TO 7s. 6d.

Very neat in cloth boards, gilt and lettered.

[TITLE.]

ILLUSTRATIONS

OF THE

THEORY AND PRACTICE OF VENTILATION,

WITH

REMARKS ON WARMING, EXCLUSIVE LIGHTING, AND THE COMMUNICATION OF SOUND.

BY

DAVID BOSWELL REID, M.D., F.R.S.E.

451 pages.

www.ingramcontent.com/pod-product-compliance
Lightning Source LLC
Chambersburg PA
CBHW030324240426
43673CB00040B/1263